The
Seasons
of
My Life

*Thank you
for your part
in my life!
Love,
Janet*

Janet E. Meyers
with Jennifer Rice

This book is a work of non-fiction. Unless otherwise noted, the author and the publisher make no explicit guarantees as to the accuracy of the information contained in this book and in some cases, names of people and places have been altered to protect their privacy.

New American Standard; About 80 Scriptures, unless otherwise indicated, taken from The New American Standard Bible®, Copyright © 1960, 1962, 1963, 1968, 1971, 1972, 1973, 1975, 1977, 1995 by The Lockman Foundation. Used by permission.

Scripture taken from the Amplified® Bible, Copyright © 2015 by The Lockman Foundation. Used by permission.

ISBN: 978-1-4834-9839-3 (sc)
ISBN: 978-1-4834-9838-6 (e)

Because of the dynamic nature of the Internet, any web addresses or links contained in this book may have changed since publication and may no longer be valid. The views expressed in this work are solely those of the author and do not necessarily reflect the views of the publisher, and the publisher hereby disclaims any responsibility for them.

Lulu Publishing Services rev. date: 02/28/2019

Previous book by Author published 06/10/2016
George H. Meyers, His Remarkable Life Story

CONTENTS

DEDICATION

This book is dedicated to the grandchildren of George and Janet Meyers:

Anna, Joel, Marie, Christine, and Sarah – children of Dan and Laurie

Lauren, Stephanie, and Eric – children of Steve and Leslie

Amy, Allison, Austin, April, and Alec – children of Jennie and Mark

I am very thankful that they all knew and loved their Granddad, and I treasure the love and honor they show me.

> *"I have no greater joy than this, to hear of*
> *my children walking in truth."*
> III John 1:4

Our grandparenting had to be done long distance while we were serving out of the country or from our missionary headquarters in Jacksonville, Florida, but our children faithfully kept us informed about their children's activities. We rejoiced when we heard that the family had all been together for a holiday celebration.

It has been a joy for me to watch our grandchildren grow up, choose their careers and start families of their own. I am in the delightful season of welcoming great-grandchildren into the world and I enjoy participating in family events and get-togethers in Oregon and California.

FOREWORD

The *Seasons of My Life* by Janet Meyers is a story of a valiant and beautiful woman; a woman I call my mentor, my friend. Her passion for God, family, and others has made a resounding impact on my life since the day we met in 1997. The first time I went to Go To Nations (at that time Calvary International), I had been told to meet with Dr. George Meyers, Executive Director. As I approached the building, I saw that the front door was out, and the "maintenance man" was repairing the door frame. This incident exemplifies the life of this beautiful couple, servants of all, because the "maintenance man" was Dr. George H. Meyers. Little did I know that his wife would become my spiritual mentor and my closest friend.

During the more than twenty years that I have known Janet, I have been personally challenged in almost every aspect of my life to come up higher. I have a comical, but true, running comment about the late Dr. George at our World Headquarters of Go To Nations when making major decisions, WWDGD – "What would Dr. George do?" I have since added another phrase that has the same true value when I make decisions, WWJD – "What would Janet do?" This comment does not discount the fact that for any decisions I make, I pray to get the wisdom of God, through the incarnate Jesus and the guidance of the Holy Spirit, but it does mean that there are wisdom "sound bites" that ring in my ears constantly from my friend, Janet.

While it would take many chapters to write all of those "sound bites," I will begin with my short list of the things that I admire about Janet.

Her love for God, shown in her desire to serve Him and honor Him all the days of her life, is at the top. Her life's work has emphasized the love of God for humanity and His desire that all be reconciled to Him.

Second on the list is her constant love for her family, her children, grandchildren, and great-grandchildren. She tells stories of her heritage, possibly dating back to the 1600s, her parents, and the things that have shaped her. She also tells me stories of happenings in her children's lives that make me feel like I know them personally, even though I have only met some of them a few times. She has told me about the hardest of times when she and Dr. George sacrificed holiday celebrations with family while serving foreigners in a foreign land. Her life story tells how she had a call and a sensitivity to foreigners at a young age and felt that God had placed this in her heart in preparation for hard places like Ethiopia and Sudan.

I have always admired so much about Janet, but her love for her husband, Dr. George, and her commitment to him rings loudly. I have never seen or heard her trying to compete with him, even though she could. She truly earned her PHT – Putting Hubby Through – during his years at Oregon State University. Janet was a leader in her own right, as you will read in the chapters ahead, but she served her husband with prayer and kindness and used her best skills for him. Her counsel to pray specific scriptures over one's husband about the character that he possesses, as well as the character that God is working in him has made a significant difference in my life. This simple truth is one that I now tell others.

I could not finish my short list without including Janet's love for her neighbors and her unselfish care for them. She is always serving others, literally. She has a beautiful gift of hospitality and has even trained our missionaries how to set a table for guests. She purchases and prepares food and serves our missionaries at their gatherings and training sessions. I have a picture of my own granddaughter impersonating her, wearing Janet's apron from Russia and holding a teapot. Janet is a consummate hostess and carries herself with such class.

Last on my short list is Janet's love for the Word of God, being obedient to His commandments and spreading His Kingdom principles for a fruitful life. Her teaching on "Keeping the Sabbath" comes to mind first and foremost. One year Janet gave everyone on our team a framed copy of the Ten Commandments, reminding us, even as we are in ministry, to keep them.

In these pages, you will read about Janet's life and begin to see how living a life for God will change not only your own life and eternity, but also the lives of many others. You will come to know Janet as I do and see the fullness of her life as she uses her God-given talents to serve Him all her days.

One of the greatest blessings that life has afforded me is the privilege of knowing Janet Meyers all these years.

Sandra Barfield, Executive Vice President of Mobilization
Calvary International dba Go To Nations
Jacksonville, Florida

ACKNOWLEDGEMENTS

I am extremely grateful for the capable editing assistance of my daughter Jennie as I have composed this sequel to George's life story. Despite her family and work obligations, she managed to carve out some time to support my goal of preparing the manuscript of my autobiography for publishing before my 80th birthday. Her extraordinary skill with language and grammar improvements has made the stories pleasant reading.

Thanks to my granddaughter Allison Leung for the cover design, skillfully employing her impressive artistic expertise. The photo was taken by George Meyers on our return trip to Ethiopia in 2002.

My children, Dan, Steve and Jennie, gave meaningful encouragement and jogged my memory with their recollection of happenings in which they were part of the story. I deeply appreciate their heartfelt tributes in the final chapter. Special thanks to Dan, who was well qualified to read the manuscript for accuracy and clarity.

Beginning with Sandra Barfield, the writer of the foreword, my colleagues and friends at Go To Nations in Jacksonville, Florida, cheered me on as I committed to putting in writing the seasons of my life, including my missionary endeavors.

I express my sincere appreciation for the honor given to me by everyone who contributed bits and pieces of their relationship with me for the book.

I am grateful to the writers of the endorsements on the back cover, Dr. Grady Carter, Nancy Lovelace and Pastor Gordon Johnson, for sharing thoughts from their connection with me to encourage the reading of the book.

Most of all, I acknowledge with profound gratitude the guidance of the Holy Spirit as He inspired me to chronical memories from the chapters of my life for my descendants and friends. It is my prayer that my Father is honored, and that every reader is drawn closer to the Lord by reading my life story.

INTRODUCTION

Although I was an integral part of much of the story of the life and times of my beloved husband, I purposed to keep his book, *George H. Meyers, His Remarkable Life Story*, centered on his history and life pursuits. It has been rewarding to receive such a positive response from the people who have read George's Life Story, published in 2016.

As a sequel, this book chronicles the seasons of my life, including some stories from our missionary experiences together that were left on the cutting room floor when his book was getting too long. Writing these books has required me to re-live our 57 years of marriage and the adventures we had together. The greatest joy of my life was partnering with George in his service to his family, his country and the Kingdom of God.

I am profoundly grateful that so many aspects of my life have the imprint of the love of our Heavenly Father, the saving grace of His Son and the guidance of the Holy Spirit. I've been encouraged throughout my life by this Scripture:

> *"My grace is sufficient for you, for power is perfected in weakness. Most gladly, therefore, I will rather boast about my weaknesses, that the power of Christ may dwell in me."* II Corinthians 12:9 (NASB)

In this sunset season of life, I desire to continue to be a good steward of all that my Father has invested in me for as long as I live.

Janet Meyers

Life's Journey Begins

"I will give thanks to Thee, for I am fearfully and wonderfully made; wonderful are Thy works, and my soul knows it very well. My frame was not hidden from Thee, when I was made in secret, and skillfully wrought in the depths of the earth. Thine eyes have seen my unformed substance; and in Thy book they were all written, the days that were ordained for me, when as yet there was not one of them."

Psalm 139:14-16

CHAPTER 1
My Unusual Childhood

For many years I worried that I might have been adopted, mostly because people would comment about my sister Marilyn, "Isn't she cute? She looks just like her Daddy." One time when I was clandestinely searching through Mama's cedar chest, I found my birth certificate. It was a relief to find that I truly was born to Richard Earl and Alice Peck on April 23, 1939, in Riverside Hospital in Wisconsin Rapids, and there were my little footprints to prove it!

My parents were older when I was born – Daddy was 32 and Mama 28. They welcomed their first baby and named me Janet Eleanor. My father, known throughout his life as Earl, or R. Earl Peck when he signed his name, was born in Juneau, Wisconsin, on June 14, 1907, to Harry and Cynthia Peck. My mother, Alice Mildred Baughman, was born in Rudolph, Wisconsin, on November 6, 1911. They were married in Nekoosa on May 25, 1938, and made their first home in Wisconsin Rapids. My mother was in the hospital for eight days for my birth, from April 23 to May 1, at $3.50 per day for her room and $1.00 per day for the nursery, for a total of $47.70.

Mama used to tell the story that as she was sitting on the davenport nursing me when I was only seven or eight months old she "felt life," and came to the realization that there must be a new baby on the way. (Davenport was the name of a fold-down sofa made popular by

1

the A. H. Davenport Company). She could hardly believe that it was true, but sure enough, Marilyn Mae was born on June 8, 1940, when I was 13 months old. Even though it was just over a year later, it was surprising to me to learn that the room charge had reduced to $2.50 per day for the seven days of Mama's maternity hospitalization. The nursery cost remained the same, $1.00 per day. That hospital bill totaled only $34.75.

Once when I was just toddling, I showed up in the living room carrying my new baby sister from the bedroom to my unsuspecting mother, who thought she had left the baby safe and secure on the bed! She told me of another incident when she poured some shampoo into a cup to use while she was giving Marilyn a bath, and when she had her back turned I drank it. Evidently, I was experiencing some jealousy over the attention the new baby was getting as I was no longer center stage!

My dad was working on a farm at that time and we lived in an upstairs apartment. When I was just old enough to ride a tricycle, one time they failed to close the door to the stairway. Not recognizing the danger, I "rode my trike" down the stairs! Somehow I lived through that experience without permanent damage, but it was a significant scare to my parents.

Daddy's Work

During World War II, my preschool years, my dad worked at the Badger Army Ammunition Plant located near Baraboo, Wisconsin, an Army facility that manufactured munitions. I don't know why my dad was not drafted, but this work was his contribution to the war effort. I know that our home was in a nearby town, Sauk City, but I have no memories at all of that period of my life. In 1944 when the war was winding down, an opportunity presented for my parents to join my mother's sister and family, Aunt Caroline and Uncle Willard Moe, who were farming in southern Wisconsin. After we moved there and Daddy worked as a hired hand for them for a short time, our family rented a nearby dairy farm in the Woodford/South Wayne area.

My Mother and Teacher

As a young woman, my mother had attended Stevens Point College and then taught elementary school in rural settings, boarding with the families of her students. After she was married to my dad, she continued to teach school. When we moved to the Rood Farm, she was hired as the teacher at Mills School, a one-room school with about 40 students in eight grades near Woodford. I started the first grade there when I was five years old, with my mother as my teacher. Twin cousins two years older than I, Philip and Elaine Moe, were also students at the school. Their younger sister Elinor and my sister Marilyn were cared for by Aunt Caroline until they were old enough to join us at school.

Teachers in rural schools in those days had many more duties than simply teaching. I went with Mama to school early in the morning so she could start the fire in the furnace, shovel snow at the entrance in the winter, bring in the drinking water and prepare the classroom to receive the students. After school one of my jobs was to sprinkle green sweeping compound on the wood floor to keep the dust down while she swept. I also cleaned off the blackboards as far as I could reach, then Mama finished them. All of this work had to be done to prepare for the next day before we could leave for home, where Mama would fix supper and begin her evening of grading papers and preparing lesson plans and tests for the next day.

Primitive Copying Technology

Among the responsibilities of teaching was preparing the class work for each grade. Of course, there were textbooks and blank exercise books, but not much was available for workbooks and tests. Using a special purple pencil, my mother would write out by hand questions or sentences, leaving blank lines to be filled in by the students. The mechanism for making the copies was the *hectograph*, a copy system consisting of a special gelatin poured into a shallow pan (like a cookie sheet). She would press the original page carefully into the gelatin, being careful not to nick it with her fingernails. That became a mirror image of the original; then she peeled off the original and laid it aside. The next step was to carefully press a piece of blank white paper onto the gelatin. After rubbing it to help it absorb the ink, she peeled it off and it was a copy of her original document.

This process was repeated until she had peeled off seven or eight copies. By the eighth copy, the ink was getting quite faint. If she had more than eight students who were going to receive that lesson or test, she had to write out another original and make more copies. To "erase" the gelatin, she soaked it with a special fluid called "spirits," then sponged away the ink, leaving the surface clean for the next master. Can you imagine the amount of work involved in this method of making copies for a school of 40 or more students in eight grades? It was especially intensive as she prepared for special programs for holidays when everyone in the school participated.

Early Education

I have realized for a long time that my early education was exceptional. In those days the school day began with the Pledge of Allegiance to the Flag and the reading of a passage from the Bible. In addition to my own grade level work, I had the advantage of being able to overhear some of the lessons of the older grades. For example, I used to take the spelling tests several grades higher than I had actually learned the spelling rules, and it made for some funny words. My mother was amused that I spelled the words *attention* and *promotion* as *attenshun* and *promoshun*.

I would get mixed up sometimes and call her Mama at school and Mrs. Peck at home! It seemed to me that she expected more of me than she did the other kids, perhaps in an effort to not show partiality to me as her daughter.

I have wonderful memories of memorizing speaking parts for plays and poems for special programs for Christmas and Easter. The Bible story of the birth of Jesus was read as part of the program. The whole community came out to enjoy our performances and the festivities. I believe I was only in the first grade when I memorized *Twas the Night Before Christmas* as a solo presentation. I also remember singing an action song that I think is called the *Shoemaker's Song*. The words of the first part are "Wind, wind, wind your thread; pull, pull, tap, tap, tap," actions that would be done by a shoemaker. More than seventy years later, that song came into my memory when my great-grandchildren Coleson and Evelyn Smith, children of granddaughter Anna and Brett, danced to it at the Scandinavian Festival in Junction City, Oregon, in 2017.

CHAPTER 2
Life on the Farm

While Mama taught in Mills School near South Wayne, Daddy managed the dairy farm. We had dairy cows and fields of grain and hay to feed them. During World War II it was very difficult to find hired men, so even though my sister Marilyn and I were very young we were "hired hands." Farming was definitely a family enterprise!

Tragedy Strikes

An accident happened one day that caused my parents much anguish because of how young I was to be doing that kind of work. I think I was about seven years old at the time. After bringing loose hay in from the field, it was necessary to put it up into the hay mow to store it for winter feeding. There was a pulley system which could be pulled by a horse or a tractor. That fateful day, I was the person who drove our John Deere tractor hooked to the rope that pulled the hayfork up into the mow. Mama was the person up on the hay wagon clamping the hayfork into batches of the hay to be lifted into the hay mow, while Daddy was up in the hay mow spreading the hay around with a fork, arranging it to get maximum use of the space.

Partway through this process, the tractor engine stalled. Daddy shouted instructions to me to let the tractor roll forward, and then engage the clutch to restart the engine. Alas, that didn't work. Instead of the engine starting, the tractor lurched and threw me underneath the tractor and into extreme danger. One of the sharp cultivators hooked into the middle of my back and carried me along.

When Daddy saw what was happening he panicked and jumped out of the hay mow. (Why wasn't he injured in that incredible long-distance jump?) While I was being dragged down the gravel driveway, he was desperately running after the tractor until it ran into a bank and stopped. When Mama arrived at the scene, her frantic question to Daddy was, "Is she conscious?" I must have heard that.

No 911 to call! My folks gathered me up in a sheet, loaded me into the car, and sped away to the hospital, burning the rods and ruining the engine. I was a bloody mass of abrasions and contusions, with a gash in my back from the cultivator, but amazingly I had no broken bones. I was told later that on the way to the hospital, I asked, "What does it mean to be conscious?"

I did not have to stay in the hospital long but had an extensive recovery period at home due to the trauma to my little body. I vividly remember having to crawl before I could walk. Family and friends brought me coloring books and other fun things to do while I was in bed recovering. One time when some special friends dropped in to check on me, they left me alone in the bedroom to go to the living room to visit with my parents. I hated to be isolated so I surprised them all by crawling on my hands and knees out to where they were to listen to the conversation.

The scar on my back is the only permanent reminder of the accident. God obviously wasn't finished with me yet!

Other Memories

The house we lived in on the Rood Farm had only two bedrooms and an outhouse. Especially my mother hated the absence of plumbing, and she instigated the acquisition of a chemical toilet which was kept in the closet of my parents' bedroom. Of course, we kids were allowed to use it, but it was our parents' chore to take it to the outhouse and empty it and re-stock it with chemicals. Our farm had a windmill, which was our source of water. For bathing on Saturday nights a large round metal tub near the stove in the living room was filled with water, heated on the stove, and one by one we all took our turn.

When we had company, such as my dad's parents, they occupied our bedroom and Marilyn and I slept on the davenport in the living room. Since we had to get up early, we were supposed to try to go to sleep while the adults were still up and visiting! Grandpa Peck had a theory that if I slept on my right side, or was it the left, it was "bad for my heart." I only know it required me to turn my face toward the wall. Because I was so social he knew this was the only way I would go to sleep, but it was very disappointing to me to miss out on any of the conversations.

Another Scare

Managing our dairy farm was a 24/7/365 occupation! Feeding and milking cows must be done twice a day, besides all of the other farm work. I remember my dad eating a large piece of Swiss cheese for a pick-me-up as he headed out to do the evening chores. Marilyn and I helped with various aspects of the chores, but we also did some fun things. We had a board swing when the weather was nice and in the winter we went sledding and ice skating on the Pecatonica River when it froze over.

We liked to climb into the stall and sit on the bare backs of our two draft horses, Daisy and Dinah. One time our huge Holstein bull somehow got out of his pen and went on a rampage, knocking over milk cans and creating havoc. Daddy hollered for us to get out of the way and we scurried up into the horse stall, safe from danger. Somehow he managed to get the barn door closed and the bull back into his stall.

Marilyn remembers our mailman bringing us a dog, which produced a litter of puppies. Most were fuzzy and roly-poly, and we named them very "original" names, obviously based on their appearance, Whitey, Brownie, and Blackie. The one that was sleek, Daddy named Dopey.

Marilyn liked to dress like Daddy with overalls, a white cap like his and a *necktie*. (He didn't wear one, but for some reason she did.) In another worrisome experience for him, she was with him when he was pitching loose hay from the hay mow down to the cows. She accidentally fell down the chute along with a bunch of hay! He nearly had a heart attack when he saw what he thought was a pool of blood while he was digging for her. He thought he had stabbed her with the pitchfork in an effort to find her quickly and keep her from suffocating. Imagine his relief when the red "something" turned out to be her red necktie.

Weather Challenges

To get from the farm where we lived to Mills School required crossing the Pecatonica River, which was subject to flooding when there was excessive rain. Occasionally it was necessary to travel a longer, more circuitous route to get to and from school when the road was covered with water. Rainstorms are challenging enough, but Wisconsin winters are harsh with lots of snow. Though shoveling snow off the walks at school was another duty of my mother as the teacher, sometimes she was helped by a school board member or an ambitious boy in the upper grades.

Reaching home the long way when it was not possible to cross the bridge was no problem in good weather, but one time Mama made a perilous decision. It was snowing, but it did not seem too threatening. Since it was Friday night, she was eager to get home for the weekend, so we started the journey in our car. The snowstorm escalated to a blizzard and along the way we got stuck in a snowdrift. Mama left Marilyn and me in the car while she walked to find someone who could pull us out. After a long time passed, she came back with a neighbor who brought his team of horses and a sleigh. We were moved into the sleigh and bundled with blankets for the ride home. My folks were concerned that we might have frostbite on our toes, but there was no permanent damage.

Community Cooperation

Summers were hot and often humid with frequent thunderstorms, making putting up hay for winter very challenging. My folks were part of a group of neighboring farmers who helped each other with the harvesting of grain with threshing machines and corn with shredding machines. Each harvest day, every farmer went to the chosen farm and worked hard, knowing that one day all of those men would come to help him harvest his fields.

I remember a horrible incident when Floyd Anderson, the hired man of Aunt Caroline and Uncle Willard, accidentally got his right hand caught in the shredder, critically mangling his hand. Almost as though she had a premonition of an accident, my mother brought out a pile of white cloths that she had sterilized in the oven. Floyd's hand was wrapped in the cloths as someone sped off with him to the hospital. Unfortunately, he lost the four fingers of his hand and later had a hook. I had nightmares about the incident, which were compounded when he would hug me.

While the farmers were working together, their wives were preparing scrumptious meals, including delicious pies and cakes, to serve their hard-working husbands and hired hands. There was a kind of friendly competition to see who could produce the most amazing dinner as the farmers moved from one farm to another. Marilyn and I had assignments to help with preparing and serving when it was our family's turn. We both loved the chance to be part of the excitement.

Norwegian Influence

The farming cooperation among neighbors was similar to the way it was done in "the old country." There was great camaraderie among the whole community in doing the farm work and in social life as well. On Saturday nights my parents took Marilyn and me when they went to the dance hall to spend the evening with their friends. We were never left with a babysitter; in fact, I don't think we ever stayed with anyone except another family member on any occasion.

The dances included waltzes, polkas, schottisches and sometimes square dancing. The music was provided by local musicians with fiddles and accordions. I think my interest in playing the accordion and encouraging our kids to learn to play instruments is rooted in enjoying the music by those men who were friends of our family. Everyone had so much fun! When Marilyn and I got tired we went to sleep on benches along the edge of the dance hall.

Those late nights on Saturday probably contributed to the fact that we did not regularly attend Sunday school or church. And of course, the cows had to be milked morning and evening. I only remember a few times, probably Christmas and Easter, when we attended a Methodist Sunday school in Woodford, a nearby town.

CHAPTER 3
The Family Tree

My Mother's Side

I t was a blessing to me to learn interesting stories of my family history. In current times people are having DNA testing done to determine their ancestry. I am thankful to my mother's sisters, Theresa Rickett, and Caroline Moe, who collected the records and stories of my ancestors and passed them down to their grandchildren and also to me. My ancestors on my mother's side were of German heritage, although both of her grandfathers, Mathias Baughman and Israel Clark, were born in the United States. They were farmers and raised large families.

Earlier ancestors of the Baughmans came from Zuyder Zee, Holland. They were a strict sect known as Amish or "Hook-eye Dutch," using hooks and eyes instead of buttons and wearing wooden shoes. Mathias Baughman's mother, Ellen Holland, was born in Utica, New York, but her older sisters were born in County Cork, Ireland. The family had emigrated in the years just before 1850 when Irish people came to America in great numbers because of famine, fever, and persecution in Ireland.

My mother's paternal grandfather, Mathias (Mot) Baughman, was born in 1847, and although he was only 17 he served in the Civil

War as a private in Co. A 46th Regiment, Wisconsin Volunteers, Infantry, from February 1865 to September 1865. His unit's duty was the important assignment of guarding the Nashville & Decatur Railroad in Alabama. When the war was over he was sent by boxcar to Madison, Wisconsin, to be discharged. According to family lore, he was so anxious to get home that he walked from there the forty miles to Monroe.

Israel Clark, my mother's maternal grandfather, made the westward move to Wisconsin from Ohio about the time of the Civil War. He had snow white hair and a long beard. His grandchildren believed that he had lived with the Indians back in Ohio because he was so knowledgeable about Indian names for plants. He was quite a naturalist, spending much time on long walks in the countryside. He used to collect nuts, fruits, and plants and he often sold ginseng roots, which were in demand by the Chinese for medicine. He had a collection of Indian arrowheads, many found at the site of the Black Hawk battlefield.

Leon and Carrie Baughman were my mother's parents. Grandma Carrie died when I was five years old. I remember being held up to look into the casket, but I have very few memories of her. Both my sister Marilyn and I remember a certain smell from her kitchen, maybe sourdough pancakes and homemade butter? Another memory is of the smell of the oilcloth cover on her dining room table. This was way before plastic tablecloths were invented. In those days, the place settings at the table did not include spoons, which were available from a jar.

Grandpa Leon was a tall, heavyset man who we saw quite often while we lived in Wisconsin. I learned from my cousin Elinor, also his granddaughter, that when he had lived with their family for two years in the early 1950s, Aunt Caroline knew that he was diabetic and had cooked separately for him. I have no memory of him taking insulin or my mother acknowledging that he should be eating differently, but I vividly remember that he had recurring indigestion after meals. Soon after eating he would come to the kitchen and say to my mother, "Ahbie, got any sodee?" Her name was Alice, but he always called her by the nickname. What he wanted was a teaspoonful of soda, which he mixed in water and drank. It evidently gave him relief from the distress he was experiencing. He must have known the cause but was apparently an uncompliant diabetic.

One time, Aunt Caroline and Uncle Willard brought Grandpa with them to visit us in Oregon. By then his gait was more like a shuffle. When we took him to the coast, he wanted to dip his foot into the Pacific Ocean. A wave came in about that time and he couldn't shuffle out of the way in time to avoid getting wet up to his knees. It was funny to all of us, but not to him!

My Father's Ancestry

My father, Richard Earl Peck, was born in Juneau, Wisconsin, on June 14, 1907, to Harry Lyle Peck and Cynthia Letitia Peck, whose maiden name was Joslin. Thanks to the preservation of records from my dad's cousin Orin Stager, I learned about Joseph Peck, the emigrant ancestor of the Pecks in this country. Known as the Massachusetts Pecks, they are now a numerous and extensive race scattered throughout the United States and Canada. Joseph was baptized in Suffolk County, England, on April 30, 1587. He had eight children, some of them born in England.

In 1638 he and other Puritans and their pastor, his brother Robert, fled from the persecutions of the Church of England to this country on the ship *Diligent of Ipswich*. The town clerk in Norfolk County, New England, stated: "Mr. Joseph Peck and his wife, three sons, and a daughter, two men servants and three maid servants came from Old Hingham and settled at New Hingham."

My grandfather, Harry Lyle Peck, was among the tenth generation from the line of Joseph Peck. Grandpa was the third child, born December 15, 1877, to Oscar Peck and his wife Henrietta (called Etta). She died in 1900 of what was then called consumption, now known as tuberculosis. They had four sons and two daughters: Ethel, Fred, Harry, William, Earl, Lela, and Oscar.

Our family had many reunions with Grandpa Harry's relatives in the Tacoma/Puyallup area of Washington State. We were well acquainted with Great-Aunt Lela Stager and Great-Uncles Oscar Peck and Earl Peck and their families. Great-Aunt Lena, the widow of Great-Uncle Will, and their children, Leslie, Raymond, Verna, Esther, Ruth, Paul, and their spouses, often joined us at the family reunions. Uncle Will met death in a tragic accident when a swinging circular wood saw came apart.

We have a wonderful relationship with Aunt Lela's descendants, Orin (age 106 in 2018) and his wife Odetta, along with Orin's son Charles (Chuck) and his wife Marilyn. There is true longevity in this family; Orin's sister Violet died at age 101. Another cousin of my dad's, Edna Fleck, daughter of Great-Uncle Fred, treated our family to ice cream cones whenever our family visited her at her café in Tacoma.

The place where Great-Uncle Oscar and Great-Aunt Elsie lived in Tacoma was not far from Fort Lewis, Washington, where George usually had his National Guard assignments. They kindly offered hospitality to us when I was able to visit him on the weekends, which gave us the opportunity to get to know them well. Grandpa Harry and two of his brothers, Fred and William (Will), fought in the Spanish-American War. Grandpa served in the 3rd Regiment of the Wisconsin Volunteers from April 1898 until his discharge in January 1899 at the end of the war. I believe it was an injury during the war that caused one of his legs to be shorter than the other so that he walked with a decided limp.

Marvin, another "cousin," came from the line of Smith Peck, a brother to Oscar Peck, Grandpa Harry's father. Marvin and Vera Peck had three children, a daughter Patricia and twin sons William Wesley and Wesley William, named for special ancestors. They lived in Portland and were always glad to join us for family get-togethers. Another relative lived in Newberg near us. Daddy called her Aunt Mary Ostrander, but I could not find her in the records. We used to take her to church with us and my sister and I found it amusing that even though she was not poor, each week she put a quarter in the offering.

Points of Interest

Smith Peck's father Hezekiah died as a result of an out-of-the-ordinary accident when crossing the frozen river. The team of horses broke through the ice and in his courageous effort to rescue them, one kicked him violently, breaking his leg and causing his death a few days later.

These notes came from the genealogical history of the descendants of Joseph Peck, by Ira Peck.

> "Our ancestor Joseph Peck took an active interest in the business of the town. He was one of the selectmen, justice of the peace and assessor. He was appointed by the court to grant summons, to see people joined in marriage and to keep the records. In 1641 he became one of the principal purchasers of the Indians of a tract that later was incorporated into the town of Rehoboth, Mass. He and three others of Hingham (which was concluded by the Commissioners of the United Colonies to belong to Plymouth) were riding and sheltered themselves and their horses in an Indian wigwam, which took fire. They labored to their

utmost but three of their horses burned to death and
all their goods, to the value of fifty pounds."

I am grateful to the people who have preserved this information. I
enjoyed reviewing it and noted how often some of the same names
came up in different generations. I have only recorded a fraction of
what is available, but I want my descendants to know our storied
history.

CHAPTER 4

The Olden Days –
Mama's Memoirs

These stories are transcribed from handwritten notes from my mother, Alice Peck, dated January 1996. This entire chapter was written by her.

One of my Christmas gifts for Christmas 1996 was a pretty book from Lyle and Melodie, Tracy and Micah, and their families. They asked me to recall some of the happenings of my childhood and write them in the book. Maybe that was a way to compliment me for my good memory at age 85. One thing I know – out of a family of six children, I am the last one. So there's no one to ask to verify anything I might write.

I was born on November 6, 1911, at the farm home of my parents, Leon Ellsworth Baughman and Carrie Israel Clark. The doctor who attended my birth arrived in a horse and buggy. I had three older siblings, who had all been delivered at home. A hired girl came to do the cooking, laundry and whatever housework needed to be taken care of while Mother took care of me, rested and recuperated.

Our family didn't get a car until 1915. It was a seven-passenger Studebaker with side curtains that could be fastened on if needed because of wind and rain when traveling. Two seats could be pulled up from the floor in front of the back seat. I remember trips to family picnics, reunions, and to the Marshfield Fair in the summertime.

I don't recall too much of what might have happened before 1915, but when I was four, my father came over to my crib and spanked me on my birthday. I started first grade that year. The school building had four rooms, plus a basement with a restroom and a playroom. There were no flush toilets. The contents were treated with some kind of lime stuff and about once a year the janitors would go down in the under part with shovels and clean them out.

In good weather, we could play outside behind the building. There were swings, teeter-totters, ball diamonds, and whirligigs. There were areas for high jumps, broad jumps and places to race. A well was being dug a little ways from the building. It was interesting to watch that and one day I was standing by the window watching and I did not take my seat when the teacher rang the bell, so for my punishment, she made me stand there all afternoon which was very embarrassing.

This was the time in history right after World War I. We would see the passenger train which ran through our farm go by with all black cars. They were bringing the dead soldiers home from the war and it made us feel very sad. Another thing that happened at this time was an epidemic of influenza that broke out all over the globe. It was reported that 20 million people died. Our father got very sick for a long time. People who came to help take care of him and help with the farm work had to be careful not to mention all the deaths so as not to make him concerned if he would live or not. My mother's father, Israel Gager Clark, lived with our family, too. His wife, Nancy Caroline, had died. Grandpa lived until 1915 and sadly his death was by suicide.

There was more to life than school. We had chores to do when we came home. We changed out of our school clothes, had a snack, and went to do our work. We carried pails of water from a well in the front yard to fill the reservoir on the kitchen range and leave a full pail of fresh water for drinking on a shelf. If we wanted a drink, we dipped some up and drank. We weren't supposed to take more than we needed, and we weren't supposed to put what was left in the dipper back into the pail.

Someone's chore was to gather the eggs. Some hens wanted to stay in the nest as if they wanted to hatch some chicks. When we would try to get the eggs they would try to bite us. If Mother wanted to get baby chicks she would put eggs in an incubator. Each day she had to turn each egg over. One day she went out to the place where the baby chicks were kept. She saw a big gray rat sitting there in a stupor from having eaten so many little baby chicks. It is amazing to me, but she went to the house and got Father's gun and shot the rat.

Our father's pride and joy on the farm was the purebred Guernsey cattle. He often had to pay high prices for a young calf to add to his herd. I can remember his getting some of his stock ready to exhibit at the Marshfield Fair. Our brother Earl grew up with a crippled hand. When he was three years old he was watching my father and mother unloading a load of hay. There was a rope running through a pulley as a fork of hay was going up into the mow. He was fascinated with the pulley moving and put his hand on the rope and it was pulled into the pulley. He didn't lose his hand but did have a serious injury.

We girls did some of the work connected with getting the meals like setting the table and washing the dishes. We didn't have running water in the house nor bathrooms or toilets. Each bedroom had a chamber under the bed to be used at night if necessary. Earl's special name for it was "chamber of commerce."

There used to be a lot of snow in the winter so that the snowplow would come and plow out a roadway. Usually, in winter, the cars were put in storage in the shed and the horses and sleds were used. Cars were jacked up so the tires wouldn't be ruined by having too much weight on them.

In 1922 a paving company came along and did some road improvement with concrete. Our father provided a place for the work crew. A cook shanty was built and another building for the sleeping place for the workmen. The horses used for power were housed in our old barn and someone took care of them when their day work was finished. The windmill furnished a tank full of water each day. I found out later that during the summer only three miles were paved. But we were glad it was in front of our place. We would ride our bikes, roller skate, and run with a ring pushed by a stick with a cross piece nailed on one end of it. Such fun! The road project was an exciting experience for us kids and I imagine it brought in quite a lot of money for our dad.

When I was 13 years old the minister of the Moravian church took a bunch of us kids and instructed us in the Bible. It was during the summer and we had to go each day and study catechism and Scripture. After we had learned all we were supposed to, we were baptized by sprinkling and confirmed. Since then I've been baptized by immersion in the Christian Church in Newberg, Oregon.

We had good, loving parents and a pretty good life. They expected us to help with the work that we were able to do. Our father bought a piano and took us to Wisconsin Rapids for lessons. I took lessons on the violin and played in the high school orchestra. I was on the basketball team. I was good at broad jumping and high jumping. I never followed up on the violin and I don't even know what became of it. We enjoyed a nice upright Edison phonograph that had to be wound up. The records were about one-fourth inch thick with one song on each side, 78 speed. It was quite a few years later that we got electric lights, but the first lights that we had were on a Delco system that ran on batteries sitting in our basement that had to be charged up every so often with a motor.

I don't know how old I was when our parents took us to the circus in Wisconsin Rapids. We parked our car and followed the animals in cages across the bridge where the big top was set up. Sometime while waiting for the acts to start up I got lost from everybody. I didn't have a ticket and no money so I was just lost. When the circus was over and the family came back to the car they found me asleep in the car. They were quite amazed that I had found my way back there all alone.

When my younger brother Mathias (nicknamed Mac) got old enough to be away from Mother he was taken to sleep upstairs with Earl. It was told that he slept facing Earl with his little hands touching Earl's cheeks. In 1928 our brother Mac got sick with diabetes and had to be on a diet, avoid sugar and use insulin, which he could give himself. He only lived until age 21 years.

The year I turned 16 my mother and Caroline gave me a party. Friday evening when I came in from milking, the cleaning was all done. I soon found out why and it was a total surprise. All my classmates and neighbor kids my age were there and I enjoyed it very much.

When I finished high school I went to Teachers' Normal School for one year. After one year we took our certificate and my first job was in a school in Carson County about six or seven miles from my home in Wood County. My salary was $90 a month and I boarded and roomed with a family for $20 a month. I taught for just one year at that school and then I was able to get a school that was open for nine months. The salary was not very good at that time, but I enjoyed teaching very much.

Our grandparents, Mathias Otis Baughman and Ellen Holland, had moved from their farm in Greene County, Wisconsin, into a big brick house in Monroe. Grandpa was a tall thin man with white hair and a white beard. He chewed tobacco and we didn't like to kiss him goodbye so when they were getting ready to leave we used to run upstairs and hide under the bed to avoid getting some of the spit from his whiskers on our mouth. Elinor Moe has mentioned that with Grandpa's name being Israel Clark maybe there was some reference to our being Jewish, but I don't know about that.

CHAPTER 5

Oregon or Bust!

T he year my dad turned 40 he wanted to surprise his mother by visiting her in Oregon on his birthday, June 14, 1947. Hiring help so that our family could get away from the farm in June was no small trick, but Daddy found a neighbor man who would milk our cows and take care of the chores, but for just *ten* days. The trip from Wisconsin to Oregon by car took four days, driving from early in the morning until late at night, including changing flat tires several times, but Daddy was determined to reach Newberg on his birthday.

His wish was granted and he greatly enjoyed greeting his mother with a hug and kiss and saying, "Here I am 40 years after my entry into your life!" Grandma Cynthia and Grandpa Harry were truly surprised and very appreciative of our family's effort to make the long trip. We stayed with Daddy's sister and her husband, Irene and Luke Weiler, who had moved to Newberg along with Grandpa and Grandma in the early 1940s. The Weilers had one son, Douglas, just 14 months old. Marilyn and I really enjoyed playing with the baby and getting to know our grandparents and aunt and uncle.

Knowing we had to allow four days to drive home, we had only two days to spend with our Oregon family. That precious time was truly memorable and planted the seed that led my parents to pull up stakes and move our family from Wisconsin to Oregon.

Trial by Turpentine

On our way west, when we had passed through Wyoming we desperately needed to find overnight accommodations in the Cheyenne area. We didn't know ahead of time that the annual Cheyenne Days extravaganza was happening at that exact time. We were exhausted after a long travel day, but lodging was almost impossible to find. After passing multiple No Vacancy signs, we found an available motel on the edge of town. It was not five-star; in fact, it may not have earned any stars at all. It didn't qualify for "the best surprise is no surprise" either. Not long after we returned home, we discovered that I had picked up head lice, probably from the night in that sleazy motel!

In those days getting rid of head lice was not as easy as it is now when a special shampoo is available that removes the lice and the nits (eggs). Having lice was considered to be a problem of very poor people and there was stigma and disgrace associated with it. Shortly after our trip, I was helping Mama with a painting project and I got a few drops of paint in my hair. She put a few drops of turpentine on a rag to get the paint out and later noticed that where she had done that, there were no nits.

An idea came to her mind to put turpentine on all of my hair to get rid of the problem all at once. When she applied that much turpentine to my hair, some got on my scalp and it felt like my head was on fire. I ran out the door and out into the field, running as fast as I could. As I ran the wind cooled my head. I ran and ran until I had no more strength and collapsed on the ground. My mom ran after me and was sure she had killed me! I was eight years old and had never experienced anything so agonizing. I have no memory of what Mama did to counteract the burning, or whether it was the end of the lice, but thankfully it was not the end of me!

From Wisconsin to Oregon

Undoubtedly, discussions of the pros and cons of moving to Oregon began on the way home from the hurried visit to Oregon for Daddy's birthday in 1947, but it was two years later before the ducks were in a row to make the move. I don't remember how our furniture made the trip, but I know we fitted everything possible into our pickup truck. The four of us, Daddy, Mama, Marilyn and I, were crowded into the cab for the long journey westward. I was ten and Marilyn almost nine. She was small for her age and fit lengthwise behind the seat on the ledge to have a rest and give the three of us a chance to spread out.

One night when we stopped at a motel, our dog Fluzz was not in the pickup. (Years earlier when we got this dog she had been named Flossie, but little Marilyn's interpretation of the name was Fluzz, so that's the name that stuck.) The dog had not been tied, and the consensus was that she had jumped out when we had stopped for a long freight train. She was deathly afraid of thunder and we figured the train had sounded threatening to her. We were all very sad to lose our pet, knowing that we would miss her, but even more not knowing what would become of her.

Our Home in Newberg

We already knew where we would be living when we reached our destination, the house where the Weiler family (along with Grandpa and Grandma Peck) had lived previously on Sunnycrest Road. They would write to our family in Wisconsin about their ranch in Oregon, saying it was like the Garden of Eden. When we were digging out of snow banks in Wisconsin, they were planting their garden and commenting on the beautiful flowers that were in bloom.

We arrived in Newberg in 1949 and were now going to see if the glowing reports the family had written us were true. We were looking forward to warmer weather and spending time with the family members whom we had seen two years ago for just two days.

The house, which had originally been built as a chicken house with a slanted roof, was a few miles west of Newberg. The original owners had evidently needed to use it as housing for their family, so it never was used as a chicken house. From the beginning of our living there, especially my mom looked forward to building an addition with the opposite roof angle to make the house look more normal. Her wish was granted, but not until several years later.

Though the Weilers and Grandpa and Grandma had been living there, they had not developed it as a farm, nor had they made any improvements to the buildings. It became available for our family when Uncle Luke took a job as a truck driver for Wilhelm Trucking in Portland. They had moved to Portland to be closer to his work. The property was 16 acres and included an area along a creek which Daddy and Grandpa called "the bottoms," where blackberries were prolific. There was a filbert orchard and pasture land for cattle. Daddy had a vision to develop the property, which included a barn and a couple other outbuildings for farm animals.

The small farm was a good setting for raising a family, though not enough acreage to make a living. Daddy found work in the timber industry, logging and sawing lumber. His work was far away, so he had to leave home in the wee hours and would return very late. He rode with a group of men in a "crummy," or maybe it should be spelled "crumby" since I think it got its name from the crumbs left from the snacks and lunches after the workers had eaten lunch in the van. My sister Marilyn and I were the ones left to take care of the animals and do the outside chores at home.

New Experiences

I was in the fifth grade and attending school mid-year as a *new kid,* which was quite intimidating. It was my first experience of school without my mother as the teacher and there were so many more students than I was used to. Once when I was asked to read aloud, I mispronounced the famous Willamette River, calling it the Willa-Mett River. Everyone laughed and I felt humiliated.

Mama continued to teach school after we moved to Oregon. I actually enjoyed cooking and cleaning in our home and there was lots to do since Mama's teaching kept her very busy. When my folks went away from home without us kids, I hated to be *assigned* a list of tasks to do. Instead, I liked to *surprise* Mama by all that I had accomplished when she was gone.

The quality of making a home comfortable and nice without much money was passed down to me by my mother. I considered her a very good homemaker even though her vocation was teaching school. I didn't realize then that my bedside stand, made from an orange crate, was not customary. I had not heard of people who decorated with period furniture such as Early American. Evidently, Mama was decorating in Early Orange Crate!

Spiritual Life

My only spiritual training while growing up in Wisconsin was from occasional attendance at a Methodist Sunday school. The summer after we moved to Oregon, a neighbor invited me to go to summer camp at Wi-Ne-Ma Christian Camp with the youth of the First Christian Church in Newberg. While I was at camp at age 11, I received the first teaching of my life about accepting Jesus as my Savior, which I willingly did.

After returning home, the pastor of the church, J. Frank Cunningham, came to our house to meet my parents and talk with me about my decision. He shared the Good News with them and they were persuaded to also accept Jesus as their Savior. He did some teaching on water baptism and later as he was leaving my mother surreptitiously asked him if it was okay for her to be baptized when she was *pregnant*. That was when I first learned that we were expecting a baby in our family. It was not a subject discussed in our home and I went to the dictionary to look up the word pregnant! My parents, my sister Marilyn, and I were all baptized at the same time. All of us were now born-again and became members of First Christian Church in Newberg.

A Baby Brother

One night in a January snowstorm in the winter of 1950, the telephone on the wall kept ringing until I finally woke up. It was puzzling to me that I was the one (at age 11) who needed to answer the phone until I realized that it was Daddy calling. His important message was to say that Marilyn and I had a red-headed *baby brother!* Mama and Daddy had gone off to the hospital without waking us. Lyle Gordon Peck was a very welcome addition to our family! My mother was so enthralled with Baby Lyle that sometimes she would rock him until he went to sleep and continue to hold him until he woke up!

Daddy was working away from home in the woods at that time and Mama got Baby Lyle onto a schedule so he would be awake when Daddy came home late at night. I got a lot of practice in childcare from taking care of my own little brother. Sadly, my mother miscarried another baby boy when Lyle was two. He would have made a nice companion for Lyle, who was stuck with older sisters and no one close to his age for a playmate.

Memories of Grandma and Grandpa Peck

After we got settled into our new home in Newberg, Grandpa and Grandma began living with us. It was our family's turn to provide a place for them and we loved having them as part of our family. Lyle was born on Grandma Cynthia's birthday, January 29, 1950. My memories of her are very vague, but I have a picture in my mind of her sitting in the rocking chair in the living room by the stove. She became seriously ill with cancer and it was challenging for my mom and Grandpa to care for her. Sadly, she passed away in the fall of 1950. It was wonderful that she got to enjoy Baby Lyle in her last year of life.

After Grandma passed away, Grandpa lived with us part-time and with Aunt Irene part-time. He was the grandparent that I knew the best, and I credit him with putting into my soul the imperative to pick berries and to faithfully preserve all of the produce God made available to us. He regularly took Marilyn and me berry picking and helped us with a unique set-up of belts around our waists with buckets attached so we could expeditiously use both hands to pick berries. Grandpa didn't let his limp interfere with his berry picking!

Grandpa's gift to Marilyn and me for our birthdays and Christmas was always a crisp dollar bill wrapped around some food item (like a jar of olives or can of beans) that he had observed that we especially enjoyed. In the wintertime, Marilyn and I would sit around the woodstove in the evening with Grandpa and Daddy cracking walnuts and filberts (hazelnuts), while Mama graded papers and made lesson plans.

I remember one Christmas at the Weiler home in Portland. After dinner, they got out some boxes of snapshots and pictures of the family in days gone by. We were having so much fun looking at the pictures that Daddy decided to drive the thirty miles back to Newberg to milk the cows and feed the animals, and then come back to the party for more reminiscing. It was a late night with lots of laughter and enjoyment.

We had wonderful times with the Weilers and also enjoyed annual family reunions with some of Grandpa Peck's siblings (great-uncles and aunts to me) who had left Wisconsin years earlier and settled in Tacoma and Puyallup, Washington. Before freeways were developed, those trips were major expeditions for our family. In addition to getting to know the elderly relatives, our family all remember visiting Cousin Edna Fleck's ice cream store. I learned from Marilyn that at one time our dad had toyed with the idea of purchasing that store, but perhaps he was not able to gain our mother's approval.

Liberty Bell

Young people now may not be familiar with the history of the Liberty Bell. Located in Philadelphia, it is most famous for ringing to announce the colonies' declaration of independence from England in 1776. In its early years, the bell was used to summon lawmakers to legislative sessions and to alert citizens about public meetings and proclamations.

I have a personal story related to this iconic symbol of American independence. In 1950, my Uncle Luke Weiler was chosen by his employer, Wilhelm Trucking Company, to drive a Liberty Bell replica to various sites around the Northwest to promote patriotism. One of the stops was in Newberg, where we lived, and we have a picture of me with my sister and baby brother sitting on the truck near the bell.

CHAPTER 6
Learning and Earning

I gratefully acknowledge my mother's teaching expertise as a major factor in my excellent early education. After we moved to Oregon, I attended Central School in Newberg through the remainder of the fifth grade. I then went on to Newberg Junior High School for sixth to eighth grades. A favorite teacher was Antonia Crater, known to my folks because she and her husband were also members of the Farmers' Union. She gave me many opportunities to help other students, similar to the role of a teacher's aide. For example, one of my classmates was subject to grand mal seizures. I was trained to tend to him if he would have an episode during school hours. I believe that assignment encouraged my compassion and desire to help others less fortunate.

Harvesting Fruit and Nuts

In our pre-teen and teen years, my sister Marilyn and I picked strawberries for a man from our church. Bob Johnston drove 20 minutes down from Chehalem Mountain each morning in strawberry season to pick us up and then brought us back home in the afternoon. Our earnings were based on how fast we could pick strawberries. It was back-breaking work, but a means of earning money for school clothes. Bob was a wonderful man and we were very sad to hear about a tragic accident that took his life some years later. He was doing some kind of mechanical work under his car when the jack gave way and he was crushed.

In the fall we picked up Italian prunes and filberts. The hazard for picking up prunes was yellowjackets. When prunes fall to the ground prematurely they often split open, creating a feast for yellowjackets. Because of the size of prunes, the bucket filled up quickly, but it was very common to get stung. We had several acres of filberts on our farm which Marilyn and I picked up, and sometimes we also helped other growers pick up their nuts.

More Earning

Beginning at age 13, my first hourly wage job was babysitting for Gene and Charlotte Knopf, earning 35 cents an hour. In addition to helping with the care of my little brother, I learned a lot about motherhood through Charlotte's instructions for taking care of their little baby, Druscilla. About two years later their son Eric was born and I babysat both children, but I don't think my pay increased.

Cafeteria Cashier

Mrs. Crater and the powers that be at Newberg High School chose me to be the cashier at the school cafeteria when I was in junior high, a job I had for many years. I missed study hall in order to eat a quick lunch, then I took the tickets and money from the younger kids at the junior high school before the senior high students came through the line. I earned 50 cents an hour, plus my lunch. I learned to eat lots of vegetables that had not been served in our home, but the real bonus was developing a relationship with George, the handsome guy who washed pots and pans and dipped the ice cream cones that were available for sale after lunch.

Extracurricular Activities

I enjoyed music class in junior high and loved my teacher, Mary Ellen Gill, an excellent trainer. I was chosen to sing in the soprano section of a triple trio. Our group of nine girls was invited to perform at various community gatherings. Mary Ellen and her sister Isabel were both teachers in Newberg. Decades later after they retired on the Oregon Coast, I connected with them for tea and reminiscing about school days.

In high school, I sang in the choir and participated in concerts. A favorite class was home economics, where I acquired skills in sewing and cooking that I had not learned from my mother at home. I was a leader in Future Homemakers of America. The beginning of my lifelong hospitality specialty was undoubtedly the training for serving at special events I received as an FHA member. Among our activities as a club, in the spring we prepared and served a luncheon for the faculty, and breakfast for the Future Farmers of America. By request, our club members were servers for banquets and other events sponsored by FFA. Another connection I had with George was through his leadership in FFA and my participation with FHA.

Shall We Dance?

I remember that our church youth group leaders were adamant that we not take part in the dance classes that were part of our P.E. training. George wasn't convinced that dancing was sinful, so he participated in the training. Although not necessarily understanding the reasoning, I was compliant and took the note from the pastor to the P.E. teacher to excuse me from dance classes. My teacher understood the church's requirement, but then she assigned me to write a paper about some aspect of physical education, while I was out of the class. I'm sure I got a high score on my paper, but it was not possible to get an "A" in P.E. without participating in the dance classes. The "B" I got in that semester of P.E. was the only grade lower than an "A" that I got through all of high school.

Secretarial Training

My high school secretarial science teacher, Ruth Cereghino, observed my special gifting in secretarial skills and encouraged me by entering me in county-wide secretarial competitions for shorthand and typing. I received high marks in these competitions, which was a feather in her cap, as my teacher. I learned to type on an Underwood manual typewriter; in fact, the whole secretarial science room was supplied with these typewriters. Typing more than 100 words per minute on a manual typewriter was quite a feat! My skills have been a great help to me and others in assignments throughout my life.

Accounting Assistant

I had done well in math in school, which helped me greatly in my jobs and throughout my life. At age 14 I began working after school, on Saturdays during the school year and full-time in the summers for Cullen T. Rist, a Certified Public Accountant. He had contracts to audit the school districts in several counties all over Oregon. The summers that I was 15 and 16 I traveled with him and another accountant to distant places. We would work all week and then return home on the weekend. We ate in restaurants and stayed in hotels, working late into the evenings. Looking back on it now, it is a wonder to me that my parents allowed me to go away with these two men for days, often more than a week at a time.

I barely remember Mr. Rist's wife Geraldine, who succumbed to cancer, leaving two young boys to raise. Besides the accounting work, I also helped in the house, cleaning and cooking, and I became very close to his two sons, Bobby (12) and Randy (10). I don't remember how much I earned, but the experience was invaluable.

Leadership Development

When I was a junior in high school I was chosen to attend Girls State, a week-long government-in-action learning program sponsored by the American Legion Auxiliary, instilling the basic ideals and principles of American government. ALA units work with local high school educators to identify girls who have demonstrated leadership qualities. Eligible female students are then recommended and selected by sponsoring American Legion Auxiliary units. Girls State "citizens" come together from big cities, small towns, and rural areas to hold ALA Girls State elections, and their varied backgrounds set the stage for a week of spirited, experiential learning.

Developing leadership skills, confidence and action-based understanding of the government process gives young women a lasting foundation for success, both personally and professionally. I was privileged to participate in this prestigious and unique educational program in Salem, Oregon's capital, between my junior and senior years of high school.

My memories were refreshed by the website and I noticed that the program is now called Boys and Girls State, with the boys and girls combined for the training. According to the website, the American Legion Auxiliary's marquee program is one of the most respected and coveted experiential learning programs presented in the United States. The program epitomizes the ALA's mission to honor those who have brought us our freedom through an enduring commitment to developing young people as future leaders grounded in patriotism and Americanism. They become knowledgeable of the democratic process and how our republic form of government works at the state and national levels.

Graduating with Honors

I took my studies seriously and got good grades, which especially pleased my mother. But I must admit that many times when I carried my books home, I did very little homework and just carried them back to school the next day. Marilyn and I rode a school bus to and from school, and I remember when an Estonian family moved into our neighborhood and also rode the bus. I did my best to help Karin and her brother adjust to life in the U.S. That was the first evidence in my life of being drawn to foreign students, which was to become crucial in the plans our Father had for my future.

On May 31, 1956, I was honored as the valedictorian of my class of 104 students. I was presented with a scholarship award for college and a certificate for a year's subscription to Readers' Digest, presented annually by the magazine. Another important celebration was on the horizon for that weekend, our wedding!

A Taste of Things to Come

As detailed in the book I wrote previously about George, our lives were woven together at Newberg High School and the First Christian Church of Newberg. Another inspirational activity we both participated in was summer camp at Wi-Ne-Ma Christian Camp on the beautiful Oregon coast. One time our pastor's wife asked me to send cards or notes to the members of the youth group who were away at camp. I remember writing a note to George, who was a camper, long before we had a romantic relationship that would lead to him becoming my husband. Later we purchased a cottage on the east side of Wi-Ne-Ma Lake that we have owned for more than fifty years, now a treasured family vacation site.

Experiencing Life Together

"And they shall be My people, and I will be their God; and I will give them one heart and one way, that they may fear Me always, for their own good, and for the good of their children after them."

Jeremiah 32:38-39

CHAPTER 7
Two Become One

O ur beautiful wedding was held at First Christian Church in Newberg, Saturday evening June 2, 1956, after my graduation earlier in the week. Many friends and relatives had come from near and far. The dramatic story of George being kidnapped as we were leaving the church was told in detail in his life story. It was well after midnight when he found a phone booth to call me and I didn't see him until the wee hours of Sunday morning. My employer, Cullen T. Rist, CPA, loaned me his car to pick up George at the Portland bus station, the meeting point we had decided on when he was able to call me.

We didn't let the ill-fated occurrence after our wedding ruin our wonderful honeymoon week as we explored special places of interest in Oregon. When we returned, we had just a week to get settled before George had to go to National Guard summer camp for two weeks.

Gibbs District, Rt. 1, Box 67, Newberg, Oregon

Before we were married, George had rented the 100+ acres of farm ground that was part of Mr. Rist's property to expand his farming enterprise. I was working in the accounting office for Mr. Rist, and he asked me to become the housekeeper and the caregiver of his two sons after his wife passed away. After our wedding, we moved into our own suite in his palatial house on the hill and I continued to do the housework and cooking for the family. After about three months of this arrangement, Mr. Rist married a lady he had met in his accounting practice; she became his assistant, and it was best for us to move away. George harvested the crops and discontinued renting the land.

212 W. Illinois St., Newberg, Oregon

Next we purchased our first home, a two-bedroom house in Newberg, from Gene and Charlotte Knopf for $5,500 in the fall of 1956. We had a wringer washing machine on the back porch that served as a utility room, and I hung clothes to dry on a line outside. We were very happy to be in our own home, but it was hard for me to adjust to cooking for just two of us since I had gone from helping with cooking for my family at home to cooking for the Rist family. With my administrative skills and experience, I got a job in the office at Newberg Community Hospital.

For the first two years of our marriage, George worked as an administration and supply technician with the Army National Guard in Portland. He was driving more than 80 miles roundtrip each day. The commute was very demanding and he began to search for a way to get back into some kind of farming enterprise.

And Baby Makes Three

I don't remember the circumstances of us learning that we were expecting our first baby. I'm sure we didn't run down to the drug store and get a pregnancy test kit. I don't know if they even existed back then! I was enjoying my job in the office at the hospital, but George was eager to move on and a baby on the way only added to that desire.

White Brothers Ranch – Route 1, Box 48, Lowden, Washington

He investigated the possibility of working on a ranch in Eastern Oregon and subsequently was hired at White Brothers Ranch, on the state line in Oregon near Lowden, Washington. It was several hours away from Newberg where we had grown up. We loved the ranch managers, Rob and Irma Lee Smith, and their family, and we developed good relationships with the Mexican workers.

One time as I was outside with the crew while George was getting a couple horses saddled up for someone to ride to check on some cattle, I was standing too close when one of the horses got spooked and reared up. On coming down, it landed on my foot and knocked me down. Since I was great with child, George was very concerned about me. Irma Lee drove me to Walla Walla to a clinic where they x-rayed my foot. They told me that my big toe was broken, and I was advised to stay off my foot, but the only treatment was a Band-Aid. Thankfully, there were no other issues from the fall.

Becoming Parents

In July 1958, about a month before the baby was due, I drove back to Newberg by myself to stay with my parents and be ready to go to the hospital when it was time for the baby's birth.

The big day finally arrived and my mother left a message for George at the ranch that I had gone to the hospital. He arrived there just before I was wheeled into the delivery room. I had been in labor for 32 hours and George was concerned that I looked so exhausted. Husbands were not allowed in the delivery room in those days, so he kissed me and went to the waiting room until the baby was born. I was so thankful to know that he was there.

Our firstborn, Daniel George, was born on August 23, 1958. He weighed 7 lbs. 7 oz., and looked like a tiny, little George! Everyone remarked about the likeness when they came to see us. George was proud to be a daddy and thankful that I had survived the ordeal. Our lives would be changed forever as we began the adventure of parenting.

> *"Behold, children are a gift of the Lord, The fruit of the womb is a reward."* Psalm 127:3

Prices for hospitalization had changed a lot since my birth and Marilyn's in 1939 and 1940. For Danny's birth at Newberg Community Hospital the room cost was $15.50 per day for four days, the delivery room was $40, and the nursery was $5 per day for a total cost of $134.30, compared to the total cost for my birth of $47.70.

In a couple weeks, we returned to the ranch and participated in the life of the team. It was a good season in our lives as new parents, and our baby was a welcome addition to the community, but another change was soon to come. Just five months later, when new management took over at the ranch, they brought their own crew and it seemed best for George to find other work. He was interested in an opportunity he had learned about at Double M Herefords with a job description of feeding, fitting and showing beef animals. The Mann family was pleased to have someone with George's experience to fill the position and we moved to Adams, Oregon.

Double M Herefords, Mann Ranch, Adams, Oregon

We first lived in a house in Adams, a village of about 100 people, but before long the original house of the Mann family at the ranch headquarters a few miles from Adams became available. Pat Mann Hopper and her husband Bob had built a lovely new home and were using this older house for housing for employees. We were thankful to have a roof over our heads that did not require a rent payment.

Living at the ranch made it possible for George to go out to do chores about 5:00 a.m. and then come in for breakfast about 7:30. He was always very hungry and his favorite meal was two stacks of pancakes, each with an egg (over easy) on top, plus meat and fruit. He had a break for lunch and often caught a short nap, but then went back to work until after evening chores. Though it was hard work, George got satisfaction from preparing the animals for bull sales and showing them at fairs.

Church Involvement

We continued to fellowship with other believers in the churches in the communities where we lived. We had been faithful members of the church in Newberg during our first years of marriage. After we moved to White Brothers Ranch, we had attended the church in Milton-Freewater.

After moving to Adams, we enjoyed being part of the congregation at the Athena Christian Church. A short time after we started attending they drafted George to be the Sunday school superintendent. We had many friends and enjoyed wonderful times of fellowship. When Pastor Paul Moore and his wife Mabel retired and moved away, Doug Priest became the pastor, and he and his wife Marge became good friends. We didn't realize it at the time, but our association with them would have incredible significance in the future.

One time George and I were asked to be chaperones for the youth group on a camping trip to the Wallowa Mountains out of Enterprise. It was August, but still very chilly in the mountains. The high school boys and girls and their respective chaperones were separated during the whole week except for meals together. That scenario was disconcerting to us as a young married couple and we vowed to never again accept such an assignment.

Adding to Our Family

We had just learned that we were going to have another baby when Danny learned to crawl out of his crib. He had cleverly piled up his stuffed toys in one end to gain enough height to put one leg over the edge and drop down into freedom. He seemed to need less sleep than I did, and his naps were short if he went to sleep at all. I was very tired and always hoping for a nap when Danny slept, but with his new skill I realized that I would no longer be able to close my eyes and trust that he was safe and secure in his crib. Just another challenge of life; but we were happily married and ready to welcome a new baby into the family.

Steven Kent was born February 2, 1960, at St. Anthony's Hospital in Pendleton, weighing in at 8 lb. 5oz. Danny, just 17 months old, quickly adjusted to sharing the attention and learned to love his baby brother. George was very proud of his two sons and I was a busy mother. My expectations that having two children would be twice as much work did not turn out to be true. Baby Steve was more easy-going and cuddly than Danny had been, and I loved my role of being the helpmate for George and caring for our children.

George's work at Double M Herefords was very strenuous with long hours and very little time off. He developed an ulcer and lost a lot of weight. Just when we realized that we had to make a change for the sake of his health, some friends from church, Bill and Doris Coppock, asked him to work on their ranch just outside of Adams during the time their son Larry was finishing his Master's degree at Washington State. When Larry came home George would need to find other work.

We moved back to the village of Adams and loved living across from the post office. That year was wonderfully healing for George, though we knew it wasn't permanent. One time George wanted to see the movie *Ben Hur* that was playing in Pendleton. His brother Bill was working in the area at the time so George asked him to babysit the boys while we went to the movie. It was a very long movie and when we came home about midnight, Danny was sitting up in the rocking chair, bumping it regularly to keep it rocking and Uncle Bill was asleep on the couch! We joked that Danny was taking care of Uncle Bill.

CHAPTER 8
Provision for Our Family

We had lots of good friends during the time we worked for Coppocks and lived in Adams. Among them were Larry and Althadel Beamer, who had four children. Their youngest child, Dick, was the same age as Danny. One time they asked us to stay with their children at their home while they went to a Quarter Horse show and sale in Texas. They were gone for nearly two weeks and we enjoyed caring for our expanded family. The Beamer kids called us George and Janet, and when we returned home our boys started calling us George and Janet. They had to be retrained to call us Mommy and Daddy.

After Larry Coppock returned from college, the job George found for our provision for the next season was with Harris Pine Mills in the mountains out of Pendleton. Unfortunately, it was so far away that he had to leave on Sunday afternoon and didn't get home until Friday evening. The family separation during the week was very challenging for George and for me. I had difficulty sleeping as I carried the weight of responsibility for caring for our little ones with my husband away from home. I was expecting a baby and we knew it would be a hardship for me with him away from home. Doris Coppock was willing to help and my mother wanted to come too.

Baby Sister

While George was away at his job, our daughter Jennifer Lynette was born on August 4, 1961, weighing 8 lbs. 9 oz. She got a warm welcome; the thermometer registered 118 degrees at St. Anthony's Hospital in Pendleton. We didn't have air conditioning at home, nor did the hospital room where I stayed.

Meanwhile, the whole crew at George's workplace was drafted to fight a forest fire. At first, he had no means of communication with the outside world, but sometime later he was able to get out to the Dale Ranger Station and call home. He learned that our daughter had been born and that both the baby and I were doing fine. The extra pay that he earned while fighting the forest fire was enough to pay the hospital and doctor bill, a great blessing for us.

We were already home from the hospital when George saw our baby daughter for the first time. We had chosen her beautiful name before either of our boys was born. I crafted a unique sign with her name in lettering that I hung on the wall above the changing table. Baby Jennie was born two weeks before Danny turned three and Steve was in between – three under three! God gave me the strength to handle the housework and care of our little ones then, and as they grew up, the closeness of age had many more positives than negatives.

300 South St., P.O. Box 732, Enterprise, Oregon

When transitioning from his job at the Coppock Ranch, George had applied for work at the Fish and Wildlife Commission, but they didn't have any openings. Later that year we got a call that a position had opened up in Enterprise. George gratefully accepted their offer and we made the move, happy for a chance to be back together as a family. George's work at the fish hatchery and on maintenance for fish screens was so much more agreeable for him, and living in an area where hunting and fishing were so common was a great blessing.

We found a house to rent in Enterprise which was being remodeled. It took some imagination to see how it was going to be when it was finished, but we were happy to find an affordable place to live. Lawrence Rowe, our landlord and neighbor, was older and retired. He loved our children and they loved him. He played the accordion, and although Danny was not yet school age, this inspired him to want to learn to play the accordion, too. Later on, we bought him one of his own and he took lessons. That hobby has given him much enjoyment through the years.

The northeast corner of Oregon was a beautiful location to live in, but the drawback was the long, cold winter. We liked the house, but the floor plan was problematic. All three bedrooms were down a long hallway off the living room. There was one tiny room in another direction that could have been an office, but in the winter we used it as a bedroom for our children because of the heating challenge. The home's source of heat was an oil-burning stove in the living room. The kitchen and dining area and that little room got nice and warm, but it was impossible to force the heat to go down the long hallway to warm the bedrooms. When it was extremely cold, we joined the three kids in this little room, with Danny and Steve in the top bunk, George and I in the bottom bunk and Jennie in the crib. True togetherness!

The backyard of our home bordered the Wallowa River, which was beautiful but also hazardous. A tall fence had been erected along the perimeter of the backyard, but I had to guard my children carefully when they played outside.

A Tragic Accident

One morning while I was doing my usual housework, I received a call that my parents and Grandpa Peck had been in a horrific car accident. We lived about six hours from the Portland area where the accident happened, but I immediately began thinking through the logistics of making the trip to be with my family in the crisis. I was in the process of washing clothes, and right then the washer overflowed, spilling several inches of water on the floor in the utility room and out into the living room. What to do? I had no way to get in touch with George and I was totally distraught. I called a friend, who graciously came and completely took over cleaning up the mess. She then helped me gather and pack up clothes for the children and me, and we were able to quickly get on the road.

My folks had been on their way to visit Aunt Irene and Uncle Luke in Portland. When making the turn from one street on to another, Daddy had misjudged which lane to take. The car straddled an island in the center of the street, causing it to lurch back and forth out of control and careen off an embankment into a trailer park. Grandpa Peck was thrown out of the car and suffered a serious back injury. Although he recovered to a degree, the amount of time he was laid up without good circulation caused him to later require amputation of one leg. Thankfully, neither my mother nor dad was seriously injured. I was grateful I could stay to help them in the aftermath of the crisis.

More Education for George

George's work assignment was outstanding in many ways, and we had wonderful family time those two years in Enterprise. Although his work was very satisfying, there was no possibility of upward mobility without a college degree. At the usual time young people go on to college after high school, George had not had that opportunity. We began considering further education for him and he decided on Oregon State University. We were determined to sacrifice and do whatever was required for him to get a degree.

I had not worked outside the home since we had children, though I took care of other people's children to supplement our family income. Now it would be necessary for me to be employed with a good salary.

Change of Breadwinner

While we were considering the possible move, we made a trip to Corvallis, the home of OSU, to spy out the land and find work for me. I arranged an appointment with the administrator of Good Samaritan Hospital, Miss Virginia Welch, to talk about my previous hospital experience and availability to work in the office. After a very nice discussion, she said that when we arrived I should submit my application, but I explained that it was imperative I have the assurance of a job as this was the last requirement needed for us to pursue George's educational opportunity. She understood our situation and hired me on the spot, with my work to begin when we were established in Corvallis.

Camellia Apartments, Columbus, Georgia

That summer before the school year began, George received orders for a training program at Fort Benning, Georgia, and we were able to go there together as a family.

Two other couples and their families from Oregon were with us for six weeks while our husbands were training at Fort Benning. Our children were of similar ages and enjoyed playing together. We wives got to know each other better, sometimes cooked meals together and were grateful for the camaraderie in the evenings.

153 Freeman Drive, Corvallis, Oregon

In August 1963, our family of five moved from Enterprise to Corvallis. George became a student at Oregon State and I was employed at Good Samaritan Hospital. The process of moving a family and household is always challenging, but we all knew this move would have great significance for our future. We were very thankful for the leading of the Lord to help us adjust and make new friends wherever we lived.

The house we rented was on the property of Jim and Barbara McClenaghan and had been their home before they built their A-Frame house. Our rent was $55 a month. The property had the feeling of being rural, but it was only a few miles from Corvallis, the home of Oregon State University. The house was small (two-bedroom, one bath) and I could plug the vacuum cleaner into one outlet and vacuum the whole house. The boys slept in a bunk bed and Jennie in a crib in their room.

Starting college at age 27 with three little children, at first George felt out of place among students just out of high school. He soon developed friendships with a couple other older students. Most of his classes were in the morning so he could take care of the kids in the afternoon after I went to work.

Occasionally, if George had an afternoon class or lab, our neighbor Barbara watched the kids. Their three children were about the same ages as our kids. Our little boys had lookalike National Guard uniforms like their daddy, and "military games" were a favorite activity in the neighborhood.

We had both milk delivery and bread delivery in those days. The kids loved it when the bread man handed the loaves to them to take into the house, and they remember him saying, "Don't squeeze."

When Danny started school at Dixie School, he rode the bus and got home before we did and was alone for a short time. Steve and Jennie were cared for at Jack and Jill, a preschool daycare in Corvallis. Jennie remembers that they took naps on mats and when they woke up they were treated to malted milk balls. She enjoyed the outdoor games such as Farmer in the Dell.

As a working mother, my nightmare was what to do when the children had pinkeye or got sick and it was not possible for them to go to their customary school. They had the usual childhood diseases and it was a great blessing to us that a saintly elderly lady in our church, Ruey Beck, graciously offered to watch the children when they were sick.

My sister Marilyn lived in a travel trailer next to our home while she, too, attended Oregon State. She helped out with childcare occasionally, and one painful incident in my memory bank is a time that I was supposed to meet her to take our children while she took an exam. I totally forgot the commitment I had made until much later. I remember sobbing and sobbing that I had been so absorbed in my work at the hospital that I caused Marilyn to miss that important appointment. I really can't remember how we reconnected, but evidently she was allowed to make up the exam at a later time. A cell phone would have been so handy!

My folks lived seventy miles away in Newberg and came to see us quite often. They blessed our children with special gifts such as a red wagon and bicycles, which we couldn't afford during that season when George was in college. Jennie remembers fondly Grandma Peck playing board games like Candyland and Uncle Wiggly with the kids and helping them learn to play by the rules.

George's National Guard unit was training every weekend to prepare for possible deployment to serve in the Vietnam War. The Guard checks provided extra income just when our bank account was running low. Thankfully, the political winds changed and the National Guard was not called up for Vietnam. We had no idea then that one day in the future George would get to preach at the International Church in Hanoi, Vietnam, when we visited missionary colleagues there.

Hospital Assignments

While George was a student at Oregon State, I was the primary wage earner in the family. I worked at Good Samaritan Hospital in multiple roles: admitting clerk, receptionist, cashier, switchboard operator, accounting and data entry, and secretary to the business manager. My first position in the office was as an admitting clerk. George was the caregiver for the children after his morning classes, so I needed to work a late shift.

I found the 3:00 to 11:00 PM shift very difficult. I was too wound up when I got home to go to sleep right away, yet I had to be up early in the morning, and I became physically exhausted. After a short time, the office supervisor and I worked out a modified evening shift from 1:00 to 9:30 PM that gave double coverage during the busy admitting time and was better for our family.

I prepared supper for the family before I left for work, then George served the meal and put the kids to bed. They knew they had to play quietly and be very obedient so their daddy could study. We only occasionally needed an outside person to look after the children. His earnings during the summers and school vacations, plus National Guard pay helped us keep up financially.

It was not long before I was promoted to work in the finance office with customary office hours, 8:00 to 5:00. My skill and loyalty earned me promotions along the way, including my position as Executive Secretary to James R. Mol, the hospital administrator. Among my duties, I took shorthand notes at the board meetings, typed the minutes and handled Mr. Mol's written communications with the board members.

Evolving Office Technology

I was known for my special ability to accurately type numbers. In those days there were manual typewriters and no means of copying. When I typed the monthly financial reports, I used five sheets of carbon paper and typed several reports twice to get the necessary twelve copies for the Board of Directors. There was no possibility of erasing, so making an error required starting over. Understandably, no one wanted to do that task every month so I had noteworthy job security.

I remember when the hospital purchased an IBM Selectric typewriter. Instead of the type bars that swung up to strike the ribbon, the Selectric had a type ball. Later a mimeograph machine, also called a stencil duplicator, was purchased. It worked by forcing ink through a stencil onto the paper. The black ink came in a tube and the whole process was quite messy, but then I could type the reports on stencils and duplicate as many as needed. Again, making a mistake required starting over.

We also had a series of Xerox copy machines, replacing old ones as new models were created. The first ones used a special solution and later the copy medium was black powder. Changing the cartridges for those left me with dirty black hands. The early technology upgrades for the copy machines were very problematic, often out of order, and when they didn't work we had to wait a long time for a repairman.

Faculty Position for George

Even before he completed his degree, George gladly accepted the offer of a position managing the Dairy Cattle Research Center at OSU. He was also an instructor in dairy cattle management and production-related courses. The Dairy Center had a registered Holstein dairy herd of about 275 cows, heifers and research cattle and a 250-acre research farm near the city. George was now busier than ever finishing his coursework for his B.S. degree, directing the work at the Dairy Center and commanding a National Guard company.

916 N.W. 33rd St., Corvallis, Oregon

With that additional salary, we were able to purchase a two-story, four-bedroom home in town. The price was $13,750; the down payment $500. The children could walk or ride their bikes to Harding Elementary School.

It was 1967. Danny was in the 4th grade, Steve in the 2nd grade and Jennie in the 1st grade, and they were latch-key kids after school. We had a strict rule that no other children were allowed to play with them when we were not home. One time when I came home from my work at the hospital, Danny was sitting in the rocking chair with a pasty complexion. He had fallen out of a tree in the backyard and, according to him, *hurt* his arm. A trip to the emergency room revealed that he had actually *broken* his arm.

Our children had more responsibilities than most kids because both George and I worked. All three of our children were taking music lessons; Danny on the accordion, Steve and Jennie on the piano. Steve suffered from serious grass allergies in the spring. We arranged for him to get weekly allergy shots and he rode his bike to Dr. Weller's office, all by himself, to get his shots.

As I was filling up my car with fuel at $2.97 per gallon the other day, I thought about the price of fuel when we lived in Corvallis. Gasoline was quite regularly 29 cents a gallon, even less when there was a price war. We could get hamburgers at Bob's Burgers for 25 cents each, and they were made with real meat. Times have changed!

Embarrassing Incident

During basketball season, we all enjoyed an inexpensive family activity of attending OSU games. One time our misplaced enthusiasm caused an awkward situation. Our little daughter Jennie, just three years old, needed to go to the bathroom. It was a very exciting time in the game, and believe it or not, we dispatched Steve, not yet five, to accompany her to the restroom that was nearby. He was directed to stand outside and wait for her. Just then, rousing shouts indicated something thrilling was happening, and just for a minute he abandoned his post to see what was so exciting.

As we pieced the story together, during that critical minute, Jennie came out of the bathroom, couldn't find Steve or anyone she knew, and realized that she was lost! Though Steve quickly went back to his post and waited, she didn't come out, and he came back to us without her. By that time, we realized what a dreadful mistake we had made and we went looking for her. Meanwhile, a couple OSU cheerleaders saw the little lost child crying and came to her rescue. They took her down to their area near the players, and shortly an announcement came through the sound system: "The parents of Jennie Meyers are lost!" Oh, how embarrassing for us as those parents!

This scenario happened more than fifty years ago. In our current society, it would be unheard of to send two little tykes off by themselves to the bathroom. Thinking back on it, I'm ashamed to think that I was so caught up in a basketball game that I put my children at risk. I'm grateful that the story had a happy ending as we collected our little daughter happily enjoying treats given to her by her doting rescuers.

Summer Fun

Childcare for the summers was a challenge. We managed the school year just fine but couldn't leave the children without a caregiver during their school vacation. One summer George had a six-week military assignment at Fort MacArthur in San Pedro, California. His sister Dorothy who lived in San Bernardino invited our kids to join their family for that time, which was a great blessing for us. George was able to make the 80-mile drive to spend time with them some weekends. I continued to work at the hospital and although I missed my family, I was grateful the kids had that fun opportunity.

Another summer, our friends Merle and Marilyn Peters, from Banks, Oregon, came to stay with us. Merle was working to finish his Master's degree at OSU and didn't want to be separated from his family for such a long time. The Peters' two sons and daughter were about the same ages as our kids. Marilyn took care of their children and ours, prepared meals, and helped with laundry and other housework, a great blessing for me. The kids had fun together and the cooperative venture was a win-win for both families.

Farm Kids in Town

Even though we lived in town, both George and I wanted our children to have the opportunity to participate in 4-H. Steve and Dan both remember that their 4-H Livestock Club was called the Blueribbonaires. They would go to monthly meetings out in rural Philomath, led by Fran Gerding. A couple things Steve recalled were animal judging and learning cuts of meat. Jennie's 4-H project was sewing, a good thing for a young girl to learn. She has some memories of going to meetings and making a cloth tote bag and an apron.

Dan remembers that they initially got involved with the Blueribbonaires through the Faxon family from Suburban Christian Church. In Dan's words,

> Jay Faxon was just a bit older than I and we would sometimes coordinate getting to and from the Evergreen Road 4-H meetings via the Faxons. We had sheep at least two summers which we kept at the fairgrounds. Steve and I would faithfully ride our bikes out through the OSU dairy property to the fairgrounds to feed our sheep. I named my first sheep after my grandmother Alice. (Janet: I'm sure my mom was honored). I later had a sheep named Wilma, but my first sheep was the best one. The next two years

didn't go so well. One year our sheep were too heavy and the next year they were too light. But it was all a good experience.

I was disappointed that George had so many irons in the fire that he didn't have time to coach our sons with their sheep project, even though he had been in 4-H himself and was very knowledgeable in raising sheep and other animals.

A reporter at the local newspaper, the *Gazette-Times*, did an article on Dan and Steve's sheep-raising operation at the fairgrounds. The article was complete with a picture and gave a nice rundown of their efforts at being farm kids while living in the city.

More Changes

Just before Christmas in 1969 we added a foster daughter to our family. Nancy Macavoy was a senior at Corvallis High School; her twin sister Susan was in college and living with an elderly lady. We knew their brother Jim through mutual friends, and he reached out for our help when their mother died unexpectedly, leaving Nancy without a home. Jim was in the Peace Corps, but besides him the girls had no immediate family and we were happy to include Nancy as part of ours.

Our family was doing well, the children were all progressing in school, and our financial picture had improved with two sources of income. George and I decided that it was a good time for him to press on to get a Master's degree. Even though he was extraordinarily busy with all of his responsibilities as a professor and manager of the Dairy Cattle Research Center, we never doubted that it was a good decision.

7616 Deerhaven Drive, Corvallis, Oregon

We searched for a home in the country to give the children a more rural life. We were pleased to find a home eight miles southwest of Corvallis, with four acres of land. The property did not have a barn, but we developed a plan early on to construct one. The three bedrooms were all on one level, and though smaller than our 33rd Street house in town, it was newer and very beautiful. George's mom came to visit for a month to make curtains and drapes. She had sewn drapes for our house in town as well and seemed to get real satisfaction and enjoyment from doing a much-needed project to help us.

It was while we were living in the country that we received the motivation to pursue international work. The stories of our mission assignments are told in other chapters.

CHAPTER 10
Our First International Venture

The year was 1971. George had finished his Master's degree and was achieving success in his career path. We were fulfilled in many ways, yet we also felt a kind of "holy restlessness" for something in our future that would have eternal value. George's assignment as faculty advisor for the Oregon State Dairy Club had given our whole family special times with foreign students. The Holy Spirit began to stir in both George and me a desire to investigate possibilities with an international scope.

Coinciding with these considerations, we received a personal letter from our friends Doug and Marge Priest, missionaries with Christian Missionary Fellowship in Ethiopia. Doug had been our pastor during the time we lived in the Adams/Athena area in Eastern Oregon. As part of our giving for the Lord's work, we were sharing in their financial support. They were coming home on furlough and were planning to share the need for more workers in Wellega Province with any couple who would be willing to consider joining them.

We had the chance to visit with them in a camping setting and to discuss the opportunities and constraints. When we were alone, George and I talked about the dynamics of moving thousands of miles away from our families. Our conclusion was that we could do it, but we couldn't force our decision upon our children, who were 12,

11 and 9 at that time. It would require putting them in the boarding school for missionary children in Addis Ababa. After learning about Good Shepherd School, our kids expressed enthusiasm about that possibility, which was the breakthrough we needed to begin exploring the steps it would take to transition our family to the mission field.

Preparation for Service

After our family decision was made in 1972 to move to Ethiopia, I left the prestigious position and good salary at Good Samaritan Hospital to give my life to mission service. Our lovely home in Corvallis on four acres in the country sold for $32,000. We were thankful that we had been able to purchase property near Wi-Ne-Ma Christian Camp on the Oregon Coast as a permanent place for our family to call home. For the next year, we were a family of five in a 768-square-foot cottage. Real togetherness! That year of preparation for our overseas adventure, George and the kids worked on remodeling our cottage, including putting flooring in the attic, which doubled the living space. The upstairs area was used as a dormitory-like sleeping area for the children.

Impact, the communication piece of Christian Missionary Fellowship, had sent out a "Call for Help" in 1970, and two years later the headline was "A Call to Praise." Our family, the Chamberlains and the Liles family had answered the call. The *Impact* gave a good overview of our qualifications and stated, "When funds for personal, field and outgoing budgets are committed, the Meyers family will depart for Ethiopia, hopefully in the summer of 1973."

This mission agency, now called CMF International, is a missionary outreach of the Christian Churches and Churches of Christ in the U.S. CMF selected Ethiopia as a field of missionary endeavor on the basis of governmental stability, openness to Western missionaries and evidence of winnable people. Kiramu station, where we would be located, was established in May 1965. Evangelism, education, and medicine were the methods of ministry to the people. The mandate of making disciples was helped through the government-required elementary school system and approved clinic program at each station.

Some local authorities were found to be uncooperative and resistant to the mission's strategies, believing them to be a threat to their power and authority over the people. Established cultural patterns and traditions often conflicted with Christian teaching. It would be necessary to spend a lot of time in building and maintaining facilities: houses, storage buildings, clinics, schools, water systems, electrical systems, generators, pumps, motors, plumbing, and vehicles. Language and cultural barriers, an unresponsive Muslim population nearby, and the separation of families with children in boarding school were very real problems. Were we up to the challenges?

Our Travels

To gather our prayer and financial support, our schedule during 1972 included several missionary conferences as well as presentations in congregations. A major goal of the year was to identify the people and churches that would be our provision for our years on the mission field. George and I traveled across the U.S. to places where we knew people and where Christian Missionary Fellowship had contacts that might be interested in learning about the opportunity to help fulfill the Great Commission by supporting our family. We participated in two Junior Camps and were thrilled by the interest expressed by the children in sharing the love of Jesus with others in a far-off land. It was gratifying to us that so many people were interested in our plans and willing to participate.

During the preparation year, Dan was a freshman at Nestucca High School, Steve was in the 7th grade and Jennie in the 6th grade. The schools had fewer students than where they had been in Corvallis, but it was a good transition to Good Shepherd School, where they would attend as day students for the first year; then they would become boarding students.

George and I were privileged to do some valuable theological study with missionary statesmen, Ralph Winter, C. Peter Wagner, and other trained missiologists at the U.S. Center for World Mission in Pasadena, California. While we were taking that training we were also getting better acquainted with Ed and Bertha Chamberlain, who would be our neighbors at Tosse, the next station over when we lived on the plateau in Ethiopia.

Another goal of that year was to acquire the clothing and supplies we would need for the next three years. It took imaginative planning to think about what sizes of clothing the kids would need as they grew. The plan was to pack those things into 55-gallon drums and ship them on ahead by sea. We had received encouraging tips from CMF missionaries on things to take that were not available in the country, or if available, the quality was poor. Our small living space got even smaller as barrels were brought into the house, and the whole family participated in innovative packing.

Cultural Adaptation

As a family, we researched and studied the culture of Ethiopia. We learned that there are more than 80 different ethnic groups, each with its own language, culture, customs, and traditions. The national dish, *injera 'b wut*, is the staple food for Ethiopians. The pancake-like injera is made from the grain *teff*, unique to Ethiopia, although it is now being grown in several states in the U.S., including Oregon. Teff is grown in their fields and harvested in methods much like was done in Bible times. The tiny seeds are ground into flour by the ladies and made into a batter, which is allowed to ferment for a few days. Then the batter is poured onto a hot clay *mitad* and cooked over a hot fire. The result looks like a gigantic spongy pancake.

No utensils are required to eat this dish. Eating with your hands from a communal dish is the norm. A piece of injera is torn off and used to scoop up different types of sauce called *wut*, usually made from vegetables, split peas or lentils, spiced with *berebere*, a hot pepper spice. Berebere is made of dried red hot peppers, herbs, spices, dried onions and garlic. At special times the sauce might include chicken, lamb or goat.

Ethiopia is famous for its *buna* (coffee), celebrated with a special coffee ceremony. While guests are chatting, the preparer roasts coffee beans over the fire and the enticing aroma fills the room. Then she pounds and crushes the roasted beans into a powder in a wooden mortar and pestle, and puts the coffee grounds and hot water into a coffee pot called a *jebena*. When finished, the strong black liquid is poured into little cups, often with salt and butter added, and three rounds are served to the guests.

The traditional Ethiopian costume is made of woven cotton. Both men and women wear a *gabbi*, similar to a light blanket, cleverly wrapped around their whole body. The costume of the women is truly beautiful. Although their everyday dress may be well-worn and the color of the muddy water in the creek, I was amazed on special occasions to see the women emerge from their grass-roofed, mud-walled, dirt-floored *gojo* in a bright white dress with a colorful border and a *netulla* (shawl) draped around their head and shoulders. How did they do it?

Language Learning

Amharic, the national language, was not offered in the United States, so we knew it would be the first thing we would have to tackle when we got to the field. Our study at the Cooperative Language Institute in Addis Ababa would include lectures by missionaries who had spent many years in the country. The decision was made that I should study the Oromo language of the Galla people to be able to communicate with the ladies who didn't know Amharic.

The first step would be to learn the *Fidel*, the Amharic alphabet, which has 231 characters, none of which looked at all familiar. The Ethiopian children learn it by a sing-song method in their first year of school. Fortunately, both languages use the same Fidel with only a few exceptions. It is mostly a spoken language, with only the Bible and a hymnbook in print at that time.

PICTURES – A

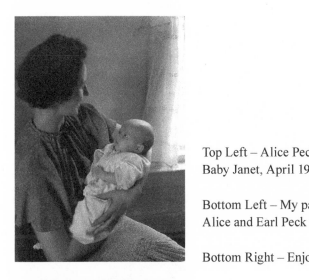

Top Left – Alice Peck with
Baby Janet, April 1939

Bottom Left – My parents,
Alice and Earl Peck

Bottom Right – Enjoying some sunshine

Sidewalk
smiles

And off
I go!

Down on
the farm

Marilyn and I all dressed up   Snow day fun

Our family

My father's parents, Harry and Cynthia Peck

Grandpa Peck, who inspired my love for berry picking

My mother (second from right) and her family

Inset – Grandpa and Grandma Baughman on the farm

Our family with Baby Lyle

My siblings and I with Liberty Bell replica

We loved our baby brother!

Our family home in Newberg, Oregon

A family gathering with Weilers

My 8th grade graduation

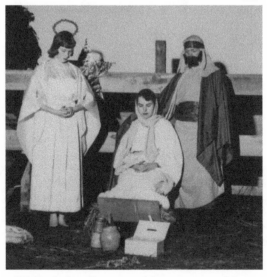

While dating George and I were cast as Mary
and Joseph in a Live Nativity Scene

Sharing our wedding cake

Our wedding day, June 2, 1956

Danny holding Baby Steve   Jennie's parasol

Our kids at Wi-Ne-Ma Beach

Our children loved to play with the nativity set

Cooling off in the sprinkler

Celebrating George's graduation from Oregon State

Missionary Adventures
in Africa

"And He was saying to them, 'The harvest is plentiful, but the laborers are few; therefore, beseech the Lord of the harvest to send out laborers into His harvest.'"

Luke 10:2

CHAPTER 11
Life in Ethiopia

W e arrived in the capital, Addis Ababa, on July 4, 1973, and were met at the airport by Tom Kirkpatrick, the mission administrator, and the Ona Liles family. For the first two weeks, we stayed at Good Shepherd School, where our children would be day students that fall. Jennie's house parents in the junior girls' dorm the following year would be Gordon and Daisy Johnson, also affiliated with Christian Missionary Fellowship. They were spending two weeks at Tosse in the countryside when we arrived and offered for us to stay in their little apartment at the dorm. We had become acquainted with them and their three-year-old daughter Christy while we were in the States preparing for our time in Ethiopia.

After two weeks we moved into our own house about one-half mile off the main road, under some trees in a nice rural setting adjacent to a dairy farm with Holstein cows, scenes very familiar to us. It was a big adjustment to accept the need for guards, day and night, and for me to have household help. The mission strongly recommended that we retain Dawit, the girl who had worked for the Baptist mission family who lived there before us.

As I got acquainted with Dawit, who knew no English, we both adapted to communicating with sign language. Her duties were washing and hanging the clothes, ironing, sweeping, mopping and waxing the floors, and washing windows. She scrubbed the vegetables and soaked them in bleach and washed the fruit and eggs. Her work made it possible for me to keep up with correspondence and language study.

The language school we attended was planning to move to a location very near our home, but we were disappointed to learn that the move had been postponed and we had to drive across the city for the first semester. At first, the hours were 9:00 to 5:30 with two hours off for lunch break, but they changed from 9:00 to 3:30, with only half an hour to eat lunch. It was so much better for us to get home earlier. After the move, we were able to walk home for lunch. One of the first things we learned was that in both Gallinya and Amharic our thank-you phrases to our support partners were literally translated, "May God repay you for me!"

Our arrival was during the rainy season and it rained morning, afternoon or night, or all three! At the elevation of 8,000 feet, it always felt damp and chilly. The only heat in our house was from the fireplace, which warmed us only if we sat in front of it. One time when George was not feeling well, after taking a bath he got into bed with his coat on! It was challenging to keep up with drying our clothes on the clothesline outside. We realized that we would have to buy some racks to dry clothes in the house, an abomination according to George. Apparently drying racks were normal in the house where he grew up. He would have to adjust or there would be no dry clothes to wear!

Evidence of Famine

While we were still living in the city, we took a trip to the Awash Game Park, 220 kilometers (137 miles) south and east of Addis. The climate was vastly different at the lower elevation in that part of the country. The drive took more than four hours on a road that had been gravel until one year earlier, shared with horse-drawn taxis, people walking, and cattle being driven. It was hot and dry there, only 500 meters (1670 feet) above sea level. The severe dry season had caused the death of many animals and some people.

Some of the scenes on the way were really pathetic; naked children in the middle of the road, begging for food, and skeletons of cattle that had died from hunger and thirst. We tried to get pictures, but we had to be very careful to not offend the people. Little boys liked to have their pictures taken, but women and girls didn't, and men sometimes would try to take the camera away. It helped us to realize that the people around Addis who seemed so poor were really quite well off by African standards.

The Village of Kiramu

While we were in language school our kids were day students at Good Shepherd School. After finishing language school, George studying Amharic for nine months and I studying Gallinya for four months, we moved as a family to Kiramu. Our children were with us for the summer and then they traveled back to GSS and became boarding students. We were thankful for grace to endure the separation as a family and looked forward to our visits with the kids at school and their visits to the countryside.

In response to frequently asked questions about what life was like for us in this country, we wrote to our partners as follows:

The old ways are beginning to give way slightly as Ethiopia pushes from its age-old customs into a modern era. Political upheavals of the past few years have had some impact on change. Under the new system, *Ethiopia Tikdem* (which means self-reliance), nearly all property and land has been nationalized.

Our life in the village of Kiramu is quiet and simple compared to life in America. Our home and area of work is about 160 air miles northwest of Addis Ababa, just south of the Blue Nile River. We usually travel by Missionary Aviation Fellowship planes, and the trip to Addis Ababa from Kiramu takes one hour and 15 minutes. Occasionally we drive the Land Rover, which takes two full days.

In December 1973, we drove into Addis Ababa to do some purchasing of school supplies and also to bring Steve and Jennie home for their Christmas vacation. We passed through the lowlands where very few people live because of the tsetse flies and malaria. In one area a group of Shankilla (Gumuz) people have established a village. Their skin is jet black and the women wear only a leather skirt. The boys are naked until they are about 10-12 years old. Many of these people have trachoma eye infections so we usually spend about a half hour treating sore eyes each time we pass through.

For those willing to make their homes in this climate, life is quite simple. The men burn off the bamboo forest, make holes with a pointed stick and plant corn. When the rains begin in March or April, they relax and watch their crops grow. They grow enough to live and build a grass house but display no sign of wealth. The other main task before harvesting is to guard the fields to keep away the baboons, monkeys and wild hogs. A wife can be purchased for about $100 these days but a .22 rifle will sell for about $300. As recently as 20 years ago, a wife could be purchased for an equivalent of five pounds of salt!

We have five students in our school from the lowlands north of us along the Blue Nile River. We are acquainted with two of the local men who used to go into these areas and capture people to take up to the highlands for sale to the Islamic slave traders. These people, who have been oppressed for centuries, make no attempt to improve their lot in life, even though slave trading ceased about 25 years ago.

Kiramu Clinic

One of the busiest places in the area was the clinic at the Kiramu mission station. About 1,000 patients per month were treated by Erketa, the national health worker. Leprosy, tuberculosis, parasites, typhoid, typhus, venereal diseases, malaria, and pneumonia were among the most common ailments of the patients who came. Accidental injuries, eye conditions, and difficult deliveries were also taken care of at the clinic. Sometimes patients were carried on a pole stretcher many hours or even days to receive treatment.

George and I discussed the pros and cons of allowing our daughter Jennie (not yet a teenager) to observe childbirths in the clinic. Most of the births in the community were attended by traditional birth attendants, so only very complicated deliveries happened in our clinic. We didn't want her to be traumatized, but she decided that she would like to watch and we agreed to let her. She has commented that she was thankful to have that opportunity and it caused her to be incredibly grateful for the excellent medical care she received when it was time for the birth of her own children.

The first time Erketa was on vacation we had determined that the clinic would be closed since our permission to be in the country did not include medical work. But people brought their sick family members to the clinic and stood there anxiously waiting for someone to show mercy. George went to tell the people waiting that the clinic was closed until Erketa came back. But just then he noticed that our neighbors had brought their three-month-old baby who was struggling to breathe.

When we had first arrived at Kiramu, I was present at the clinic when this baby boy was born, making him very special to me. Father God used that baby to change our minds about treating the sick in spite of the constraints. George came to the house and talked to me, and together we determined that we could not let that special baby die when we had medicine that could help him. We were convicted that we must have mercy and treat him and also others who might not survive until Erketa returned. I am very thankful for the training and experience George had with animal medicine that helped us as we prayerfully treated the most serious cases.

Regassa

Our clinic nurse Erketa was helped by a fellow named Regassa, whose duties included organizing the patients coming in and out, dispensing oral medications, and cleaning the clinic at the close of the day. Another responsibility of his was to come to our house to get the rabies vaccine, which had to be kept in the refrigerator. When a person was bitten by a rabid animal, the remedy at that time was a series of injections over a period of time.

Regassa's reputation was less than stellar; he was known as a drunk and had avoided the expense of a proper marriage, bypassing the bride price system by bringing a lady into his life that everyone referred to as his "cooker." Very early one morning the dog barked incessantly and George went to our bedroom window to see what the problem was. Regassa was afraid of the dog, but he ventured into the yard far enough to shout an appeal to George. He wanted us to bring the Land Rover to Kiramu village to transport his wife to the clinic to give birth. We were glad to help him, and the birth of the baby seemed to legitimize his relationship with the baby's mother and improve his standing in the community.

Culture and Customs

We learned a lot of things NOT to do in that country. For instance, it was not good to have little girls play with dolls, as is common in America. We found out that both the Galla and Gumuz ethnic groups believed that dolls were babies that had had the life sucked out of them by evil spirits. And some of the gestures that are common in our culture are taboo, even obscene in that culture. All of our cultural study in preparation for moving to Ethiopia was well worth it.

A funny thing happened when we flew to Yasow in the lowlands among the Gumuz to visit our colleagues, Ray and Effie Giles. The people were curious about the foreigners, often examining our clothing and wanting to touch and see way more than we wanted them to see. Their men do not have hair on their arms or legs. Especially the children loved to rub the hair on George's arms. When we packed for Ethiopia, I had taken some nylon stockings in my luggage, not knowing if or when I would have occasion to wear them. I learned how valuable they were to keep the flies off my legs when my hands were occupied, such as when I was hanging up clothes. I had the idea to wear them to the lowlands for just that purpose. Soon after our arrival, a little girl who was evaluating everything about my person noticed that I had two sets of skin on my legs. She could actually pinch and pull one away from the other. In an amazing bush communication system, that news traveled far and wide. All day long people came to check out the two skins on my legs!

A Lesson in Psychology

Homeschooling was not popular when we went to Ethiopia in 1973. Had our children been younger, we definitely would have educated them at home, but they were already in junior high and high school and in many subjects, especially math, ahead of my capability. George could have taught them, but he had many assignments in ministry, and we had decided even before going to Ethiopia that it was best to take advantage of the wonderful provision of Good Shepherd School for their education.

The first time we visited our children at GSS where they were boarding students was a shock and trial for George and me. We weren't prepared for their response to our visit. They came and greeted us, spent only a few minutes with us, then hurried off to play with their friends. It felt to us like we were visiting someone in prison, with only a limited time of connection.

What we hadn't learned in advance and later found out from professionals was that their reaction was a mechanism to avoid getting reattached, as they still remembered the pain of separation. When they came home for their spring break for only ten days, they didn't settle in and reconnect; however, when they came for the summer (2½ months) it was totally different. We loved having them with us at Kiramu and they enjoyed being a part of our work.

An Outing with the Kids

In March of 1975 when we were in Addis Ababa visiting our children at GSS, we had an opportunity for a family getaway about 2½ hours south of the capital at a natural hot spring called Sodere. There was an Olympic-size swimming pool fed by the hot springs. The water was almost too hot to enjoy swimming, but we went in anyway. We camped in a tent and enjoyed time with our children and other CMF missionary friends.

One evening just as we were finishing eating, a strong wind came up. I hurried to finish washing the dishes as it became windier and started to rain. Just as I walked away from the campsite to throw out the dishwater, the folding metal utility table we had been using was picked up by the wind, flew through the air and whacked me squarely in the back. It knocked the wind out of me but didn't knock me down. We realized that it was really fortunate that it came at me squarely; a corner of it could have broken my back or even worse. Among other complications, we had car trouble and had to return to Addis by bus. Our vacations were never particularly relaxing and quite often our guardian angels had to work overtime!

CHAPTER 12
Travel and Transition

J esus told many parables, earthly stories with heavenly meaning, using as examples the common things of rural life. These took on added meaning for us as we associated them with the culture of Ethiopia. Plowing, preparing the soil, sowing the seeds, cutting and bundling the stalks, threshing, and winnowing were being done without benefit of machinery, in the same way as during Bible times. The admonition in I Timothy 5:18 about not muzzling the ox while he was trampling out the grain was quickened to us as we watched the harvest process.

One of George's concerns was the lack of interest by many mission organizations in helping to increase food production as part of their work. It had been estimated at the time we were there that about one million people had died or been seriously affected by famine in four provinces of Ethiopia. Missionaries introduced medicine and health care that was a great blessing to the people; however, the resulting increase in population in the arid areas was beyond their food production capability and led to food shortages.

George's background in agriculture and animal science was a great benefit to the community and our ministry. We were grateful to have shared in the tremendous task of sharing the Gospel with the people on the plateau. We thanked God for the times of reaping and harvesting that followed the preparation of hearts and sowing of the seed.

Special Visitors

On the last leg of their trip to Israel in 1974, my parents spent the month of December with us at Kiramu. Their arrival time in Addis Ababa coincided with our need to bring Dan back to Kiramu to recover from hepatitis. He was on the Good Shepherd School cross-country running team, which was very taxing at the elevation of 7,700 feet in Addis Ababa. We thought that his overexertion might have contributed to his catching the virus. Although he had a mild case, he was jaundiced and extremely weak, and the doctor wanted him to have at least a month of rest and recuperation.

I was glad for the chance to give Dan some needed TLC, but it was a challenging time for me to manage his need for isolation and at the same time show my parents our life and work. Hepatitis is highly contagious and I was very concerned that my folks might contract the disease. We already were boiling our water for drinking, but during that month I also carefully boiled all of the dishes and utensils used by Dan.

George and our guard Getahune had some tasks lined up for Daddy to do to help him feel a sense of purpose. We have a picture of him swinging a hammer on a construction project. He enjoyed getting to know the nationals, but the language barrier was extremely frustrating for him and George was not always available to translate.

One of the tasks my parents did to help us was counting and rolling the *doombaloes*, the coins people used to pay for their treatment and medicine at the clinic. They are the color of a U.S. penny, but nearly as big as a quarter. The value of five dollars was rolled in a page from a Readers' Digest and would eventually get to the bank. One day they rolled $600 worth, the proceeds from ten days at the clinic.

On purpose, we kept the prices very low, but we also knew that if the people didn't pay anything for the medicine, they didn't consider it valuable and often didn't follow the advice of Erketa in taking it. They always begged for a *murphy* (an injection); somehow they believed that the best medicine came through a needle. Especially children in the U.S. will do almost anything to *not* get a shot, but the opposite was true there.

Miraculous Protection

Our air travel in Ethiopia was challenging because of the high elevation, requiring exceptional skill by the pilots. At one point on the flight from Addis Ababa to Wellega Province, the ground would disappear as we traveled out over the Great Rift Valley. We booked a flight with MAF to take my folks back to Addis Ababa after their month with us. Since we were not able to travel with them, Tom Kirkpatrick, the CMF administrator, agreed to help them catch the international airline that would take them back to Oregon.

A scary and extremely dangerous occurrence happened on their way to Addis. Just before the Great Rift Valley part of the trip, the engine of the single-engine plane sputtered and quit. The pilot was David Stavely, our British friend, who managed to make an emergency landing in a field. In the course of his investigation of what had caused the engine problem, he suspected contamination of the fuel. He strained the remaining fuel and found evidence of sabotage; some insects had apparently been put in the tank.

He was able to start the engine, take off from the makeshift runway, and fly back to the capital. We were unaware of this frightening turn of events until they were back in Addis and MAF could contact us on the radio. We all praised the Lord for the miraculous timing, place to land, and extraordinary expertise of the pilot. Minutes later they would have been over the valley floor, thousands of feet below!

Family Separation

George and I experienced empty-nest syndrome way too early in life by choosing for our children to be educated at the boarding school. We saw them about every six weeks and they joined us in the countryside during school vacations. The next stage was even more challenging when Dan left for the States to enroll at Oregon State University in August 1975. The summer before he left, we planned a special vacation with our children in Kenya. We had a great time visiting several game parks and watching wild animals in their natural habitat. It was truly a memorable time before our family would be separated and living on two continents.

Political Disturbances

When we were researching Ethiopia as part of our preparation to join the CMF missionary team, the public relations narrative referred to 13 months of sunshine (due to their calendar system) and the country as being the most politically stable country in sub-Saharan Africa. However, we had not been there long before there were signs of serious political instability. At the beginning it seemed patriotic, offering hope of justice for the poor, but it soon became clear that it was the beginning of a Marxist revolution which ultimately overthrew Emperor Haile Selassie and contributed to his death.

While we were in Addis Ababa to meet my parents and bring Dan back to Kiramu, we had stayed at the Baptist Guest House near the campus of Good Shepherd School. We actually heard the machine gun bursts that executed 60 high-level government officials and military officers. Although the perpetrators had promised a bloodless revolution, it escalated into one of the bloodiest military takeovers in modern African history.

We would hear rumors of uprisings in Addis Ababa where our children were boarding students and they would hear of disturbances in the countryside and be concerned for our welfare. We were very uneasy about being separated from our children during those times.

Travel Is Hazardous

We learned of a bloody incident when the plane was on its way to Tosse, the station where our CMF colleagues lived. The plane hit a large bird that broke out the windscreen on the right side and cracked it across the left side. The passenger in the seat next to the pilot was actually uninjured even though he was splattered with blood from the bird. The impact damaged the cowling on the leading edge of the wing and it was rendered unable to fly. MAF was able to make arrangements to send another plane with a new windshield and a mechanic to install it on the damaged plane.

In April, Steve and Jennie came home for ten days for Easter vacation. We were looking forward to having them with us, even though the time was short. As the plane was landing on our airstrip, it broke a brake line, did a ground loop and smashed up one of the tail wings. Our airstrip was too short and required a 35-degree dogleg to gain enough length for the pilots to land and take off. At the elevation of nearly 8,000 feet, there wasn't much margin for error, so we were really grateful that no one was hurt. George helped the pilot remove the front and rear wings and send them overland by Land Rover to Addis Ababa for repair. This raised the number to four of the six (MAF) planes being out of service for various reasons at that time.

A month after that accident, a mechanic came to do basic repairs on the crippled airplane, and later a pilot came to fly it as far as Jimma, where the remaining things in need of fixing would be taken care of before putting it into regular service. The mechanic was *my* guest for two days – a bit awkward since George was gone, but not as outrageous as the time Marge Priest hosted the MAF pilot and *not* her husband Doug on their wedding anniversary.

Another pilot had an accident down in southern Ethiopia that tore off a wing and did severe damage to the plane. It was caused by a freak storm at the end of the airstrip just as he landed. He had three children on board, but fortunately no one was injured.

Grueling Trips

When it was possible to drive to Addis Ababa from Kiramu in the Land Rover, it took two full days. The first day was on entirely unimproved mountain roads which could only be traveled in the dry season and even then only in four-wheel-drive. We stayed the first night in Nekempte and continued on to Addis for about 225 miles on narrow mountain roads. The last 75 miles was asphalt, but most of the way it was gravel. Buses and trucks, plus donkey caravans and people driving cattle and horses made that trip incredibly strenuous. We made that nine-hour journey together several times and we loved to visit our children and friends in the city, but the trip to get there was exhausting and dangerous.

Traveling with the Kids

On one occasion we did the reverse of that trip to take our children home with us to Kiramu for their summer vacation. Just before we left, George bought five apples in the market, an expensive luxury in that country. We discussed along the way whether to each eat an apple or to divide them up. The consensus was to cut one apple into slices to share and have a treat for five days. To this day, I hate to see a child take an apple, so plentiful in our state, eat a few bites around the middle and throw the rest away.

Temporary Dorm Parents

George served on the board of directors of Good Shepherd School during our time at Kiramu, which required trips to Addis Ababa for meetings. Those trips made it possible for us to visit our kids at the school. Our good friends, Gordon and Daisy Johnson, left for the U.S. before school was out in 1975 because Daisy was seriously ill. Her sickness was later diagnosed as typhoid fever. We were asked to step in as dorm parents during the last two weeks of school that year.

Back to the U.S.

In addition to missing our son Dan, who had returned to the States for college, the political upheaval was weighing heavily on us. We began to plan to return to the States for furlough in mid-July of 1976. One morning in April, we were notified on the radio that my dad was seriously ill and in the hospital. That news and the intensifying political instability caused us to move our departure date up to June.

Entering Ethiopia had required a protocol of procedures but getting permission for our family to leave the country was an even more complex process. George began trying to get exit visas for our family in April for the proposed departure after the kids were out of school. In an apparent attempt to get a bribe, he was accused of starting a forest fire in an area he had never been in. It took two months, multiple letters, and numerous trips to government offices for George to obtain the required documents for our departure.

We had made many wonderful friends both in our mission community and among the nationals. We trusted that the seeds we had sown would be watered by others and that there would be eternal results. There were tearful times of saying goodbye to our Ethiopian friends, especially because we didn't know whether we would be able to return.

CHAPTER 13
Defining the Next Step

Our Dairy Farm Venture

When George told me that he loved me enough that he would even let me milk his cows, he really meant it! Before we left Ethiopia in June of 1976, a dairy operation at Othello near Moses Lake, Washington, had been identified as our next step. I told the whole story in George's book in the chapter "Re-Entry Challenges," but I want to share my perspective and some of my experiences. We moved to the farm in mid-August, a few months after returning from our first missionary journey, after we had reported on our work in Ethiopia to the churches and individuals who had been our financial support partners. Because of the risk of censorship, the news we had shared from Ethiopia was sketchy and we purposed to fill in the gaps as we met with people face to face.

The dairy enterprise was a family venture with George's brother Bill and his wife Lorre as partners in the purchase. They had a farm in Newberg, Oregon, which they were willing to use as part of the down payment, and we agreed to invest our life savings into the venture. Dan, Steve and Jennie were all involved in helping with the work in this huge operation with 350 Holstein cows and 160 acres of farmland. Bill took on the responsibility of raising and harvesting the hay and grain, and George focused on feeding the animals, artificial insemination and the business affairs. Steve drove the tractor to scrape the manure out of the loafing shed and Jennie took special interest in the baby calves, feeding them with the oversize baby bottles. Steve and Jennie were *new kids* at Royal City High School and they completed their farm assignments before and after school. Dan chose to postpone his studies at Oregon State University for a season to lend his invaluable assistance.

Dan and I shared the milking shifts, starting early in the morning and finishing late at night. With a herd of more than 300 cows, there were only a few hours in the day when no cows were being milked. We had a double-8 herringbone milking parlor with state-of-the-art milking machines, eight cows on each side for a total of 16 in each group. The cows were not fastened when they came in to eat their allotment of grain, which was computer matched with the tag around their neck and based on their milk production. The milker's responsibility was to wash each cow's udder and attach the milking machine. The cows usually finished eating at about the same time the machine automatically came off when they were milked out.

Unique Dilemma

One night when I was alone on the late shift, I had a dreadful experience. One of the cows collapsed and died just as her milking machine came off. Besides being a shock to me, it threw the rest of the cows into confusion. The animals behind the lifeless cow didn't know what to do. Cows are incredible creatures of habit and they sensed something was terribly wrong. After a few minutes of bewilderment, one of them got up the courage to jump over the dead animal, followed by the other cows in the parlor that were already milked. They took their normal route to go to the loafing shed, but there were still about 150 cows in the waiting area that were waiting to be milked and fed their grain ration.

What to do? George was asleep in the house after an exhausting day of helping Bill with harvest, plus his usual work. He had confidence in my ability to get the cows milked so he could sleep and be ready for the next day. When I had this bizarre challenge, I somehow got word to him that I needed his help. (Neither Dan nor I can figure out how I contacted George, more than a block away at our house.) In about ten minutes he came to my aid and went to get the tractor with a cable to drag the dead animal out of the milking parlor.

There was great consternation for the waiting cows because they hadn't been milked and knew something was wrong with their routine. George had a hard time driving them back so he could bring the tractor in to remove the dead cow. Besides the disruption of that night, the loss of a producing cow was a great economic loss. Based on his dairy cattle training at Oregon State, George believed she had a heart attack, which is rare for dairy cows.

Disappointing Outcome

We had been managing the farm for less than four months when trouble began brewing. When the owner of the farm realized he made a mistake and didn't really want to sell, he made life miserable for us. The price of cows had gone up and he accused George of robbing him in the price paid for the cows. We learned that he had some serious mental issues, and his irrational behavior caused George to be concerned for the safety of our family.

We spent a lot of time in prayer and discussions with the whole family to determine the best course of action. At the advice of our attorney, we began negotiations to return the dairy farm back to the previous owner. Extricating ourselves was an incredible challenge, but we were all thankful that Bill's farm was returned intact. Because we had used mostly family labor, we did not have any residual debt. Even though we had plenty of reasons to pursue a lawsuit, we chose not to rack up any more attorney fees and to put this chapter behind us.

Re-Entry Issues

Our mission organization, CMF International, asked us to share information about our re-entry experiences to help others. Now books have been written and whole ministries address the issues missionaries face both before and after going to the field. These were the things we thought of that had impacted us:

- Life in the U.S. is too fast-paced.
- We can't get used to getting to appointments and events on time.
- Our clothes are out of style, but there is so much variety in the shops that we can't make a decision about purchasing new ones.
- Our friends are too busy with their own affairs to care that we are home.
- We have the sense that the churches we visit are only superficially interested in what we have to share or what we experienced.
- We are disgusted with the materialism in North America.
- We are horrified when taken out to an all-you-can-eat restaurant; people are often overweight and eating too much when so much of the world is hungry. There is too much waste as children are allowed to take food they don't eat.
- As returning missionaries, there is so much uncertainty about the future.
- There is much less family time available in the U.S. than on the field.

Star Route, Box 34A, Cloverdale, Oregon

In November 1976, after we disengaged from the dairy farm, our family moved back to our cottage at Wi-Ne-Ma to rest and regroup. In January 1977, we partnered with Laurie's parents, Dr. Loren and Edith Bliese, for a ticket for Dan to Ethiopia to renew his relationship with Laurie that had been continuing by airmail correspondence. While he was in Addis Ababa, he and Laurie became engaged.

Gordon and Daisy Johnson, who had been dorm parents for Jennie at Good Shepherd School in Ethiopia, had returned to Oregon and were now pastoring a church, Christ's Center, and overseeing Christ's Center School. After returning from his trip, Dan was offered a position as a teacher's assistant at Christ's Center School and he moved to Junction City.

Steve and Jennie braved the stigma of being *new kids* another time when they enrolled mid-year at Nestucca High School in Cloverdale. They had been in a Christian school in Ethiopia, and then a public school in Royal City and now in Cloverdale. It was a shock to them to discover the lack of morals among their peers in the U.S.

Steve had been a star basketball player at Good Shepherd School in Addis Ababa, and he went out for basketball at Nestucca. After a few practices he came home from school one day and informed us that he would not be continuing the sport. He said the coach was ruthless with the players, using profanity and demeaning terms, and despite his love for basketball it wasn't worth it to him to be on the team.

We were being restored as a family and felt the Lord directing us back into missions. For the first months of 1977 we visited churches and support partners and began to plan for another term of service with CMF in Africa, perhaps Kenya. In May 1977, the rest of the CMF Ethiopia team returned to the States due to the Marxist takeover. We were privileged to share in a meeting and reunion in Indianapolis to praise God together for His special protection and guidance during the political unrest. We prayed with the other team members, as we all were seeking our Father's will for the future.

The return of the CMF team from Ethiopia and several other factors combined to prevent our return to Africa at that time and to direct us to our next place of ministry. Steve and Jennie were invited to participate in a spring break camping trip with the students at Christ's Center School. They had such a good time and were so touched by the love and acceptance shown to them that they appealed to us to be allowed to attend that school the next year. We agreed to honor their wishes and made plans to move to Junction City.

235 S.W. Laurel St., Junction City, Oregon

It is not common to move to a community when the breadwinner of the family does not have a job there, but we didn't have clear direction for the future and were willing to take this major step of faith. Our re-entry into the U.S. had been a year of numerous challenges and our teenagers' wellbeing was a major concern. We knew we were not finished with our missionary assignments, but we felt it was important to stay in the U.S. for Steve's senior year and Jennie's last two years of high school. Although Dan didn't live with us, it was a wonderful time of bonding and healing for our family to be together.

We decided to look for a house to purchase in Junction City. It is a small town and we drove all the streets looking for a For Sale by Owner sign. Our family was pleased with the house we found for sale on S.W. Laurel Street, within walking distance of Christ's Center. Before the ink was dry on the sales contract, George had been offered a job as administrator for the church and school. I agreed to work at the school one day a week to help with the tuition for Steve and Jennie. The need for my administrative skills increased, and I usually worked three or four days.

Researching Options

We realized that wherever we went our children would not be going with us on our next missionary venture. While we were still in Ethiopia, George had been researching the possibility of working in

Sudan among the Dinka tribe. We stayed in touch with close friends who prayed with us to discern the will of the Lord for the next step.

We were hoping for a door to open for ministry in Sudan. Our attempts to communicate with the leaders of ACROSS (Africa Committee for Rehabilitation of Southern Sudan) from Oregon had not been successful, and our pastors recommended that we go to Kenya to explore in person options for service in Sudan or wherever the Holy Spirit would lead us to work.

In August of 1979, we shared with potential partners that our prayers for direction were being answered. Two churches and several families committed to our financial support, and on August 12th we were commissioned by Christ's Center for another assignment in Africa in a place that was not yet identified. With the blessing of Christ's Center pastors and the board of Frontier Ministries International, the missionary sending agency we had launched, we submitted our application for visas to go to Kenya.

We made plans to depart in mid-December 1979. The date of departure came and went, but we couldn't follow through with our travel plans because our passports and visas were apparently lost at Menno Travel Service in New York. We had to postpone our flight and we had "the last supper" with our children several times. We finally got on our way December 26th and never did find out where our passports had been hiding while we waited.

CHAPTER 14
Interim Stay in Kenya

Daystar Communications in Nairobi was our home base from January to May 1980. While we were getting acquainted with the leaders, we took a two-week course called Community Health Development. We moved into a small room, pushed the cots together, put up a picture of our kids and called it home. There were 14 in our class, and we and the teacher were the only white people. They told us that in the last term, Christian leaders from 18 countries had been trained in various aspects of communications and development.

The director of the school approached George about teaching there, and he was open to teaching occasional short courses, but he didn't want to be tied down and unable to take advantage of other opportunities for evangelism. We started studying the Swahili language on our own but were considering a formal class if we weren't able to go to Sudan.

A Trip to Kitale

After two weeks in the city, we followed up on an invitation and traveled north and west to Kitale to spend time with our friends, Dick and Jane Hamilton. Their home was at 6220 feet elevation, but the major part of their work was among the Pokot people down off the escarpment in the lowlands. Their home was "grand central station" with lots of guests, including Diane Messik, a single nurse who worked with them in their medical outreaches. We slept on two single mattresses in their utility room.

Another guest was a four-year-old boy, Epoo (A-po), who had contracted polio as a baby. He weighed only 25 pounds but seemed quite healthy except for weak muscles in his back and one leg. Diane and a physical therapist at the local hospital were trying various casts and braces to stiffen his back and make his bad leg cooperate. They knew that he must learn to walk with a brace and crutches so that his people would let him live. If he wasn't able to "keep up," they would probably not preserve his life. He had been with the Hamiltons for one month and had adjusted to the food and lifestyle amazingly well.

One time we went together to a service in the countryside. When we got there at 10 AM we had a meal of boiled eggs, bread and chai (tea), followed by singing and George preaching. After that, we had *ugali na kuku* (thick, white cornmeal mush, served with chicken.) As was the practice in Ethiopia, it was eaten in a communal dish. Here the guests squeezed a ball of ugali and soaked up the broth and chicken before putting it in their mouth. We appreciated their hospitality and enjoyed the chance to visit.

Several of the Kenyans who were associated with Hamiltons pleaded with us to come and work there, but we did not have the revelation that this was the place for our future ministry, so we continued to pray for God to show us His plan for where we were to work.

To return to Nairobi, the Hamiltons drove us as far as Eldoret and we enjoyed a train ride from there to the city. There were no second-class seats available, so we went first class, a compartment with seats that made into a bed, a wonderful option since the train went at night from 9:00 PM to 9:45 AM. It took twice as long to go by train because of the many stops, but it only cost $16 per person, less than the cost of petrol to drive a vehicle, and cheaper than a hotel.

Can We Get into Sudan?

We were finally making progress in our communication regarding the possibility of working in Sudan. We visited with the ACROSS administrator and found that they did have a need for an agriculturalist in Sudan. Since that country did not accept missionaries, it was necessary to have some kind of professional credentials to enter the country, even for relief and development work. George was confident that his university degree and past experience would be our ticket to get in and we continued to pray for an open door.

More Transportation Challenges

We did all our traveling in Nairobi by bus, rain or shine. We had some real thriller rides, actually terrifying because the bus drivers drove so recklessly. One day, we went together by bus for an appointment with ACROSS. There was going to be a delay in meeting with the right person, so about 3:00 PM we decided that I should go on home. I waited quite a while for the bus to our guesthouse, but then it started raining and soon was a downpour. The shelter didn't begin to hold the number of people trying to get under it. I went into a shoe store, pretending to browse just to escape the torrent.

I went back to the bus stop and tried to get on Bus 7, but I was nearly trampled to death and the bus left before I could get on. A few minutes later I was able to board Bus 6, which would also stop near the guesthouse where we were staying. The trip home should have taken 15 to 20 minutes, but the storm had caused an incredible traffic jam. It took two hours to travel just the first four blocks! I was standing wedged between people during the entire trip, way too up close and personal. We eventually covered the several miles and I reached my destination at 7:15 PM.

Apparently while I was in the shoe store, George had finished the visit at ACROSS and had gone back to the main bus stop and boarded Bus 7 to go to the guesthouse. We had just missed each other. George had arrived home about 5:30, just a bit ahead of the worst part of the traffic jam. When I got off the bus, he was coming down the lane to meet me at the bus stop. He had been in enough of the traffic snarl-up to realize what was causing my delay. According to the newspaper the next day, in 40 minutes it had rained almost three inches, causing the streets to become rivers.

In the rainy season, we continued to have heavy rains every day, mostly late in the afternoon and evening. We went out one evening to see friends, and while we were there it really poured. When we started for home about 6:00 PM, the buses were tied up in traffic, so we had a long walk home in a downpour. The streets were like rivers, the manholes were geysers and we continually had to wade through water. Fortunately, it wasn't cold, so even though we were totally soaked, no harm was done. We realized that the majority of the population had never ever known any kind of transportation besides a bus or *matatu,* an oversized taxi.

George had an interesting conversation with a girl on the bus Easter Sunday evening. In polite conversation, he asked how her day had been and she admitted that she had been out drinking with her friends. She had gone to Nairobi Baptist Church in the morning and drinking in the afternoon. He said, "Didn't you know this was Resurrection Sunday?" Just before he got off the bus, she asked him to meet her the next day for an after-Easter beer!

Getting Prepared

While we were in Kenya that spring of 1980, we enjoyed worship services and fellowship with other believers at Valley Road Church. One time when we had walked there from our home away from home at the Pentecostal Assemblies of Canada guesthouse, I had become quite sick during the service, and although I was feeling a little better, the thought of a long uphill walk to get back home was daunting.

When the service was over, as we walked outside and away from the building, a running boy crashed into me. He was enough shorter that his forehead hit my chin and either his hip or knee struck me in the lower abdomen/groin area. I was stunned and struggled to keep my balance but wasn't knocked down. The hosts of the guesthouse where we were staying saw the incident, came to my rescue and took us home in their car. The incident reminded me of my mom getting hit on the playground and breaking her hip, which prematurely ended her teaching career.

We had committed to several projects at Daystar and were on the countdown to get them completed before our departure. I had volunteered to do some typing while we waited for news from Sudan. One day I typed the entire day, 30 pages of lecture notes and handouts for Eddie Elliston's class scheduled for the last two weeks of June, plus research papers and term papers for the African students as they were finishing the semester. Only a few got their papers ready in time to take advantage of my offer.

Friends from Christian Missionary Fellowship, Phil and Gwen Hudson, stopped by just before we left for Sudan to give us their washboard. They no longer needed it after purchasing a washing machine. I never thought I would be happy for a washboard, but it truly was helpful when washing clothes by hand was the only option.

The year before, we had enjoyed Thanksgiving with the Hudsons, Gwen's parents and three other families, making a total of 16 for dinner. One of the couples had splurged to purchase a turkey from a military group in Nairobi. When it was cooked and the lid taken off the pan, the smell was horrific. It had apparently spoiled and been re-frozen, so they didn't realize it was not edible until after it was cooked. The menu was quickly changed, everyone had plenty to eat and we all had a wonderful time of fellowship. Missionaries get a lot of practice in adapting to challenging situations!

Destination Sudan

We considered working in Sudan a higher priority than working in Kenya because Sudan was only accepting personnel with experience in agriculture, medicine, construction, and water development. Kenya was so open that people with only Christian training were welcomed to work there. In April 1980 it looked favorable for George to become the agricultural projects coordinator for Mundri District in Sudan. If approval was granted to us and our mission organization, Frontier Ministries International, we would soon be on our way to Sudan.

By June of 1980, we had jumped through all the hoops and were finally granted permission to enter Sudan based on George's professional credentials. We received news that our documents had been validated by the Ministry of Agriculture in Sudan and we were scheduled to travel there by the end of the month.

More Missionary Experiences

"Now all these things are from God, who reconciled us to Himself through Christ, and gave us the ministry of reconciliation, namely, that God was in Christ reconciling the world to Himself And He has committed to us the word of reconciliation. Therefore we are ambassadors for Christ."

II Corinthians 5:18-20

CHAPTER 15
Life in Sudan

Can We Live in a Sauna?

T he capital, Juba, was our entry point when we finally reached southern Sudan in June 1980. When we landed at the airport, the tarmac was wet since it had just stopped raining and steam was rising from the runway. The small air terminal did not have air conditioning, and the power was out so the fans weren't turning. We perspired profusely while we waited in line to have our papers processed.

When we reached the ACROSS guesthouse, we discovered that it was 117°. We realized that with 100% humidity, it would take us a long time to become acclimatized. The British hostess, Dr. Gene Johns, welcomed us and showed us to our room. We were exhausted, but it was impossible to sleep; we just lay on the bed sweating and discussing whether we could ever adjust.

Mundri Village

We settled into our home at Mundri about 125 miles north of Juba and 50 miles west of the Nile River. Our home was on an ironstone plateau with sandy, red soil with a high iron content. In the heavier rainfall area, the soil was very fertile, but it was not good quality where we lived. Familiar food items were scarce or non-existent; eggplant, okra and *dura,* a type of millet, got monotonous.

George had a very hard time eating food made from the staple grain dura. It often went "off" and smelled and tasted terrible. When dura was in short supply, sometimes the United States donated wheat to prevent famine. Alas, the officials combined the ground wheat with the spoiled dura, causing it all to be practically inedible. I tried to improve the taste by adding vanilla to things such as pancake batter, but George still couldn't choke down anything made from dura flour. He lost so much weight that he was down to his high school wrestling weight.

Snake Deterrence

When we first got to Mundri, we were advised that it was good to have a cat to ward off snakes, and we were given an orange tabby named Benjamin. When "he" gave birth to kittens, we realized that whoever had named him was not knowledgeable in determining the sex of animals. For the delivery place, Benjamin chose the bottom of the standing closet in our bedroom, where my nightgown was kept. All our efforts to relocate the kittens did not work.

The tiny kittens were cute, but before long they were underfoot, and it was easy to trip over them. As they got older they ventured out into the kitchen, where their mother would bring lizards in to feed them and train them to hunt. Sometimes the growling and snarling occurred under the table as we were eating breakfast. We got attached to the kittens and it was hard to give them away, especially to the nationals who we knew wouldn't feed them. To survive they would have to eat insects and lizards.

Exhausting Meeting

In September 1980 George and other leaders in the community were called to a meeting of the Sudan Socialist Union. He said it felt odd, being a capitalist like he is, sitting in on that meeting. It started at 9:30 AM and didn't stop until 6:00 PM! During that time, he only had one glass of lemonade, so he came home extremely tired, thirsty and hungry. He was asked to speak several times to defend ACROSS and explain various programs.

There was misunderstanding and mistrust of ACROSS due to lack of knowledge of the purposes of the organization. Some government officials thought it was just a service organization sent to transport them, provide all kinds of assistance, and see that all their needs were met. They had no concept of the bubble-up kind of development, where the people acknowledge that they have needs and are willing to help themselves with a bit of facilitation by people such as ACROSS personnel.

The opposite is the trickle-down method, where officials in places of authority think of development ideas and offer them to the peasants. Rarely do the people feel really involved in that method; as soon as the outside help stops, the whole development scheme grinds to a halt. For instance, if the pump breaks down on the community borehole, the villagers go back to the river for their water; or if the chief authorizes latrines to be built in the community on the advice of development workers, the people rarely use them, referring to them as the chief's latrines.

Horrific Smell

One of the challenges we faced in Sudan was long periods of time in church services and other meetings when it was dreadfully hot with no air moving. Buildings in Sudan, especially churches with tin roofs, were often nesting places for bats. The extreme heat and humidity combined with bat urine and excrement created a horribly nauseating smell. Sometimes it was so bad that I would have to hold a handkerchief over my nose to keep from being sick. People learning English pronounced the word manure as "manur-e-a." A custom developed that was related to the disgusting bat odor. When believers were provoked to swearing, the expression often used was an emphatic "bat manur-e-a!"

Lodging in Yei

After our first year in Mundri the ACROSS Program Director, Keith Gingrich, sent a radio message asking George to come from Mundri to Juba for a special meeting with an officer from the United Nations High Commission for Refugees (UNHCR). There was a desperate need to provide a solution for the humanitarian crisis of Ugandans escaping into Sudan from the hostile regime in their country. At the meeting George agreed to the assignment of managing the project, which required us to make a quick move from Mundri to Yei.

We embarked on this adventure knowing that we would be "roughing it." Our first place of lodging was in a hotel that had been brought into Sudan on a truck, piece by piece, from a location in Uganda. The accommodations were extremely primitive, but we were together and determined to make a difference for the Ugandan refugees who were coming across the border, desperately seeking security and provision.

Poisoned by Hospitality

One evening on a trip to one of the Ugandan refugee settlements, we drove 40 minutes to the settlement in our Suzuki Jeep. We took two Ugandan workers with us to assist George at the meeting with the leaders of the settlement. After our arrival, I was invited to go with some of the ladies to an impromptu ladies' meeting. As part of the hospitality, I was given some brown liquid to drink that we learned later was the residue from soaking cassava. It tasted terrible, so I only sipped a little to be polite. The other ladies appeared to be drinking it, so I didn't suspect that it was poisonous. Apparently, they were used to it and got some kind of "high" from it. We later learned that improper preparation of cassava can leave enough residual cyanide to cause acute cyanide intoxication. I was literally poisoned by the tiny bit I consumed.

I began to feel sick quite soon after tasting a very small amount of the liquid. After George was finished with his meeting, I rejoined him for the trip home, but I didn't feel comfortable explaining why I was feeling so sick since we had English-speaking nationals riding with us. Bouncing along on the corrugations on the roadway made me feel worse and worse.

By the time we got back to our home at the hotel, I was in desperate condition and George thought for sure I was dying. He had me lie down on the grass behind our room, semi-conscious between episodes of violent vomiting. He put wet washcloths on my face, tried to comfort me and prayed that I wouldn't die. Although I felt sick unto death, in a couple days I recovered from the incident. Evidently, God was not finished with me yet!

Challenging Living

After a few months in that no-star hotel, which I described in detail in George's life story, a house became available through the Episcopal Church in the town of Yei. We were looking forward to moving in, but our move was delayed when a violent windstorm caused serious damage to the roof. In addition to being our residence, one part of the house was set aside as the office for the refugee project.

Maybe it is more accurate to say that we camped in that house while we waited to have some furniture made. George contracted a carpenter to build some chairs and small tables. The primitive process took a long time and we thought he would never finish the task. Before the furniture could be created, it was necessary for that craftsman to cut down a tree and in a pit with a partner and a two-man saw, saw some lumber. Meanwhile we "made do" with a piece of tin over a cardboard box and a couple primitive stools.

I was extraordinarily challenged in preparation of meals for us and offering hospitality to others. We did not have a refrigerator or stove, too few other necessities, and limited food supplies, yet situations regularly came up that required me to prepare meals and offer hospitality. One time, a TV film group of 12 men from World Concern came for three days. It is probably hard for you to picture a country with no restaurants, but there literally was no place for them to eat except with us, an exceptionally tricky assignment for me.

Rewarding Work

George really enjoyed his work with the UNHCR. We both considered that assignment to be the most physically and mentally demanding that we had ever experienced, but also very rewarding. George's skill of organizing people and resources had been called into service immediately, and he was able to hire qualified people who themselves were refugees. The system he developed to help the refugees raise their own food was very successful. Within three years, 26 of the 28 refugee camps became self-sufficient in food production. We later learned that the strategies George developed were used by UNHCR for work in other countries.

We handed the leadership of the program off to a Dutch project manager. It was a pattern for us to have pioneer assignments, and then when we got things going well someone else came to take over. We moved back to Mundri but remained available for another assignment that was being considered by ACROSS leadership.

New Airstrip

In January 1981 we had an incident on our new airstrip in Mundri. I wrote to our family as follows:

> It happened that everyone on our team went to the airstrip since we were expecting one of our nurses to come home from leave and our doctor, Elizabeth Baines, was coming around on what we called the "Milk Run" to see everyone. The landing was okay, and the pilot said our strip was in good condition, but later when he went to take off with four onboard, somehow he didn't get up enough speed and had to abort the attempt. He thought perhaps the air was too still because of the heat. He started trying to stop about two-thirds of the way down the strip, but still skidded into a bank at the end and bent the tip of one of the propeller spokes.
>
> We were all thankful that no one was hurt and there was limited damage to the plane. We ended up with two guests for meals at our home; two other guests ate with the nurses and slept in the guesthouse. Our guests were with us two more nights until the repair part came. I wasn't really excited about taking off on that strip until it was tested a few more times. It is a good thing our joy doesn't depend on circumstances!

Tonj District

It wasn't long before a high priority assignment to initiate a work in Tonj required us to move yet again. George and other ACROSS leaders had been considering a new opportunity among the Dinka tribe in Tonj District, a mostly unreached tribe of three million people with only 1/10 of 1% Christian. Together we made several exploratory trips on undeveloped roads from Mundri to Tonj, investigating the possibility of deploying people in the region. We pioneered the opening of that region for other ACROSS professionals to use their expertise to help the people and promote the Kingdom of God.

We lived in three different places during our time in Tonj. First was a house on the Kenaf farm, an Italian-based project that had been a large-scale attempt to produce burlap bags. Corruption and greed in high places had caused the project to fail at about 80% completion. Had it been thriving, the house would have been occupied by supervisory workers and not available to us. We were glad for a place to live, but we were not able to stay there long before it was needed for Dan Kelly, his wife Daphne, and their three sons. Dan was an agriculturalist from Australia and we were very happy to have them join the ACROSS team and our work in Tonj.

Village 7 Stone Cottage

A house in the center of town was being renovated for us, but it wasn't ready when the Kellys came, so we moved to a tiny cottage in a communal setting with other expatriates at Village 7 at the edge of town. The individual cottages did not have kitchens, so we ate our meals with the others under a shelter. There was no refrigerator, so food preparation and preservation were extremely problematic, and we often had different opinions among the group on what was safe to eat.

The only redeeming factor about this place was that George and I were together! Creature comforts were totally absent. At this location, the outhouse was a long way away from our one-room cottage. It had a seat over a bucket that had to be emptied and George took his turn at doing that unpleasant chore. Pit latrines were not allowed in Tonj because of the shallow, hand-dug wells, and there was a well in the compound.

One time while we were in our cottage, we heard what sounded like machinegun fire and George yelled for me to get down, lower than the glass-less window. Almost immediately I felt *sick* and the only option was to hurry to the outhouse about a block away! I risked getting shot, but it was an emergency! We learned later that what sounded like gunfire was a celebration at the edge of town, so we never were in danger, but it was a frightening experience.

Our Own Home

Thankfully, we only had to live at Village 7 for two months before our newly renovated house was ready for occupancy. We greatly enjoyed our new living quarters, meals that I prepared, and the privacy we Americans treasure so highly. George created a small solar lighting set-up that gave us dim RV-type lighting to help us endure long, dark evenings.

He also cleaned out a small building on the other side of town for an office and our radio set-up. I rode my bicycle to participate in the twice-daily radio communication with the other ACROSS locations. When our colleagues on the other side of Sudan were taken as hostages, I stayed on the radio to monitor the situation while George developed plans to protect the team that was our responsibility, to avoid a similar situation. I detailed the dramatic rescue of the hostages in George's life story.

Our determination to make a difference in the life of the people of Tonj District was cut short by acts of war. Our hurried departure from Tonj after receiving the warning message of George's threatened assassination is chronicled in the chapter "The Incredible Journey."

CHAPTER 16
A Taste of the Culture

T he church was first established about 1950 in the region where we lived in Sudan and the country gained independence in 1956 from the joint British and Egyptian government coalition that administered the country. Then during the first civil war (1955 – 1972) masses of people fled the country or into the bush or were killed. When there were political problems, the people moved across the borders into Uganda, Ethiopia, and Somalia. The 17-year war decimated the infrastructure and left the country in ruins.

Quoting from an article by Mollie Zapata on Enough 101 website December 13, 2011, *Sudan: Independence through Civil Wars.*

First Civil War: 1955-1972

In the first civil war, from 1955 to 1972, southern insurgents, called the Anya Nya, fought against the Government of Sudan (GOS) for greater autonomy. By 1969, Anya Nya controlled most of southern Sudan. In 1971, the reel group integrated into the Southern Sudan Liberation Movement, or SSLM, the precursor to today's Sudan People's Liberation Movement/Army, or SPLM/A.

The war ended with the 1972 Addis Ababa Agreement between SSLM and GOS, which granted significant regional autonomy to southern Sudan on internal issues, and also promised the Abyei area, located on the north-south border, the right to hold a referendum to determine whether they would remain a part of northern Sudan or join the newly formed Southern Region.

It was into that setting that we entered the country in June of 1980. The church operated the schools in the early years, and many of the regional government officers were educated in Christian schools and had a Christian commitment. The older leaders, who spoke English, considered the time of British rule to be the Golden Era, and told us that it ended too soon. George found it difficult to have any motivation for learning the local languages, Moru or Arabic, because most of the officials he dealt with were fluent in English.

Even though the years we were in Sudan in the early 1980s were considered to be a time of peace, there was constant tension between the Arab north and the black African south. We felt blessed to know many Christians, although we didn't see the kind of righteous living and fruits of repentance that we know our Father desires from His people. The people were usually pleasant and easy to work with. Their culture was more centered on people-to-people relationships than is common in the Western world. A man's worth was measured by his family and the relationships he had established in the community.

A Weekend at Lui

This story describes a weekend in Sudan that demonstrates aspects of the culture. We drove our Land Rover to Lui, a village 14 miles from Mundri. When we arrived at the church compound we heard the youth group singing choruses to welcome us. Pastor Thomas, his wife Wilma and his family came immediately to greet us. They had five children of their own – three little girls, ages five, four and three, an 18-month old boy, and a one-month old baby girl. Living with them were three older girls and two older boys, children of relatives, who were going to school in Lui. The older children were a great help in duties such as carrying water, preparing food, working in the garden, and childcare in exchange for the opportunity to live with the pastor's family.

We were directed to go inside a small mud-walled house with a grass roof that was to be our home for the weekend. An older girl brought us each a glass of lemonade. After we drank that, she brought a tray with cups and saucers and a thermos of tea prepared with milk and sugar. Pastor Thomas asked us to go with him to see the church garden down near the Yei River. We were able to drive about five miles on a bush trail and then we walked the last mile after crossing a creek. The site for the garden was beautiful, but due to lack of workers, it was badly grown up to grass and weeds. About an acre in size, there were 75 pineapple plants, 25 citrus trees, and 25 banana plants, which were then producing. The potential was great, but if the project were to succeed, the congregation would need to either provide labor for cultivating or enough money to hire some workers. The lack of emphasis on stewardship in the church there was a real problem.

Later we were served a supper of thick dura porridge and stewed chicken with broth. We ate with our hands, dipping the thick porridge in the soup and putting it to our mouths. Another dish of vegetables was served, primarily okra. It was nearing the time that had been announced to the community as a "cinema."

About 600 people turned out to see the cinema. Even people who don't go to church will come out for something special like that. A major problem was the lack of an appropriate place to show the pictures so people could see. The projector required the battery from the Land Rover to power it, so George drove the pickup into a large area near the church building, hung up a large sheet to serve as the screen, and began the service with singing and a prayer.

We had brought some slides from our time in Kenya among the Turkana and Pokot people, a few slides from the survey among the Dinka people in Tonj, some pictures of scenery in the Pacific Northwest, and pictures of our family. The reaction of the crowd to various pictures was fascinating. Mostly there was so much talking and laughing that it was not possible to do much narration or explaining. After some singing and a closing prayer, the crowd was reminded of the times of the Sunday services and dismissed to go home.

We returned to our "tukel" where beds were provided for us. We had brought our sheets, but the one thing we really needed which we didn't remember to bring was mosquito nets. We didn't sleep much; if we covered our heads with our sheets it was too hot and we couldn't breathe, and if we didn't cover our heads, the whine of the mosquitoes was too annoying to allow us to sleep. Once during the wee hours, there was some whirring of either a bird or a bat flying around. The last time we talked to each other and looked at the time, it was 3:20 AM. Fortunately, we both slept some after that.

We woke up to the sound of someone sweeping the ground outside. We got up and dressed and Eva, one of the older girls, brought us some doll-dish-size cups of Moru coffee, strong enough to wind up on the spoon! We drank two cups of that and within moments she brought another tray with larger cups of tea mixed with milk and sugar, and the pastor joined us.

Right after tea, Pastor Thomas asked us to go with him to the village of one of the members of the church whose mother had died. Again we drove partway and walked the last mile since there were swampy areas that we needed to pick our way through by stepping on spots of dry land. The man whose mother had died was quite overcome that we had come all that way to visit him and share his sorrow. We stayed only a short time, greeting all the family and neighbors, and left a gift of money before returning to the Land Rover.

As we reached the pastor's compound, our hosts directed us back into our tukel and brought breakfast. This consisted of boiled cassava (much like a large piece of sweet potato, but white, with not much taste or food value), eggs scrambled in chicken broth and some boiled rice, a very satisfying breakfast!

We then hurried off to the English service at the church, where George was to preach. In that service there were about 80 secondary students who understood English. For the later Moru service, about 350 people were present and a translator was needed. George preached a really good message explaining redemption by using the example of a slave being set free by his master, building on the fact that Lui has a tree that is known all over the region as a slave tree, where Arabs had bought slaves to take to the North. After church, we greeted all the people and took some pictures of the new church building which was nearing completion.

Lunch was more dura porridge, called *linya*, and another chicken gave its life for the cause. Many people came by to express their appreciation for the time we spent in Lui and our fellowship in the Gospel. We considered it a blessing to have been invited to share and we greatly appreciated their hospitality and friendship.

Another War

Continuing the quotation from Enough 101 noted on page 1:

Second Civil War: 1983-2005

> The second civil war erupted in 1983 when President
> Jaafar Nimeiri introduced Sharia Law and reneged

on the Addis Ababa Agreement's provision for a referendum in Abyei. The SPLM/A fought against the Government of Sudan until 1989, when the parties reached a peace agreement and suspended Sharia Law. However, on June 30, 1989, a military coup led by Omar Al-Bashir overthrew the Sudanese government and repudiated the peace agreement.

The Southern Peoples Liberation Army (SPLA), led by John Garang, was founded as a guerrilla movement against the government of Sudan. It was this disturbance to peace that led to George's threatened assassination and our miraculous escape from Tonj.

The second civil war lasted 22 years, well past our time of serving in Sudan. George's PhD thesis, *The Effect of Conflict in the Horn of Africa on Development in the Region,* emphasizing how nearly continuous war has continued to impede progress in development and modernization, was again being played out in Sudan.

CHAPTER 17
Ambassadors for Christ

Our Father looks at the world as a mosaic of different people groups, each with its own language, culture, and distinctives. There are still thousands of these groups waiting for their first taste of the Bread of Life – our Savior. In our work with Calvary International, we participated with agencies in various networks and alliances to use missionary manpower and resources to achieve measurable results.

This is a favorite quote from the late Dr. Ralph Winter at the U.S. Center for World Mission:

> People who are lost are just as lost if they are citizens of Anytown, USA, or jungle tribesmen, citizens of Asian megacities or dwellers in a remote rural mountain vastness. People who are equally lost may not be equally difficult to find. Populations equally needy may not have equal opportunity to hear.

In our work as missionaries, we came to realize that most North Americans don't realize how rich they are in comparison to the rest of the world. According to the Office of International Programs in Portland, Maine, in 2019 the world population has reached 7.7 billion people. The researchers commented: "If you keep your food in a refrigerator, your clothes in a closet, if you have a bed to sleep in and a roof over your head, you are richer than 75% of the entire world population."

If the World Were a Village of 100 People

If we could turn the population of the earth into a small community of 100 people, keeping the same proportions we have today, it would look something like this...

50 would be female
50 would be male
25 would be children
There would be 75 adults,
9 of whom would be 65 and older

There would be:
61 Asians
13 Africans
12 Europeans
8 North Americans
5 South Americans & the Caribbean
1 from Oceania

33 are Christian
21 are Muslims
13 are Hindus
6 are Buddhists
1 is a Sikh
1 is Jewish
11 practice other religions
11 are non-religious
3 are Atheists

70 non-whites
30 white

17 speak Chinese
9 speak English
8 speak Hindi
6 speak Russian
6 speak Spanish
4 speak Arabic
50 speak other languages

30 would always have enough to eat (15 would be overweight)
50 would be malnourished
20 would be undernourished (1 would be dying of starvation)

48 can't speak, act according to their faith and conscience due to harassment, imprisonment, torture or death, 52 can
20 live in fear of death by bombardment, armed attack, landmines, or of rape or kidnapping by armed groups, 80 do not

12 are unable to read
1 has a college degree
12 own a computer
8 have an internet connection

12 are disabled
1 adult has HIV/AIDS
43 live without basic sanitation
20 have no clean, safe water to drink
80 live in substandard housing

68 breathe clean air
32 breathe polluted air

6 people own 59% of the world's wealth (all of them
from the United States)
74 people own 39%
20 people share the remaining 2%
21 people live on $1.25 (US) per day or less
The village spent $1.24 trillion (US) on military
expenditures, and $100 billion (US) on development aid

Source: Office of International Programs, Portland, Maine

Encountering Starving People

On January 6, 1981, as we prepared to return to Sudan after a trip
to Nairobi, we were asked by ACROSS officials to drive a Land
Rover to Juba for the Minister of Religious Affairs. We departed in
convoy in our vehicle and a pickup driven by Eddie Elliston and his
wife Donna, our Christian Missionary Fellowship colleagues years
previously at Kiramu in Ethiopia. They were planning to do survey
work for about six weeks in Sudan for CMF. We knew it would be
a long, hot, dusty trip, but we also knew that God would protect us
and give us strength. Our vehicle was loaded with ACROSS freight,
but we were able to include some of our own needed supplies (more
than we could have taken by plane).

We traveled five days and nights in very hot weather, camping out
at night. We bounced and jolted along on some unbelievably poor
roads, but it was good to be able to give the Ellistons support. We
also gained more appreciation for the lorry drivers who transported
our supplies from Kenya to Sudan.

The hardest part of the extremely difficult trip was seeing the suffering
humanity in the Turkana region of northern Kenya, where people

were starving. When we stopped for our evening meal and to set up to spend the night, numbers of people surrounded us, watching our every move. Although we knew we had to eat to sustain ourselves, it was really hard to do because we didn't want to eat in front of starving people. Another difficulty was the incredibly annoying gnats buzzing around our faces and biting us. We gave away a lot of food, but our help was only a tiny contribution in the face of the looming humanitarian crisis.

At one of our camping sites, a lady begged me to take her baby, who was already quite lethargic and would undoubtedly die because of the famine. We realized how little we or anyone else could do about the complex problems of overgrazing, tribalism, cattle raids, and graft and corruption in high places, culminating in great distress at the village level. We talked to a Catholic priest, who said they needed 83 lorry loads of grain each month in the area where he worked, but each of the last two months they had only received 12. They still had some milk powder and oil to give out, but the people looked severely malnourished and were facing even more drought and famine.

Messengers of Hope

> *Therefore, we are ambassadors for Christ, as though God were entreating through us; we beg you on behalf of Christ, be reconciled to God.* II Corinthians 5:20

It was a joy for us to work in Sudan with committed Christians from many countries and church backgrounds who shared our goals for evangelism and development. We found our colleagues to be very cooperative and helpful, and the Sudanese people were easy to work with and responsive when we shared the love of Jesus. We were able to open two new areas for evangelism and development, which involved considerable road improvement to get equipment into the area.

George organized construction of simple buildings for Sudanese evangelists and medical personnel to live in. He also supervised the drilling of wells and installation of hand pumps for clean water sources. He especially enjoyed teaching agricultural extension workers, using his expertise from previous training.

He was very involved with helping the local church, preaching many times in different congregations in the area. Once when the Bishop of the Episcopal Church of the Sudan was present for George's sermon, the bishop was very complimentary, commenting that George was obviously being led by the Holy Spirit in his message.

One Sunday we took two carloads of people from the church and the nearby Bishop Gwynne College to Bahr Olo, 41 miles west, for the dedication of their new church building. Money for materials had come from the Swedish Pentecostal Church, and eleven men had done the majority of the work on a volunteer basis. It was a grand celebration and a beautiful day up until 3 PM, when we were to be served tea under the mango trees. It was sunny one minute, then a few drops of rain fell, and within moments a full-force storm was upon us. We all dashed for the church building but got wet before we could get inside. The wind blew the rain halfway into the building and it poured for about 40 minutes, absolutely deafening on the metal roof. We didn't get home until after 6 PM and found it had rained hard at Mundri, too.

Serving Others

One Friday night in Mundri in March of 1981 we hosted a "feast" for our workers and their wives. With a few children thrown in as extras, we served 45 people in our house. We served *kisera*, the local version of Ethiopian injera (pancake-like bread). I had a Sudanese friend make the kisera and I made one kind of sauce for dipping from eight chickens and another kind with five pounds of lentils. I served fresh mangoes and peanuts for dessert, along with hot tea.

The people ate with their hands from communal dishes, so we only had pans to wash.

George and I were glad that we had invited them, and even more glad that it was over! I was too tired to do anything about the disaster in the sitting room that night. The floor was about an inch thick with bits of kisera and bones, so I had the two girls I had hired to help serve come back in the morning to help clean up. Our sitting room had large window openings with screens, but no glass. Right after we got the house all cleaned up, a terrible windstorm came through. Fortunately, it didn't take the grass roof off, but it did deposit an awful pile of dirt in and on everything in the house. I could have cried!

More Travel Challenges

During the next years, we were in and out of Juba from time to time, staying a night or two in the guesthouse on our way to Nairobi or some other location. One time I rode on the back of George's motorbike all the way from Mundri to Juba, a four-hour journey, on an extremely hot day. He took me off at one point to lie on the side of the road while he poured water on me to cool me down. Besides nearly having heatstroke, I was so stiff and sore when we arrived that I could barely walk.

ACROSS leaders encouraged regular vacations out of Sudan into cooler locations. One time we were scheduled for a vacation and were booked on Sudan Airways to Nairobi. The airline was also known in the expatriate community as Inshallah Airlines, *insha'Allah* being the Arabic language expression for "God willing" or "if God wills."

Usually the plane flew from Juba to Nairobi three times a week. We were to take our luggage to the airport in the evening to be weighed and left for the flight the next day. Unfortunately, the timing of this vacation coincided with Ramadan, and if the plane was full of Muslim pilgrims heading to Mecca, it didn't land in Juba. Several times we left our luggage at the airport in the evening, only to be told to come retrieve it the next day. We were in Juba eleven days before we were finally able to get on the plane out to Kenya for our holiday!

Making a Difference

George's ACROSS coordination work required judicious diplomacy in international and inter-denominational relations. We prayed that our work would produce eternal benefits as we allowed the Holy Spirit to lead us each day. The objective was a great harvest of souls as a reward for our labors. George commented many times how thankful he was to have me with him during those years and how much he appreciated my help and valued my companionship.

CHAPTER 18
The Incredible Journey

Winds of another civil war were blowing in southern Sudan in August of 1983. Having evacuated our team of missionaries to safety at the direction of our international leadership, George and I had stayed behind in the village of Tonj to assess the situation. The pro-Christian rebels in the South were suspicious that the United States was providing weapons to the northern Sudanese, so Americans were suddenly suspect.

Our construction supervisor rode his bicycle 26 kilometers from his outpost in Thiet at the break of dawn to deliver to George the frightening words, "Tonight you will be assassinated!" He shared with us that the rebels had taken over the outpost and had plans to kill George and a government official from Khartoum who was stationed in Tonj. What disturbing news to get before breakfast!

More details of our escape from this horrendous threat were told in Chapter 26 of George's life story, but I will summarize here.

Realizing our peril, George dispatched workers to get the Suzuki Jeep ready for travel and load our Land Rover pickup with barrels of fuel and jerry cans of water. Complicating our departure plan was our determination to honorably pay our workers. When we had sent out our other team members, each of the five project leaders had given us his cash box. George and I sat down with the payroll records and counted out the cash for the termination pay for each of the 240 workers assigned to the five projects. We worked as fast as we could and by early afternoon all of our employees were properly paid.

To reach Juba, the capital of southern Sudan, we needed to travel about 400 kilometers east, but we knew that the roads were impassable due to rainy season flooding. We were also concerned that the rebels might have those roads blocked, so we headed west toward Wau, a town in Bahr el Ghazal state along the border with the Central Africa Republic.

As we headed out, George driving the Land Rover pickup and I the Suzuki Jeep, we avoided the Tonj Police Post where we would have ordinarily checked out to depart the town. George was familiar with the jeep trail across the airstrip through the bush that would connect with the dirt road, now muddy in the rainy season. For a few miles, I kept up with him even though the road was very slippery and my vehicle fish-tailed every little bit. Then he increased his speed and disappeared from my sight. I could not figure out why he would drive at breakneck speed and leave me behind.

From time to time I would meet trucks heading towards me with soldiers standing in the back. I had no way of knowing if they were friends or enemies. I alternately cried and prayed, but kept driving. It had been a long time since I had seen George's vehicle, but when I finally reached the bridge at Wau, there he was – waiting for me! He had remembered that the bridge closed at 6 PM and he had been driving as fast as he could to beat that deadline. He had persuaded the bridge attendant to hold the gate open until I arrived about half an hour later.

We stayed at the German Blind Mission for two days to allow three of our employees who were driving two additional vehicles to join us. From Equatoria Province further south, they were as foreign in Tonj as if they were expatriates from abroad and were also in jeopardy. As those men and the lady who cooked for them became part of our convoy, the dynamics changed and we were never alone as a couple.

The next day we drove our four vehicles onto a pontoon ferry made from 55-gallon drums and watched incredulously as the men pushed us across the wide river with long poles. On the other side, we had to drive off from the ferry into the water and onto the shore. We continued our challenging journey. A few miles later we came to a bridge construction camp where the workers lived while away from home on their assignment. After we shared our situation, those Kenyan workers kindly received us, prepared a wonderful meal for us and allowed us to spend the night in their guest quarters. That turned out to be the only welcoming hospitality we had for the next five nights.

The roads were more like trails, almost impassable in some places. We had to ford streams and drive around huge boulders. We slept in government rest houses, churches and once under a building overhang. It was dreadfully hot. Although our appetites were depressed, we knew we had to eat to keep up our strength. I had brought a few cans from our pantry and heated the food on a charcoal jiko (a stove made from a 5-gallon can) to give us some nourishment.

I had blisters on my hands from the hot steering wheel, but the physical suffering was minor compared to my agony of soul. Although George had always been very kind and loving with me, on this incredible journey he showed none of the tenderness I was accustomed to. He treated me more like a truck driver, which was very bewildering.

We were both totally exhausted but pressed on early each morning to try to reach safety. By the evening of the fifth day, we arrived in Yei, a place of safety where we could rest a few days before continuing on to Juba. ACROSS had an office in Yei, where we had previously lived when we initiated the administration of the Ugandan refugee program. We were thankful to be alive and in safe territory!

It was only after we arrived in Yei that I got an explanation for George's unusual behavior. He told me that he was sure if he showed me tenderness and compassion, I would fall to pieces and not be able to continue to drive the Suzuki Jeep alone day after day. He began to try to make up for the emotional suffering he knew he had by necessity caused me to endure.

After recuperating a few days in Yei, enjoying some good food and fellowship, we traveled one more day eastward to Juba, the capital, the end of our incredible journey. There we learned that the government official from Khartoum who was targeted along with George, but was not forewarned as we had been, was killed by rebels and his house burned down around him that fateful night. We were thankful to God for favor and protection as we fled the extremely perilous circumstances.

Another Assignment

George worked on wrapping up the affairs of Tonj and sorting out the finances of the separate projects. He was asked to help the Dan Kelly family get relocated into the refugee project where Dan would be the ACROSS project manager for the five new settlements on the Yei-Bahr Olo road. George went with Dan on the 420-mile journey to orient him to the area and refugee administration. It was almost more than George could do to even start out on the trip, just a week after our arduous 840-mile escape journey, but Dan did the driving and they ended up having a great time together.

Unrelated to the refugee work, we had a delightful meeting with Dr. Sam and Ginny Cannata from the Southern Baptist Mission at the ACROSS guesthouse. We had been colleagues in Ethiopia and had many things to share with each other. While we were visiting with them, our friend Jim Powell from Rumbek came in. Jim is a black American, so it was easier for him to blend in than for us, but we still were concerned about his safety. A month earlier he had been held up at gunpoint as he took salaries to his workers out some distance from Rumbek. The robbers shot at his feet and relieved him of several thousand Sudanese pounds. We thought that the incident would be enough to get him to leave the area, but he waited until his mission organization actually ordered him to get away from Rumbek.

The ACROSS directors were proposing a new role for George of managing all of the refugee work for the United Nations High Commissioner for Refugees (UNHCR) in Sudan from an office in Juba. But first, his assignment for the next two months was to fill in as Acting Director of ACROSS for all of Sudan. All three directors were needed in England due to various extenuating circumstances. Though their intention had been to stagger their trips, that had not worked out, so George was asked to assume the leadership of ACROSS at that crucial time in the life of the organization. He was also in demand as an informant for the German Embassy and other agencies that were wondering what to do about security.

Social Life

Our social life changed dramatically after we got to Juba. We weren't used to being out in the evenings, so we struggled to keep our eyes open when we needed to attend an event. We couldn't seem to break our pattern of waking up about 5:30 AM, and then we were in no shape to stay up in the evenings.

We represented ACROSS at a reception for the United Nations International Children's Emergency Fund (UNICEF) representative to Sudan. It was held in an outside recreation hall near the United Nations swimming pool. The dignitary being there seemed incidental to the fact that the U.N. community liked to get together and drink beer! We didn't know very many people and the mosquitoes were thick and hungry, so it would be a lie to say we had a good time. We realized that if George took that job in Juba permanently, we would have to do that kind of thing too often.

We were blessed by our fellowship with ACROSS colleagues in Juba and friends from other like-minded agencies. The predominant church was the Episcopal Church of Sudan, but there were pockets of ministry among the Presbyterians, Catholics, African Inland Church, and more recently Juba Christian Center. George had been significantly involved in the birth of that work and it was rewarding to reconnect with the leaders and hear their stories of victories and challenges. We learned that there were now many new branch churches, some strong and others quite fragile. African Inland Church also had five new branch churches in the Juba area. Even though there were renewed efforts to Arabize and Islamize the South, we knew that God would be victorious.

As George completed his interim assignment, we assessed our situation. We reasoned that if we stayed in Juba we could find our lives in jeopardy in a similar way as we had experienced in Tonj. We knew we had been called to Sudan, but now the conflict between the North and South had escalated again. Americans especially were targeted for hostile incidents, and there was a real danger of us being taken hostage. After considering all the circumstances, we believed that our ministry in Sudan was coming to a close.

We had only been in Juba a short time when the mailbag from Kenya brought an amazing letter from Dr. Ray Kliewer, George's Animal Science professor at Oregon State University who was working at the Holstein Association in Brattleboro, Vermont. Though Ray had no way of knowing that serious disturbances in Sudan were forcing us to leave our work there, he was obviously led by the Spirit to offer George a position with the Holstein Association. The letter was dated August 25, 1983, the day we reached Juba, and gave us hope for the next step.

We were thankful for the privilege of using our giftings for the work of evangelism and encouragement of Christians in Sudan during those three years. We left ACROSS with good memories of our associations with the Sudanese people and colleagues from many different countries and backgrounds. We recalled with great gratitude God's special protection during the treacherous final days in Tonj and the escape journey and told others that we had "come this far by faith" and that we continued to trust the Lord for His direction. We acknowledged with great gratitude the miraculous timing of the letter and the job offering, just when we needed to know our Father's plan for our future.

CHAPTER 19
Update on Ethiopia and Sudan

Ethiopia

B y the end of the 1980s, the Marxist regime in Ethiopia was losing financial and military support from the Soviet Union. Long-standing liberation movements consolidated forces, forming the Ethiopian People's Revolutionary Democratic Front, according to the Office of the United Nations High Commissioner for Refugees. In 1991, the EPRDF entered Addis Ababa and took control of the country.

From Garry Brock, CMF missionary colleague from our time in Ethiopia, July 2018:

> The new president of Ethiopia is doing some interesting things. He is an Oromo named Abiy Ahmed. He is reportedly a strong Christian. He apparently has the backing of the ruling coalition, the EPRDF (The Ethiopian People's Revolutionary Democratic Front). This front consists of four political parties. The parties are the Oromo People's Democratic Organization, the Amhara National Democratic Movement, the Southern Ethiopian People's Democratic Movement, and the Tigrayan People's Liberation Front.

The military wing of the EPRDF effectively controls the army and therefore they have controlled the country. The past few years have brought many riots and fighting between the Amhara, Oromo, and Tigrinya (EPRDF) people. Having an Oromo as president makes the Oromo happy and keeps the Tigrinya and Amhara from fighting each other. Much of the tension these days is about Addis Ababa and the annexation of land which mostly belongs to the Oromo. The appointment of Abiy is seen as a way to cool the tensions and keep the Amhara and Tigrinya from dominating the political scene.

Abiy has done some pretty radical things like stopping the annexation of land for Addis, releasing political prisoners, offering to make peace with Sudan and South Sudan and now making peace with Eritrea, including opening the borders. He evidently has the backing of some strong people in the EPRDF. There are rumors that some of the old generals are not happy but none-the-less Abiy continues to move forward.

Christians seem to be very happy with the appointment and Abiy's references to faith. The Amhara and Tigrinya folks seem OK with having an Oromo president for now to keep the peace. So I guess time will tell.

What About Sudan?

After we left Sudan in 1983, the second civil war lasted 20 more years, ending in a cease-fire in 2003. More than two million people were killed and a substantial part of the population of the region was internally displaced or became refugees in neighboring countries. Through the years, we received bits and pieces of news regarding the situation in southern Sudan from former colleagues when we worked with ACROSS (now known as Association of Christian Resource Organizations Serving Sudan). Sadly, the news was grim with many of the people suffering from lack of food, isolation, and other effects of rebel activities.

Early in August 1986, the city of Juba was in an uproar. It started when an estimated 50,000 head of cattle were driven by Mundari tribesmen into the city. The Sudan People's Liberation Army (SPLA) was in hot pursuit. This initiated three weeks of tension, with the airport being closed as well as all roads in and out of Juba. During those weeks, two Sudanese ACROSS staff members along with three other people were shot while running an SPLA roadblock. Two American Catholic sisters were captured a few miles out of town and held for five days in the city of Juba, which became an armed camp.

A Sudan Airways plane was shot down near Malakal, killing 60 passengers and crew. One of the Episcopal Church bishops whom we knew well and had hosted in our home was killed when the helicopter he was in was shot down near Rumbek while he was trying to arrange for a food shipment to that distressed area. We also heard that one of our former radio operators was killed when the truck he was riding on was ambushed by rebels.

Wau, the provincial capital of the area including Tonj District, 400 miles northwest of Juba, the capital of South Sudan, became a refugee center for Sudanese fleeing the chaos in their own villages. Thousands of people swelling the population quickly exhausted the existing food supplies. The continuing struggle between the Islamic North and pro-Christian South prevented aid from getting to the suffering people. The rebels refused to allow aid groups to transport food by any means to the cut-off areas.

ACROSS Expelled

In 1988 the following information came to us from Executive Director Daniel Bitrus just prior to his turning over the directorship of ACROSS to our former colleague, Dan Kelly. The Council of Ministers of the Sudan Government expelled four voluntary agencies, including ACROSS, from Sudan. The reason given was that they had worked against the security interests of the country and had undeclared and illegitimate objectives. But when the truth was revealed, the accusation was that the four agencies had been involved in propagating and spreading Christianity in the South rather than carrying out the relief work for which they were originally permitted to come to the country.

New Country

On July 9, 2011, the South successfully seceded from the North, forming a new country called South Sudan. The nationals were encouraged, but oil remained the challenge to true peace. There are incredible oil reserves under the Sudd (swamps) of South Sudan. The North claims a share of the oil and the resultant dispute continues to prevent ongoing peace.

George wrote about current events on the first-year anniversary of the country of South Sudan in his Cascade Commentary, October 2012.

> After decades of civil war and neglect, South Sudan remains one of the poorest and most undeveloped regions of the world…It has been said that if one ever drinks from the waters of the Nile he will always return to drink again. There are many humanitarian aid groups working to improve the economic and social infrastructure that was left in ruins from so many years of war.

Southern Sudan was clearly the hardest of any of the missionary assignments of our 40-year missionary career. Infrastructure was totally absent and disintegrated even further after we left. During our stay there, we led projects from homes in Mundri, Tonj, and Yei…It became impossible to keep teams of development workers safe in the region because of hostage taking.

When we lived there, we were asked by the United Nations High Commissioner for Refugees (UNHCR) to establish a program to help the Ugandan refugees coming across the border in large numbers. They needed assistance to get started raising their own food supply. Usually, the U.N. does not work with Christian organizations, but they had experienced so much financial loss from working with local governments that they implored ACROSS to help. We were representatives of ACROSS but on loan to the UNHCR. The project was well funded and began with nine settlements and 9,000 refugees. A year later it had increased to 28 settlements with a total of 168,000 refugees.

We've learned that there are now 30 camps and nearer to 200,000 people, but the encouraging news is that all but three of the camps are now raising adequate food for their own people. The Ugandans are very industrious and some of the settlement areas have good soil and adequate rainfall. We are thankful to have had a part in setting up the agricultural extension network that has allowed such an encouraging success story.

If Westerners do not understand the requirement of educating the next generation of Africans of the price paid for freedom, it will surely be lost and there is 100% probability that their descendants will be Muslims. We must not allow our opinions and actions to be based solely upon our American upbringing and Western orientation...Remember, Islam is an anti-Christ religion. It is a totally integrated, holistic system that sweeps entire societies into its net from which there is no escape...The South Sudanese must stand firm in faith in Christ, in the unity of purpose, and be ready to war against the next Jihad that will undoubtedly come.

Mollie Zapata wrote in her article on the Enough 101 Website: *Breaking Out of the Spiral in South Sudan: Anti-Money Laundering, Network Sanctions, and a New Peacemaking Architecture:*

The metastasizing crisis in South Sudan requires a new strategy for achieving a sustainable peace. Conditions on the ground are unbearable for large swathes of South Sudan's population, and regional peacemaking efforts are not delivering results.

Absent any new variables, the parties to South Sudan's war, particularly the government, lacks sufficient incentives to make the necessary compromises for peace. Since an outright victory by any party does not seem realistic in the short run, the variable that actually could alter the parties' incentive structure is much more effective, focused, and meaningful international pressure.

I receive current information about Ethiopia and Sudan through the Life and Peace Institute. George always looked forward to receiving their Horn of Africa Bulletin, and read it from cover to cover. According to the LPI website, their work in Ethiopia dates back to the late 1980s, when it supported several locally driven post-conflict initiatives through partnerships with traditional leaders, NGOs (Non-governmental organizations) and faith-based institutions.

The Life and Peace Institute program in Sudan contributes to building peace in partnership with active and knowledgeable participants from academia, civil society and local communities. This is done through the provision of organizational and technical capacity-building support to partners as well as directly accompanying their partners as they engage in peacebuilding activities.

Family Missions Connection

It has been wonderful for me to become friends with my grandson Joel's in-laws, Michael and Esther Gray. Their mission organization, Grace Extended Ministries International, is active in East Africa, including South Sudan. In November 2018, they reported that their associate, Pastor James from Uganda, had been able to get into South Sudan and had taken a team in to train leaders. Pastor James shared that he was heartbroken to visit churches in the bush area that were started before the war. The pastors and leaders had been killed, and others had fled to refugee camps in Uganda.

Michael wrote:

> The need for biblical teaching is great in this war-torn nation. Despite all the people have already been through, the ongoing fear of attack and the desperate need for food, medicine, and supplies, there is a genuine openness to the Gospel. We know the most effective way to reach this nation for Christ is through our Timothies teaching the pastors and leaders. [Timothies is the name GEM has coined for

the men they have trained, using the example of the Apostle Paul teaching Timothy in the Bible.] Despite the obstacles, GEM has felt a call into this region for many years. The door is open and the way back from war and lawlessness is through Jesus Christ. We realize that the pastors are starved for training and are thankful for the opportunity to respond to that need.

Pastor James had written to Michael and Esther:

As I crossed from Uganda into the eastern region of South Sudan, I stopped seeing houses, vehicles, shops, and markets. There was no electricity. We had to hire a vehicle and security personnel to accompany us on the three-day journey across very bad roads to reach our destination. We taught for four days. Food was scarce. Bible understanding was limited. There had been no formal biblical training in the area for 70 years.

One of the pastors said, "I have taken so many years pastoring a church and I have planted more churches, but I have never received training such as this from the Bible. This teaching has transformed our lives and our ministries." Another pastor stated, "This training has made me know the need to have an ongoing faith that will take me through the difficult times and to see my future of ministry and family in God. I was about to quit ministry due to the difficulties we are going through in this nation, but your coming to teach has changed me completely."

Interestingly, when we were working in Sudan, people from Uganda were coming as refugees to Sudan, and we had a project to help them. During the crisis of the second civil war, Sudanese people traveled to Uganda. There is a well-worn path between the two countries due to incredible political turmoil and disturbances at various times through the years.

George and I personally knew many of the people trapped in those circumstances and we continually prayed that divine intervention would allow help to reach them before it was too late. We helped some of our close Sudanese friends with our own resources, but for the past decade I have not had a good means of giving to help the people in South Sudan. Now with my connection with the Grays, I again have the opportunity to invest in the lives of the Sudanese people by supporting the fruitful missionary endeavors of Grace Extended Ministries International.

Serving Other Organizations

"It is a trustworthy statement deserving full acceptance. For it is for this we labor and strive, because we have fixed our hope on the living God, who is the Savior of all men, especially of believers."

I Timothy 4:9-10

CHAPTER 20
Life in New England

W hen we were forced to leave Sudan, George accepted a position at the Holstein Association and we moved to Brattleboro, Vermont. We knew that we were not finished with our missionary work, but he was very knowledgeable about the dairy industry and had much to contribute. The position was perfect for him and he quickly got oriented into his role on the Research and Development team with Dr. Ray Kliewer.

When we first arrived in Brattleboro, Dr. Kliewer and his wife Marian offered us a place to stay in their home. It was bitter cold and they kept their thermostat very low. We had come from the Sudan where the temperatures were over 100° so our bodies were in shock. The Kliewers asked us to housesit for them while they had a winter vacation in Hawaii, and we set the thermostat a bit higher. We were thankful for a place to live while we searched for an apartment, learned the area, and began house hunting.

409 Western Ave., Apt. #5, West Brattleboro, Vermont

We moved into the apartment on Western Avenue when it was cold and icy in January 1984. The moving van parked on the street and the movers brought the furniture down the treacherous, icy driveway using dollies. Four boxes and a heater did not arrive with the moving van, but after we had filled out the insurance papers and given them up as lost, they were located. We much preferred to get our belongings rather than money for their value.

Although it was a very nice apartment, we did not have laundry facilities there and I had to wash clothes in the bathtub or at a laundromat. Neither did we have a vehicle at that time, but a small bus that came past our apartment met our transportation needs until we could acquire a car. I didn't have a job at first and enjoyed being a housewife and helpmate to George. In spite of the sub-zero weather, our apartment stayed warm and comfortable. Thankfully, the cost of the heat and hot water was incorporated into the rent.

Employment for Me

I signed up for a five-week computer class in the office building next door to our apartment. Before I registered, I asked if there was any chance of earning part of the cost of the tuition ($80). The director of Continuing Education for the University of Vermont assured me that he would be glad for my help. He proposed that I oversee the computer room on Thursday nights from 6:30 to 9:00 PM so that students in the three computer classes could come in to practice. I was very pleased to have the training and the tuition paid.

When that class finished, I applied to a Kelly-girl type company called Secretarial Services. I knew the owner of the company from the church we attended, so the hiring process went quickly. My first task was to type the manuscript for an author who was writing a novel, requiring me to travel 18 miles each way to his home three afternoons a week. The son of Italian immigrants, he chose settings in Sicily and Sicilian communities in New York and New Orleans. Though written in English, the book was peppered with Italian terms, which he asked me to underline. When the book was published, the foreign words would be italicized.

When that job concluded, for three months in 1984 I worked in the Outbound Department at the Experiment in International Living to help with the sending out of high school and college young people on their way to a summer abroad in the home of a family from another country. During the year, about 650-700 people were sent out in various programs, including mountaineering in Switzerland, biking in France, and homestay/travel projects in India, Mexico, and the Scandinavian countries. The application deadline was May 15th, so the peak period for work in this department was from March through June. Later, George had a chance to do some Spanish study at that same school.

Real Estate Secretary

I was hired as the receptionist and secretary for Martocci & Henry Real Estate, a large firm in Brattleboro. George's work with the Holstein Association required international travel about 60% of the time, which made my job a great diversion for me. I was the first face for people coming in to the agency and I enjoyed interacting with the public. This was before computers, and besides answering the phones, I typed the contracts for more than 20 brokers and salespersons. I was very much appreciated because most of them hated typing or used the hunt and peck method.

Hit from Behind

One day after work I made my usual stop at a mailbox close to the office to drop off the day's outgoing mail. I had pulled off the street into the space set aside for the drop box. Just as I unbuckled my seat belt, I was hit from behind by a car traveling at a high rate of speed. I was thrown forward and upward and hit my head above the window. Someone who witnessed the accident called 9-1-1. My indelible memory of the accident is of the 17-year-old driver of the other car admitting that he had been distracted by lighting a cigarette. He didn't seem at all concerned about me, but kept yelling over and over, "My dad is going to kill me!" An ambulance came and took me to the hospital, where I was x-rayed and tested for a concussion.

George was on an international trip and there was no way to contact him, but it really wasn't necessary. My boss, Frank Martocci, came to the hospital and waited through all the testings. When I was released, he took me home. Later that week when George returned, we went together to the place where our car had been towed after the accident. We both were amazed that even though the left rear fender was accordion-pleated, the trunk bent and the left rear door damaged, the heavy springs prevented more serious injuries to me and the car was able to be repaired. The young man's car was totaled, and his father's insurance covered my medical expenses and the collision repair for our car.

RFD 1, Box 288, Hinsdale, New Hampshire, Corner of Prairie Road and Meetinghouse Rd.

In the spring (called mud season) we began to look for a place to purchase. Through my work at the real estate agency, we found a large, two-story house, a fixer-upper with lots of charm and potential, just across the Connecticut River in New Hampshire. We worked on improvements as we had time and money concurrently. The heating system George created was ingenious and became a great help for the long cold winters. The main source of heat was a wood furnace and there was also an oil-burning furnace. Each night he filled the wood furnace with wood before we went to bed and it would burn down to coals by morning. With a timing device, he set the oil furnace to come on early in the morning for a couple hours to warm up the house while he got the wood furnace going. With this combination, we had a warm house while we got ready for work.

The oil furnace was also set to come on to warm the house for a couple hours before we got home from work and were able to restock the wood in the wood furnace. Each fall we purchased six or more cords of wood, already split, and had it delivered and dumped near the opening to the basement. The wood stacking project was most often my task. I was glad to have a project to do while George was traveling, and he purposely made the heating system easy for me to manage in his absence.

I wrote to my parents in January 1985:

> George is taking a course in Conversational Latin American Spanish at the Experiment in International Training where I worked last year. He had to be there by 8:30 AM and had to take me to work first; then he got finished about 3:30 PM and went back to his own office at the Holstein Association to check on the mail before picking me up at 5:00. Our day was a little longer, but we were prepared for it and were so glad we could make our schedules work together without having to have a second car.

> It is snowing right now but is predicted to be only a light dusting. We can remember one time when a light dusting was predicted and we got 26 inches! We hired a neighbor with a snow plow on the front of his truck to plow our driveway. Unfortunately, the garage at this older home is detached, requiring shoveling of a walkway to get to the house.

> It has been really cold, in the single digits and down to zero, but today warmed up into the 20s. There is predicted to be quite a lot of wind today and tomorrow with wind chill temperatures below zero. We are pleased that we are doing so well at keeping our large

home warm. Sometimes we look at the woodpile and wonder whether it will last, but we trust it will. We have an order in for four more cords of wood. The guy who supplied our wood promised to deliver the new supply way back in October and still hasn't brought it. The wood would be green anyway and it would be best to hold it over until next fall.

Social Life

We made many new friends among George's co-workers at the Holstein Association and had many enjoyable gatherings for fellowship. One year in December as a gift, the Holstein directors contracted a bus to take the executive leaders and their wives to the Broadway musical *Chorus Line*. We had never been to New York City except in the airport, so it was fun for us to join our associates in some sightseeing and walking the streets before the play started. There was no plan to overnight there, so we got back to Brattleboro in the wee hours after a delightful experience.

The Holstein Association had been formed in 1885, and George and I were chosen to be hosts for the international guests for the 100-year anniversary celebration. The nearest airport for them to arrive at was Hartford, Connecticut. On May 25, 1985, we drove to Hartford, checked into the convention hotel, and spent the day welcoming visitors from various places in the world. George already knew many of them from his travels. Although I had not met them, it was a gratifying time of getting acquainted with the guests. One of the days during the convention, international visitors were invited to travel by bus the two hours to Brattleboro to tour the Holstein Headquarters.

Our camaraderie with friends at Agapé Christian Fellowship was especially fulfilling. George was an elder and we both served on the Missions Committee along with close friends Carl and Verlaine

Brown. They caught the missions mandate and later joined us as missionaries with Calvary International. After their initial time in Guatemala City, they were posted in Oaxaca, Mexico. They brought together a networking group from several different agencies that were targeting the unreached Indian tribes in the area. We visited them there on our multi-country trip in the spring of 2000 and met their national partners and missionary colleagues from other agencies.

Prophetic Words

As missionaries, at various times both George and I received prophetic words. We were worshiping at Agapé Christian Fellowship in Brattleboro, Vermont, when a prophet named Charles Browning came for a special meeting. He spoke this word over me, someone taped it and transcribed it for me. At that time, we had already had missionary journeys in Ethiopia and Sudan, and we knew there would be more in the future. As is often the case, this man whom we did not know was very perceptive of our spiritual walk.

> Precious one, as you seek the Lord amazing things are going to come about. You're looking at some distant places and the Lord paves the way for that, not only prepares the way, but goes with you. So you might have some reasons in mind, but God has His special reasons.

> We speak of that peace that is like a river, a peace not only that comes to you from Him, but through you going out to others that makes you a peacemaker. Just let that peace flow out from you. The Lord is going to have a ministry there that as you go and even in the midst of people that are upset and people that are shaken by certain things, they will begin to feel your peace and began to settle in their own hearts and lives

as you are in their midst and the Lord is with you ministering that peace that passes all understanding.

You are going to need even more in the way of physical and spiritual strength, not just ordinary strength, but extra strength. The Lord promises that as you need it the strength will flow, but there will be times you feel weakness. At the times you feel it, let that openness to the Lord, that praise to the Lord ascend and let joy bring forth. In that joy there is strength, even extra and super strength just bursting forth to finish things that you will need to finish using the physical strength he gives. And also there is spiritual power going to come forth. He will show you and give you that wisdom to express that, as well is discerning of the certain ones that should be receiving those benefits that flow out from you.

See the Lord change people's minds and hearts and even take away at least a good part of contrariness and opposition. God goes before you and he says,

"When a man's ways are pleasing to the Lord, even his enemies will be at peace with him." Proverbs 16:7

So Father, lead this one as the shepherd leads the sheep and open up green pastures and let her hear again the invitation to those still waters that speak of peace. Let her drink and eat abundantly of the Spirit's meat and drink which is so wonderfully provided for her. In Jesus name.

Restoring the Grandeur

In spite of his intense travel schedule, George was eager to do some renovation on our house, built in 1825. The house was spacious and we weren't using it all, so he had the idea of creating a rental apartment on the back part of the house. By adding a bedroom and using our existing kitchen and the large back porch, a one-bedroom apartment was created. The porch was not very useful to us; in fact, I used it as a freezer in the winter.

There was a large room in the center of the house that was kind of like a family room. The previous owner had worked on his motorcycle in front of the wood stove in that room in the winter, so the carpet had major oil stains when we moved in. It didn't take long for us to get rid of the carpet, but because there were so many doorways and window openings it was a puzzle to figure out how to use that space in the renovation. With incredible ingenuity, George created a lovely new kitchen in that space.

Tenant Friends

After we finished the new apartment in the back, I met Harold and Becky Porterfield in my work at the real estate office. They were seeking an affordable place to live and were happy to move into our new apartment. Although she was much younger, I had a lot in common with Becky, who came from a missionary family. They both became delightful friends. Their first baby, Daniel, was born while they lived there.

When we purchased the house, there was already an upstairs apartment, which we rented to friends from Agapé Christian Fellowship, John and Sheri Parker. They were newly married when they moved in, but while they lived in our apartment John Michael was born. Since our own grandchildren lived far away, we enjoyed the little ones who were our very close neighbors.

George was pleased for me to have friends close by when he was traveling.

The previous owners had converted what would have naturally been a formal dining room into a bedroom. (Bedrooms don't usually have a chandelier!) We both wanted to restore that space into a proper dining room and to be able to access it from the living room. To our amazement, when George took down the wallboard on that wall, there was the framework for the original doorway, making the conversion very easy.

We also wanted to make a sunroom on the east side near the side entrance (another space that had been converted into a small bedroom). When George began the demolition, he discovered in the wall a picture of the house in its earlier days that showed that room as a sunroom with a wall of windows. It was a rewarding project to restore the house to its earlier splendor, even though we lived "under construction" for quite a long time. With two rental units, our cost of living in that large house was exceptionally low.

On the Road Again

George had a busy travel schedule during 1985, including several trips to Puerto Rico and islands in the Caribbean. On a European trip, he had an enjoyable stopover in England visiting with Romney and Sandie Jackson, friends and coworkers from our time in Sudan. Before his trip, we hosted a young lady from Turkey for ten days. She was an economist with the dairy company there and was training for five weeks in Brattleboro and other places in the U.S. We enjoyed cross-cultural contacts such as this very much.

Although he had trips to Algeria and Venezuela, most of George's travel in 1986 was in the U.S. He took separate foreign delegations from Algeria, Turkey, and Hungary on tours of various dairy farms and facilities in Vermont, Arizona, Wisconsin, and California, ending each trip in Washington, DC. The bonus on those trips was getting to visit Steve and Jennie's families in California.

George served with the Holstein Association for five years, traveling about 60% of the time. We realized that we had been separated an equivalent of three years! There was a reorganization of the international department and he was concerned that his position might be eliminated. We decided it was time to explore options for mission service again.

CHAPTER 21
East Coast – West Coast

MAP International

As we considered mission service at the beginning of 1989, we explored possibilities with *Intercristo,* an organization in the Seattle area that matched openings with qualified applicants. We submitted our credentials and reviewed many opportunities, but none of them seemed to "have our name on them." We didn't know that MAP International, based in Brunswick, Georgia, had been notified of George's availability until I received a call one day from Larry Dixon, the president of MAP. George was traveling, but I answered the questions he asked. A date was set for George to meet Larry in the Philadelphia airport. After a few weeks of relationship building and negotiations, a job offer was made for Vice President of Program.

I had enjoyed my work at the real estate office in Vermont, but we decided to accept the position at MAP International, requiring a move to Brunswick. When I left my job, I got a card signed by all the realtors that said, "As you go on to new places and new faces, remember this: All the old faces at the old place will never forget you!" The note with the bonus check stated, "Given in appreciation for the many years of unselfish and faithful service to the employees of Martocci & Henry Real Estate and the insurance companies that shared our building."

As I was driving down the road near our home one afternoon, I was contemplating the moving process and I heard these words in my spirit – Eliminate and Concentrate. That concept helped me then as I sorted what to take, what to give away and what to throw away, and I have kept those words in my mind through the years, trying to avoid accumulating too much baggage to carry along the way.

In April of that year, a large moving van paid for by MAP International moved our belongings from New Hampshire to Georgia and we transported a few precious things in our car. I remember being incredibly exhausted at the end of the day the truck was unloaded, even though my main task had been to show the movers where to put things. The president of MAP had emphasized that George should be available for the annual meeting of MAP International the first week after our arrival. There was no time to rest from the move because of all the events surrounding the meeting with MAP personnel, who had come from many places in the world.

51 Sunset Blvd., Brunswick, Georgia

Within days after we moved into the beautiful two-story house with a large hospitality room, George offered our home for one of the social events. More than 50 people came for a smorgasbord meal and visiting. I'm sure it was not a potluck, and I must have done a lot of the food preparation, but undoubtedly others helped. People were amazed that we were able to host the large group so soon after moving in. We weren't completely unpacked, but there was a large walk-in attic room where we were able to store boxes to unpack later.

MAP's mission is to advance the total health of people living in the world's poorest communities. George enjoyed his work of supervising an international staff of about 70 people, including doctors, health professionals, trainers in international development and national workers.

We quickly developed relationships with George's MAP International colleagues and with new friends from Christian Renewal Church. Our time in that home included many opportunities to host people. We developed some wonderful friendships that have continued through the decades. Later, when we were back in mission service, Christian Renewal Church served as our sending church, and was exceptionally committed to our well-being as missionaries.

Two years later, our time in Brunswick ended too soon when George was laid off at MAP International to avoid a potential financial catastrophe. His offer to go on a reduced salary was not received. He knew the organization had serious issues to be addressed because of a downturn in the economy, but he had no idea his job would be part of the solution. It was a great disappointment to us because we had quickly put down roots in the community and at Christian Renewal Church.

Although George's job with MAP International had a good salary and benefits, I had been supplementing our income by working as office manager for the Physical/Occupational Therapy Department at Glynn Brunswick Memorial Hospital. I recently re-read my job description and was amazed to realize how extensive my duties were in that position. I loved working with the PT/OT staff, and my supervisor, Elizabeth Daniel, became a dear friend. The letter she wrote for me to provide to potential future employers was very complimentary and blessed me greatly.

George received a generous severance package and I continued to work at the hospital. We put out feelers to consider other mission possibilities, but we didn't receive any that we considered feasible options. He applied for other jobs in the area, but the responses he received indicated that they didn't want to hire him because he was overqualified, and they thought he would undoubtedly get a better offer and not stay.

While we prayed and waited for direction on the next step, George used his construction skills to build an apartment over the garage in our home, which we were able to rent out for extra income. We were making it financially, but he was seriously underemployed and discouraged.

Smucker Manufacturing, Inc.

At the same time that we were seeking employment for George, our long-time friends at Smucker Manufacturing, Duane and LeeAnn Rawlins, were looking for a manager for their agricultural equipment company in Harrisburg, Oregon. They learned that George was available and presented him with an opportunity to be the general manager of the company while mentoring their young son, Rob Smucker, to take over that role in the family company.

Neither of us was eager to move across the country again and we both knew that we were not finished with our commitment to the Great Commission, but we accepted this opportunity as divine guidance. The bonus was to be near our families, and especially to help our aged mothers. Although it was not technically a ministry job, we felt like it was an assignment from the Lord. We knew that we would be returning to mission service when Rob was trained and ready.

We had purchased a home in Junction City in 1977 and lived there while Steve and Jennie finished high school at Christ's Center School. Through the years, it became a family resource with several combinations of the family living in it according to their needs. Jennie and Mark lived there before and after baby Amy was born, Steve lived with them for a time when he was a college student at Oregon State University, and Dan and Laurie made it their home for a time as well.

We were thankful to still own that home on Laurel Street, which had been a rental for some time. We gave the renters six weeks' notice that we needed the house ourselves. Now here we were back in Junction City in 1990 living in that house again. It was good to be back with family and friends from church and the community. My mother had a hip replacement soon after we moved back to Oregon, and I was glad to be able to take care of her in our home. We truly enjoyed get-togethers with our family during those years.

Plates in the Air

While working full-time at Smucker Manufacturing, George was also writing the dissertation in fulfillment of his PhD. We only had one car, which he drove to work, and I rode the bus to Eugene (16 miles) several times a week to check out resource materials from the University of Oregon library. In the evenings he reviewed the pertinent literature and I typed his preliminary drafts.

We had an electric typewriter but not a computer, so each time he made a revision I had to type that section over again. By the time we were ready for the final draft of the 180-page document, our son Dan arranged for me to use a computer at Christ's Center. Wow! If that option had been available sooner, it would have saved me hours of typing!

George always had ongoing projects and he expected me to keep them going while he went on to something else. It was an honor to serve him in his career and ministry aspirations and help him reach his goals. When writing the acknowledgments for his doctoral thesis he wrote: "I express sincere appreciation to my wife Janet who encouraged and assisted me for nearly a decade of service in Africa and subsequent international development assignments."

After he completed his dissertation, I got a job at the Junction City Medical Clinic as a receptionist, appointment scheduler, cashier and file maintenance manager.

Another Transition

In 1990 after three years in Oregon, George was contacted by Bill Shepherd, a former colleague at MAP International. He had been laid off also and was currently working as a consultant at Calvary International in Jacksonville, Florida. He knew of the need for a person with George's qualifications at the ministry. We explored the opportunity and determined that it would be a good fit for us when Rob was ready to take over at Smucker Manufacturing

In September 1992 we attended a missions conference on Jekyll Island in Georgia, and at the same time we were following up on an invitation to be interviewed for a position at Calvary International. While we were at the conference, we met with leaders of the worldwide mission organization. They reviewed George's qualifications to fill the role of Vice President of Ministries and determined that his background was a match for the opening.

It was possible for George to participate in some of the missionary leadership meetings at Calvary International when he was traveling in the Southeast for Smucker Manufacturing. Rob appreciated the mentoring he had received and looked forward to taking the reins. George counted it a privilege to have a part in launching him into the leadership of the company. The Smucker family gave their blessing as we moved on to our next assignment.

CHAPTER 22
Florida, Here We Come!

I don't remember how we acquired multiple copies of a AAA map of the Southeast, but I had the idea of using them as wrapping paper for special gifts for the family after we made the decision to get back into mission service. It was a fun way to announce to them our plans to join Calvary International and move to Jacksonville, Florida. In our research of the area, we learned that Jacksonville is the most populous city in Florida and the largest city by area in the contiguous United States. Most of our lives we had lived in rural settings, so moving to this large city was a bit intimidating. After living there, we joked that we needed to pack a lunch if we had occasion to drive across the city.

The population was nearly a million people, about 60% white and 40% African American, Latino, and other ethnicities. Jacksonville is home to the 10th largest Arab population in the United States, as well as the largest Filipino American community in Florida.

From our cottage on *Pacific Drive* in Oregon to an apartment on *Atlantic Boulevard* in Florida, once again we were moving from coast to coast.

5201 Atlantic Blvd. Apt. 201, Jacksonville, Florida

We wanted to live close to the office when we first moved to Jacksonville in August 1993. We thought that renting for a year would give us a chance to learn the area prior to purchasing a home. The location of Colonial Point Apartments was just ten minutes from the Calvary International office, where George was assigned as Vice President of Ministries. The two-bedroom apartment was adequate, but we needed to use the second bedroom for our home office, and this prevented us from having a place to host overnight guests, an important part of our lifestyle for our entire married life.

6045 University Club Blvd., Jacksonville, Florida

After living in the apartment for about ten months, we began to look around for a house to purchase that would be large enough to accommodate guests. After church on Sundays, we would drive around looking for signs that advertised For Sale by Owner. One time when we were in Woodmere subdivision north of Jacksonville University, George commented that he liked the look of the brick house on the corner of University Club Blvd. and Dawnridge Road. Alas, it had no sign and did not appear to be for sale. We did a curbside look at a couple houses for sale in that neighborhood and we liked the area, but we weren't interested in either of those houses. A few weeks later we went back to that same subdivision and were excited to discover a For Sale sign on that special corner house that George had been drawn to previously!

We noticed a car in the driveway and knocked on the door. A lady was painting in the living room, and she shared that her mother who had lived there had recently passed away. She invited us to tour the house and gave a good sales pitch. In addition to three bedrooms and 2½ baths, there was a large Florida room (glassed-in porch) across the entire back of the house. We really liked the house and decided to call the real estate company the next day to discuss the price and other details. We qualified for the mortgage and were able to negotiate a sales agreement for $90,000. We especially appreciated the Florida room, which we turned into an office with desks for each of us.

Even though the city was large, we carved out a corner that included the Calvary International office, a 20-minute drive, and the necessities of life – grocery store, cleaners, doctor and dentist offices. Our church, New Life Christian Fellowship was a 30-minute drive toward the beach.

Calvary International World Headquarters

When we moved to Jacksonville, at first I supplemented our missionary income by working for Watson Realty, a large real estate company. My work was to hire and train personal assistants for the highest producing real estate salespeople. This was a part-time job, about 30 hours per week. They cooperated with my need to travel with George from time to time as part of our ministry. I tried to keep up with George's administrative needs during that period of outside employment, but it was almost overwhelming.

When our missionary donations increased, I discontinued my part-time employment and worked full-time in the office of Calvary International (now called Go To Nations), serving as George's executive assistant and helping with other duties to keep the office running smoothly. Another major aspect of our work with Calvary International was hospitality. In addition to having a series of people living with us, we hosted many missionaries and guided the social life related to training events.

We owned our home in Jacksonville almost twenty years, 1994 to 2013, and lived in it between mission assignments. We were the defacto guesthouse for Calvary International and hosted guests most of the time. We also hosted many enjoyable events for friends and colleagues. At the end of the sessions of Missionary Preparation

Orientation, the 10-day training for new missionaries, we invited the participants to our home for a meal and fellowship. When we hosted groups, George helped me learn to delegate some of the household tasks to guests who were willing to help, and I flourished in my hospitality role for the ministry.

We sometimes heard that Calvary International was the best-kept secret in Jacksonville. To make it better known, I initiated a program I named *Taste and See* to showcase the scope of the ministry and to expand our reach in the local community. I prepared lunch and served as hostess for small groups of people our staff identified who were not knowledgeable about the ministry. I also trained other team members who were interested in learning the art of hospitality.

Always Thoughtful

Dateline April 10, 1995, Calvary International, in George's handwriting:

> As I was writing thank you notes to some staff members, I want to say thanks to you in a special way as the most important person in my life. I appreciate your commitment to me, our marriage, family and ministry. You are special to me in every way and a blessing to many. In sincerity and love, George

One year when we were serving in Guatemala, my birthday greeting from George was in Spanish.

Feliz Cumpleaños con Todo Mi Amor
(Happy Birthday with All My Love)
Signed, Jorge

Unfortunate Incident

In 2008 George had an unusual situation occur that seemed like it could have happened in Africa, but not in a resort city on the coast in Florida. While we were on a consultation project with Christian Adventures International in Daytona Beach, he was bitten on the foot by a brown recluse spider. He didn't feel it at the time, but later a blister developed and upon close inspection we saw the fang marks. He had a serious reaction – pain, itching and discoloration –and it took months for the effects to wear off.

My Father Knows My Name

In May of 2008, I responded to this message from Dr. Grettel Wentling, Missions Director, New Life Christian Fellowship, Jacksonville, Florida.

> Dear Janet, I'm sure you've had a bunch of people ask you about this, but can you tell me what happened Tuesday night at Lakeland? I was told that Todd Bentley was calling out your name, and Paul Stock went up on stage and explained that he lived with you and that you were like a mother to him. What can you tell me about this?

We were visiting George's brother's family in Hermiston, Oregon, when I began getting phone calls from friends and coworkers who were watching the special revival program from Lakeland, Florida, on God TV. I didn't get to talk to Paul Stock (our friend who lived in our home) that night but did talk to him the next day. We did not know that Paul had taken some extra days off work after Memorial Day to attend the revival meetings in Lakeland, Florida. Had he not been there, no one would have told Todd who we were and that we were missionaries with Calvary International.

As best we could piece it together from the many accounts, Todd heard my name in his spirit several times over the night and finally said, "Janet Meyers, who is Janet Meyers? Is she here in the arena?" Paul knew I wasn't there, so he ran up to the front and told the screeners that he considered me his mother and George his father and has lived with us for seven years. They escorted him up on the platform and he told Todd Bentley that we were missionaries with Calvary International and traveled all over the world. Todd said, "Yes, she is the one! God has amazing grace for her and their ministry!"

My Go To Nations co-worker Sandra and her husband, Don Barfield, from New Life Christian Fellowship were watching. They were so excited and called me on our cell phone in Oregon. I was not in a setting in which I could truly respond like I wanted to at that time, but I did share with the group what had happened. They are all believers but did not have the background to understand or appreciate the magnitude of what had happened concerning me. To Yahweh be the glory! I was humbled by this unique occurrence and wondered what it could mean for us and our ministry.

I am the good shepherd, and I know My own, and My own know Me. John 1:14

I responded to Dr. Grettel:

We all know that our Father knows us by name and loves us unconditionally, but I am in shock and awe that He would announce to the whole world on God TV that He has planned some amazing grace for me and for our ministry. I have asked the Lord how I should live in light of this occurrence. So far, I have only been assured that I'm to continue to be faithful to what I already know and understand.

Remembering Paul

Paul Stock lived with us from 2004 to 2011 to help his financial situation, and he helped us by looking after our house and grounds when we were away. His father had died before he was born, and he had looked to George as his father from the time they met, when we first moved to Jacksonville. He was the same age as our son Dan, and he loved for us to say we had adopted him. One time when we returned from Guatemala, Paul was in the hospital recovering from the injuries of a serious accident, and he did not seem to be right mentally.

We discovered that the peculiar symptoms Paul was experiencing were due to Pick's disease, similar to Alzheimer's. I was able to take care of him in the initial stages, but eventually we made the tough decision to place him in a nursing home for around-the-clock attention. Sadly, after a year there, he passed away in September 2012. We chose to remember Paul as a physically fit, energetic disciple of Christ, finding ways to bless others along his pathway of life. He was a hardworking, highly-committed person of good character and faith. We loved him like a son and are thankful that the Lord allowed us to have a part in his life.

CHAPTER 23
Life in Guatemala

O nce when we lived in New England and I was feeling cold and miserable, I whined to George, "Take me to a warmer climate." I should have been more specific, such as pleasantly warm, because our next time of ministry out of the U.S. was in northern Guatemala, where it was extremely hot and humid, much like Sudan.

We arrived in Guatemala City in December 2002, on special assignment from the president of Calvary International to take over when the directors of the Timothy Project in the Petén region were not able to continue. Once again, the extreme temperature change was hard on our bodies. George experienced some altitude sickness in the mile-high city, but the eight-hour bus ride north took us down to about 300 feet and he was fine after we got to the lower elevation.

The area is known for its heat and dust, but mercifully we had arrived during the coolest season so were able to adjust more gradually. The Global Training and Ministry Base was a significant asset of Calvary International and was needed to provide training for new missionaries and to continue community development in the area.

Director's House, Building 3, GTMB, San Benito, Petén, Guatemala

The house prepared for our arrival was easily the most beautiful we had ever lived in on the mission field. We had arrived with just our suitcases, knowing in advance that furniture and household items had been left for our use. We had one week with Jason and Leah Noble, the couple who had been overseeing the project for the past six months, before they departed for a well-deserved furlough. We worked hard to catch the baton. We were the only expatriate staff on site until Julie Jorgensen arrived the following February. She had been on the GTMB staff previously and we were extremely grateful that she was willing to return to help with financial and accounting issues for the Base.

We knew it would be incredibly hot, but there was an air conditioner in our bedroom and in one room of the office building where we could go to cool off. I thought back to our time in the Sudan, where it was much hotter, and we had no electricity for fans or any means of stirring the air. Here we set our bedroom thermostat at 80°, but the rest of the house stayed about 95°. We began our workday early to take advantage of the cooler temperature in the morning.

The market in Santa Elena (30,000 people) and a smaller market in San Benito (25,000 people) were great produce markets with lots of vegetables and fruits. Both were stocked on Tuesdays and Fridays and we were delighted to have such great food options for our own use and to serve to others. Our first guests came mid-January for a week, flying in a private plane from Colorado Springs to explore possibilities of assisting in the evangelism aspect of Calvary's community development project.

Mercy Ministry

Shortly after our arrival, we met our neighbor Ruth just outside the main gate of the complex. She asked if she could get some powdered milk for her mother and invited us to visit her. Ana lay on her bed in the primitive hut that housed the extended family. She was seriously crippled by rheumatoid arthritis and suffered greatly, wincing in pain as I gently touched her misshapen hand when we prayed for her. Aspirin for her pain and milk for her to drink seemed such small gifts but were a blessing for Ana in her remaining days of life. When the disease took her life about two months later, we went for a courtesy visit and helped the family with burial expenses. The box (casket) was still in the house pending the burial that afternoon. The lady was a Christian so we were able to encourage her family that their loved one's suffering was over.

Construction Continued

The remaining building to be completed at the GTMB was the L-shaped building with nine apartments for staff and interns, along with dormitories for short-term teams. As we walked from our house to our office less than a block away, we would regularly hold out our hands toward the building and pray for its completion for the glory of God. As more funds came in, construction proceeded, but much more slowly than in the U.S. due to lack of modern equipment.

Because there was no possibility of ordering a truckload of prepared concrete, we had to make our own. Workers, including our grandson Austin, put gravel, sand, cement, and water into a small cement mixer that had been donated to the Base. I have a vivid memory of him sweating to keep up with the Guatemalan workers with their empty wheelbarrows waiting for the next load to come out of the cement mixer. (He and our granddaughter Stephanie had come together for a summertime mission experience in the Petén.)

The workers made surprising progress considering the primitive systems for all aspects of construction. The project was done without acquiring debt, on a pay-as-we-go basis, with lots of volunteer help. I had amazing favor as I worked on raising funds to complete the building. Many of the donors gave in honor of their loved ones and we put name plates on the doors of the apartments they had paid for.

It was rewarding to see the L-building come to completion. Ours was the first apartment to be ready for occupancy and gradually other apartments were finished and occupied by staff missionaries. A kitchen, dining room and the women's and men's dormitories were a great blessing to the short-term teams who came to help with community development.

Apartment 401, GTMB, San Benito, Petén, Guatemala

In March of 2005, we moved across the complex at the GTMB to our apartment with a combination living/dining/kitchen, tiny bedroom, and an office/reading room. We were able to move most of our goods in a wheelbarrow! Our colleagues joked, "This is perfect for a couple just starting out!" Actually, it was the first new home we had ever lived in during our 49 years of marriage!

Our move made the large director's home available for Dave and Dorothy Henry and their three children. Just prior to their arrival, the Henrys had completed Spanish school in Guadalajara, Mexico, and we were tasked with mentoring them for the director role.

Holidays in the Petén

Many of the saints' days and beliefs of the people were based on the complicated syncretistic blending of the Aztec and Mayan cultures with the Catholic religion, brought in by the Spanish invaders. Sadly, in our neighborhood many of the evangelical Christians continued to celebrate those holidays with their pagan relatives.

November 1st and 2nd were called *Dia de Los Muertos*, the Day of the Dead, when families visited, cleaned and decorated the graves of their loved ones. At first glance, the decorations, colored paper, and little skeletons performing daily tasks reminded us of Halloween. Many families honored their ancestors with home altars laden with harvest fruits and traditional bread with crossed bones of dough on top. Special food was put on the graves, awaiting the spirits to come and devour it. No one seemed to notice that the dogs were feasting!

December 7th was the "burning of the devil" ceremony, an ancient tradition called *La Quema del Diablo.* Guatemalans would use this holiday as housecleaning day. By late afternoon families had cleared their homes of all unwanted bits and pieces and erected vast heaps of rubbish outside on the streets. At around 6:00 PM the piles were set on fire and onlookers gathered to celebrate. They strongly believed that by burning the rubbish they were purging their homes and towns of evil. Scarecrow-looking beings intended as an effigy of Lucifer were also burned.

Christmas and New Year's holidays were celebrated comparably to the rest of the world. Tamales were the preferred food, often served with spiced fruit that reminded us of crab apples. Pickup trucks with loud megaphones advertising tamales for sale were driven around the community. The firecrackers were deafening, heard off and on for most of December and into January, especially at night.

Community Transformation

Among the projects we accomplished while in Guatemala was assisting the Evangelical church leaders in Integrated Community Development. We implemented the Nutrition and Health Project for the Children of the Petén (NSP) and hosted several events bringing the Evangelical leaders together for prayer and fellowship.

Concurrently with the program for children was ministry to *ancianos,* elderly people, most of whom were destitute and had no option to be cared for by their families. My Sweet Refuge was the name of the combination nursing home/hospice center. The staff at the Global

Training and Ministry Base visited with the residents at the nursing home and helped in practical ways. When short-term teams came from the U.S., there was always a project to be done at MSR. George was very involved in the business affairs and I enjoyed praying with the patients and participating in special programs to help them feel respected and valued.

Church planting and demonstrations of various aspects of community transformation were part of the integrated model village program. Included was nutrition and health emphasis through home gardens, farm crops and orchards, water filtration and clean-up, disease prevention, treatment, and clinical care. We were pleased to have a part in getting Community Health Evangelism started in the Petén. CHE is a program for training and empowering village health promoters in the rural areas and is being used successfully by many mission organizations in various parts of the world.

We initiated a regular gathering of all the missionaries serving in that region, which was much appreciated. After we turned the GTMB over to other leaders, the community development projects we had begun were continued and more were started. Tim and Nancy Lovelace received the supernatural inspiration for GloDev, Inc. (Global Development) while they were participating in a community development project in the Petén.

Sanitario

Quoting Candace Gammon, Regional Director of the Americas for Go To Nations:

> Dr. George and Janet came to San Pedro Sula, Honduras, to visit Wyly and me. They came on the bus from the Global Training and Ministry Base in the Petén region in Guatemala. A long trip on the bus includes stops at various times for food and restroom

breaks. Janet told me that George's first thing to do was to find the most trustworthy lady on the bus to help Janet find the best possible option for using the restroom when they stopped.

After they got home to the Base, Janet wrote the most wonderful note of thanks, which included a description of their bus ride home. "A lady from the bus helped me find the bathroom that was misnamed the *Sanitario* (sanitary it was not!). It was so bad that she warned me to not touch anything by repeatedly saying with emphasis *AIRE, AIRE!* (Spanish for air)." I, too, have experienced many less than sanitary Latino restrooms, and I laughed and laughed over Janet's account of her bathroom experience on that bus trip.

Roatan, Honduras

After we left the Global Training and Ministry Base, before returning to the States, we followed up on an invitation from our friends Bob and Sara Phillips from Georgia to visit them on the island of Roatan. In a previous season of ministry, they had worked among the Miskito indigenous people in Honduras. Now Bob's building skills had been called into service to build a medical facility on Roatan, with a plan for Sara, a registered nurse, to oversee medical personnel when the clinic was completed.

It is possible to get from the coastal city of La Ceiba to Roatan, one of the Caribbean Bay Islands, very quickly by plane, but to save money we traveled by ferry. About 300 people, including many children, boarded the ferry and waited for it to start the 80-minute journey. The first ten minutes of the ride were calm and the children were all excited, but then the ferry accelerated and we hit the waves of the ocean. We should have been clued in when we were each handed an airsick bag as we boarded, but we quickly learned why the nickname of the ferry was the Vomit Comet! The ride was a horrific experience for everyone. Children were screaming, both of us were seasick, and we thought we would never reach our destination.

Bob Phillips wanted George to take on a supervisory role for the clinic, and we listened intently to his impassioned appeal. We enjoyed the visit with them and appreciated the tour of the island, but despite Bob's best effort at recruiting us, the job he proposed didn't match what we were considering for our future mission service.

Sara flew with us back to the mainland of Honduras for a visit at the hospital and clinic facility, Hospital Loma de Luz, 37 miles (1-½ hour drive) from La Ceiba, operated by Dr. Jefferson McKenney, a surgeon, and his wife Roseanne, a nurse. We had been following this work for a long time and were pleased for the opportunity to tour the facilities and discuss the challenges with Dr. Jeff and Roseanne. I am always happy to receive the Cornerstone Foundation newsletter with reports and stories from their ministry. Recently, I was pleased to learn that Hospital Loma de Luz is now a cooperating ministry with Samaritan's Purse. I am receiving regular updates from Jerry and Linda Kuykendall, friends from Georgia. They served on the board of the hospital for several years and "just happened" to be there when we visited the facilities. They have since moved there and now have important roles at this exceptional ministry, which includes a bilingual school for both missionary and Honduran children.

Another Transition

After three years in Guatemala, in February 2006 we returned to the World Headquarters of Go To Nations in Jacksonville. Re-entry from Central America was quite different from what we had experienced when we came home from both Ethiopia and Sudan. Those two assignments were three years each, without the benefit of telephones, electricity, email, and computers. By the time we served in Guatemala, communications were so much improved that returning from there we did not experience the problems we had experienced earlier.

Though communication options had erased many of the challenges we faced in our service in Africa, some new dilemmas had been added with instant communication possibilities. I remember an issue when email was first being widely used. One day at the Calvary International office in Jacksonville we received 80 email messages from field missionaries in various places in the world, most requiring a reply and some action on the part of someone at the World Headquarters. The expectation of a quick reply was unreasonable, and we had to appeal for a realistic timeframe for our limited staff to respond to the requests. The present administrative leaders have created a workable system to identify priorities for missionaries to use when requesting a response.

PICTURES – B

Our family in
the Ethiopian
countryside

Taking my language test in Addis Ababa

Receiving the gift of a large squash

My turn to ride the motorbike

Ethiopian national dress

Working in the Kiramu Clinic

Our family in 1977
(leisure suits were in!)

House in Junction City where our family lived at various times

Receiving the gift of a live chicken from a friend in Sudan

My primitive kitchen in Mundri, Sudan

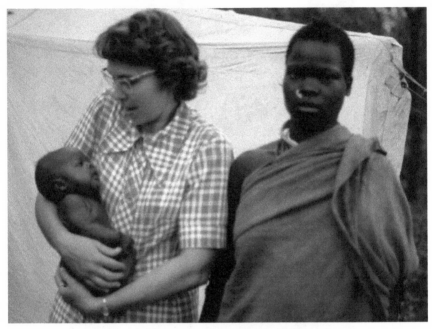

Holding a precious African baby

Crossing the river in a pontoon boat on our escape journey from Tonj

After Sudan, our 1825 house in Hinsdale, New Hampshire

At my desk at Martocci & Henry Real Estate (Note: no computer!)

Enjoying our return to Ethiopia in 2002

In front of the house we had lived in 30 years earlier in Kiramu, Ethiopia

Melted butter being poured on chumbo by our hostess to honor us

With Tarike Olana, an Ethiopian girl who had no arms, a birth defect due to her mother taking Thalidomide during pregnancy

With evangelist Negeri and his wife Messalu, friends from decades earlier, still faithfully serving the Lord

George talking with a Sudanese pastor on our return to Sudan

Sharing with some students in Uganda

On our visit with missionary colleagues Ed and Barbara Louton
in South Africa, Ed took us to this spectacular lookout point

On our trip to Russia, George was asked to preach

In Hong Kong on our way to China

Creative transportation in the Philippines

209

Dispensing medicine in Nicaragua

With Mayan lady and baby in Petén, Guatemala

With a dear lady at My Sweet Refuge, chosen by her peers as Queen for a Day

Along the Path of Life

"Thou wilt make known to me the path of life; In Thy presence is fullness of joy; In Thy right hand there are pleasures forever."

Psalm 16:11

CHAPTER 24
Stories from Our Travels

Military Assignments

We were usually separated during George's National Guard camp commitments, but the summer of 1978 was different. He left in June for a two-week assignment at Fort Lewis, Washington, near Tacoma, but the project he was working on was not completed at the end of that period and he was asked if he could possibly stay to finish it. A disappointing change in personnel at Christ's Center that summer made it possible for him to extend his time at Fort Lewis, and I was able to join him.

We rented a studio apartment (a *bedsitter* according to the British) at Steilacoom Woods, an apartment complex in the town of Steilacoom near the military base. The Murphy bed was stored in the wall during the day, changing the bedroom into a sitting room. I wasn't used to so much time with very little housework, so we decided I should get a job to be productive and contribute to our family finances.

I applied at a temp agency and was hired at Monitor Products, a company that manufactured parts for office furniture. From June to September I worked as a typist and vacation relief in various positions. I was gainfully employed, but we still had evenings to enjoy the swimming pool and be together. We both greatly enjoyed our five months of physical and emotional restoration at Steilacoom Woods. On the way home, we stopped in Salem at Jesus Northwest, a Christian music concert where Keith Green was featured. Our friends Ed and Mona Glaspey from Christ's Center were there, too. Although not pre-arranged, we had a good visit with them.

Another time I was able to join George for a month in Indianapolis when he had a military assignment at Fort Benjamin Harrison. I volunteered at the office of Christian Missionary Fellowship during the day and we often enjoyed meals with friends in the evening. I helped with the typing and assembly of *The Flavor of our Fellowship*, a missionary cookbook, which all of the CMF wives keep handy in their kitchen. It was a wonderful time of renewing relationships with the staff who worked in the office while we were missionaries in Ethiopia.

Budapest, Hungary

In 1987 I joined George in Budapest, just after a seminar he had conducted in the Hungarian countryside as part of his work for the Holstein Association. After a few days of sightseeing in the city, we took a trip on a hydrofoil boat up the Danube River to Vienna, Austria. We had a delightful time enjoying a Family Day Festival, much like a country fair, and an evening of Johann Strauss waltzes expertly performed by professional concert musicians and dancers.

From there we went by train to Nuremberg, Germany. To reach the village of Mühlhausen, the birthplace of George's grandmother, required a 40-mile drive on the Autobahn. It was harrowing for both of us, but especially for George who was uneasy driving the rented Opal at 80 mph in the slow lane, while cars passed by at 100 mph or more in the fast lane. It was worth it though, and we both enjoyed the time exploring the village and interacting with the people there. We caught the train again in Nuremberg and continued through East Germany to Berlin for three days of visiting points of interest there, concluding a wonderful week of vacation together.

The year 1988 required much travel for George in his role at the Holstein Association, developing markets and delivering dairy and livestock technology. The time in Mexico, Guatemala, Honduras, El Salvador, and Venezuela all helped his continuing Spanish studies. He also traveled to Hungary, Turkey, Tunisia, Algeria, Ghana, and Nigeria and there were a few trips in the U.S. I was able to accompany him for two weeks in Madison, Wisconsin, when he represented the Holstein Association at the World Dairy Exposition. As a bonus, we had the opportunity to visit my relatives who lived in the state.

In September of 1989, I took a leave of absence from my work as office manager for the physical therapy department at Glynn-Brunswick Memorial Hospital to accompany George on a trip to East Africa. We were blessed to have four weeks together getting acquainted with the work of MAP International in Kenya and Uganda and renewing our friendship with many colleagues from our previous mission assignments.

A Visit to Scandinavia

Close colleagues in the Sudan were our Swedish friends, Leif and Britt Zetterlund. In addition to working together on various projects for ACROSS, we enjoyed some fun times together. Leif played the accordion and we enjoyed singing together. Several times the four of us were invited to share special music for events and ACROSS get-togethers. One time when we were heading back to the U.S., we accepted their invitation to visit them in their home in Sweden. We enjoyed meeting their family and had some great fellowship. We also went to Denmark and Norway on that excursion.

Guatemala Trip – 1994

Although I was not part of this trip, I must share this family story. In November 1994, George went from Florida to Guatemala on mission business for Calvary International. By pre-arrangement, he met up with our son Dan and granddaughter Anna, who were with a short-term missions group from Christ's Center in Junction City. Both of them had key roles in presenting the drama *Zion* as an evangelistic outreach in various locations.

While the group was traveling in the countryside, an incident occurred that was humorous to some, but not to George. When the vans stopped out in the boonies for a primitive "pit stop," unbeknownst to him he was standing on a hill of red ants. He noticed some specks on his pants that looked like some type of weed seeds, and then he started to feel some bites. He cried out for help and danced around while Dan and other guys were swatting the ants and trying to get them off his legs. In the heat of the moment, it seemed best to get out of his slacks, now covered with ants, to try to stop the vicious attacking ants from getting to the upper part of his body.

The humor happened in the van when one of the ladies exclaimed, "Don't look! George has his pants off!" Can you imagine the pandemonium that ensued? Before the episode was over George had about 80 angry poisonous bites, which could have been a death sentence. Thankfully, he recovered from the trauma and was able to continue the trip. Pastor Jon Bowers at Christ's Center couldn't help himself and told the funny story (at George's expense) at the Sunday service when the team returned to Junction City.

Africa - 1997

We called it *Encore in Ethiopia* and rejoiced all along the way on our two-month trip to Africa February 25 to April 25, 1997. Our Father had put it in our hearts many years before that someday it would be possible for us to return to Ethiopia. It was a great blessing to be able to renew friendships with people we already knew and to develop new relationships.

A major purpose of our trip was to participate in an AIMS (Accelerating International Mission Strategies) conference in support of the strategic alliance targeting the 41 known unreached people groups in the country. George was asked to provide training in how to start a missionary sending agency. He considered it a great honor to share in the training process for the 286 trained Ethiopian nationals who were in various stages of preparation for reaching out to the more rural areas of Ethiopia, which were predominantly pagan or Muslim.

Ethiopia will quickly stretch out her hands to God. Psalm 68:31b

As we traveled to various places in the world, certain people made an indelible impression on us. When we were at Tosse, a tiny village in Ethiopia, we celebrated the goodness of the Lord with believers there. George was one of the trainers in a course where the local Christians had been invited to sit in on the instruction and join in the singing and fellowship. I was attracted to a little girl, Tarike Olana, whose arms and hands were malformed – just little nubbins coming out from her shoulders, a tragic result of the drug Thalidomide. Her daddy, Olana, had been the nurse at the Tosse Clinic, but he had died from AIDS. An uncle brought Tarike with him to the training course. She seemed starved for affection and tucked herself in close under my arm wherever I went that whole day. In a tearful, emotional moment for her and for me as we were leaving the area, she begged me to take her home with me. It was hard to explain to her tender heart that it was not possible, and we had to leave her with simply our promise to pray for her!

More Africa Travels – 2002

In 2002 we had a very rewarding trip to South Africa plus four countries in East Africa. On this six-week, five-country missionary journey, many different methods of transportation were employed. We flew on a Jet airplane from Atlanta to Johannesburg, and a Russian

Anatov plane from Arua to Kampala, Uganda. Overland, we rode in a down-country, incredibly overloaded bus partway, then transferred to a freight truck carrying people and goods to Kiramu, Ethiopia, where we had lived in the 1970s. Our trip home to Florida was on a Boeing 747 for a total of 30 hours – 17 hours flight time and 13 hours of waiting time in airports before we reached our destination.

On that multi-country trip, we had a challenging time sorting out the money: South African Rand, Kenya Shillings, Uganda Shillings, and Ethiopian Birr. What does it really cost to take this taxi? How much is a hand of finger bananas? We enjoyed delicious tropical fruits – papaya, pineapples, guavas, mangoes, and passionfruit. In the places where there had been British or Indian influence, chai (strong tea with milk and sugar) is regularly served. And yes, Coca-Cola is everywhere, no matter how remote, though it is warm and not at all thirst-quenching. No matter how thirsty we were, water was not recommended!

Visiting Former Colleagues

We had the emotional experience of spending a week in the house we had lived in at Kiramu from 1973 to 1976. It was not occupied at that time, and we were on our own. Our Ethiopian friends were so glad to see us! We were invited to eat with some family at least twice a day. It was so great to meet their families and to see how the gospel had prospered after we had left, despite the hardships. For their safety during the Marxist rule, we had not been able to communicate with them.

In our absence, the evangelists had become government school directors, a source of income for them. Getahune, our guard and the man George had trained in animal medicine, was continuing to help the local men with medical issues with their cattle and mules. Once when George was in Russia, he risked sending a letter to Getahune using a Russian address. Getahune proudly showed us that the letter was a prized possession.

Asefa, a special friend of our sons who had also worked for us, was a teacher in the Kiramu school. He invited us to come to his home for a meal and to meet his family, which included two wives and fifteen children. Taking a second wife had ostracized him from the church, but he explained to us what had happened. His first wife had not conceived in the first year of their marriage. He was the only son of his parents, who were not believers. They had insisted that he take a second wife to raise children to help them in their old age, the common system of social security. He took a second wife and shortly after she started producing children, his first wife also began to conceive and Asefa's family multiplied rapidly!

Update on Regassa

In a previous chapter I told about Regassa, the clinic helper whose reputation was less than excellent when we lived there. We had a part in the birth of his first son, which validated his marriage relationship with the lady he had been living with. While we had been away for two decades, he had become a Christian and was now an upstanding member and leader of the Kiramu congregation.

> *Therefore if any man is in Christ, he is a new creature; the old things passed away; behold, new things have come.* II Corinthians 5:17

Regassa proudly brought his wife and six beautiful children to meet us. It was incredibly rewarding to witness the transformation of this man we had known in his previous circumstances, confirming the truth of Scripture.

CHAPTER 25
Practicing Hospitality

W hen I was growing up there was a plaque on the wall near the dining table that read: *Christ the unseen guest at our table, the silent listener to every conversation.* It's true, but do we remember it in our everyday life with our family members? Every family has traditions that mean so much and help to preserve the memories. Jesus often broke bread with His disciples at the close of the day, using the occasion to teach them important things about His Father. The Israelites were fervent tradition-keepers, enjoying their celebrations, feasts and holy days.

Scripture reminds us to tell the next generation the praiseworthy deeds of the Lord, His power, and the wonders He has done.

> *Listen, O my people, to my instruction: Incline your ears to the words of my mouth...We will not conceal them from their children, but tell to the generation to come the praises of the Lord. And His strength and His wondrous works that He has done...That they should teach them to their children; that the generation to come might know, even the children yet to be born, that they may arise and tell them to their children, that they should put their confidence*

in God, and not forget the works of God, but keep His commandments. Psalm 78:1-7

The Bible is explicit that the older are to train the younger. I have been a mentor most of my life and in many situations, beginning with my own children. Each one of us is responsible to God for sharing what we have learned. Great blessing comes from teaching what you have learned to those who are younger, maybe not in age, but in the Lord. The command is not gender specific. Both men and women have a responsibility to pursue our Heavenly Father's character in our lives. The Bible also instructs that training is to be done with grace. Graciousness is characterized by showing kindness and compassion, being thoughtful of others.

> *Older men are to be temperate, dignified, sensible, sound in faith, in love, in perseverance. Older women likewise are to be reverent in their behavior, not malicious gossips, not enslaved to much wine, teaching what is good, that they may encourage the young women to love their husbands, to love their children, to be sensible, pure, workers at home, kind, being subject to their own husbands, that the word of God may not be dishonored.* Titus 2:2-5

Turkey on the Menu?

While we were living in the little town of Adams we were members of Athena Christian Church. When we moved there, the pastors were Paul and Mabel Moore. One Thanksgiving we invited them and the visiting evangelist Willie White to our home for dinner. Willie had been our pastor in Newberg and had performed our wedding ceremony, so it was very special to have him come to our home for a meal. I was the last one to start eating and had not yet noticed anything amiss.

Willie sheepishly said, "Did you plan to serve turkey? I think I smelled it." In the rush of getting the food into serving dishes and onto the table, I had failed to get the turkey out of the oven. George quickly sliced it up and we enjoyed the meal, with turkey added to the trimmings. I surely would have noticed its absence in a few minutes, but it was embarrassing to have the guest of honor be the one to mention it. This was a good reminder to me that practicing hospitality is not about serving a perfect meal, but about fellowship and loving others.

Cold Turkey?

One time when George and I were visiting our supporting congregation in Mesa, Arizona, we were hosted by a couple who wanted to take us to their vacation home in the Flagstaff area. We knew there would be many other guests besides ourselves on Saturday. Our hostess could have been described as a health food nut, but that terminology was not used then. Some of her concepts are practiced more widely now, but at that time her practices seemed quite radical to us, and even to her husband and son.

As was planned, we arrived at their home the evening before the main event and we noticed the tantalizing aroma of turkey cooking. George could practically taste a traditional turkey dinner. The meal served to us that evening was soup and sandwiches with no sign of the turkey. The next day when the other guests had gathered, turkey was on the menu, but it was simply cold sliced turkey, which was very disappointing, especially to George. (We were sad to learn that despite her valiant efforts at healthy eating, our hostess was diagnosed with cancer and passed away a couple years later.)

Raw Turkey?

One time when we lived in the countryside near Corvallis, I experienced a true hostess nightmare. We had invited George's parents and extended family to our home for the noon meal after church on the Sunday after Thanksgiving. I was looking forward to serving a delicious turkey dinner. In the morning I prepared everything I could possibly do in advance and put the turkey in the oven before we left for church. Upon arriving home, we were all looking forward to that enticing smell of turkey almost ready to eat. To my horror, the oven was OFF and the large turkey was cold and raw.

I had apparently failed to turn the oven ON after putting the turkey in and setting the temperature. What to do? Our guests were on their way. In those days, turkeys did not cook as fast as they do now. George chopped up the turkey, cutting off the legs and wings and dividing the breast portion into several chunks. He turned the oven to 500 degrees and determined that the best thing for us to do was to visit with our guests while we waited several hours for the turkey to cook. Unfortunately, we were not well stocked up on snack foods to offer our guests when they arrived, and we had to break the news to them that dinner would be later than planned.

Later, George's Aunt Vinie Place told us that it was the best Thanksgiving she ever had. Uncle George was short on patience and she was accustomed to his always being in a hurry to leave for home right after the meal. This time he couldn't leave because the dinner had not yet been served, and she got her wish for an extra-long visit with the family.

In Season and Out of Season

We were faithful to use our gifts of hospitality to serve others, both friends and strangers. It was my pleasure to help George with the practical side of hospitality by preparing meals and welcoming people into our home, no matter how humble our living situation. I have practiced hospitality since being a young girl, first at home with my parents and later as a wife and mother. In our time on various mission assignments, I often lacked the most basic requirements for meal preparation, but I did the best I could. I didn't always know the Scriptural mandate below, but I gratefully acknowledge that I have been given hospitality as a spiritual gift. However, Romans 12:9-13 encourages us all to practice hospitality, whether or not it is a spiritual gift.

> *And since we have gifts that differ according to the grace given to us, let each exercise them accordingly... Be devoted to one another in brotherly love; give preference to one another in honor...contributing to the needs of the saints, practicing hospitality.* Romans 12:6,10,13

Francis A. Schaeffer, an American theologian and pastor, is most famous for his writings and establishment of the L'Abri community in Switzerland. In his book *How Should We Then Live,* he wrote:

> Pray that the Lord will send you people of His choice. But don't pray that way unless no matter who these people are, you are willing to take them into your home, have them eat at your table, introduce them to your family and sleep in your beds...There is no place in God's world where there are no people who will come and share a home as long as it is a real home.

Houseguests

Through all our years of marriage, we almost always had someone living with us. Both my brother Lyle and sister Marilyn lived with us at separate times when they attended college at Oregon State University. Most often our houseguests stayed with us for their convenience, but we did have other situations in which our guest was a great help to us. Paul Stock lived with us for eight years, initially because he was in serious debt and couldn't afford housing.

Paul was with us at the time when George's heart condition prevented him from doing our yard work and Paul was very happy to help. His own father died before he was born and he loved and served George as a father. It was a great blessing to have him living in our home, keeping the yard looking beautiful, and providing security when we were serving in Guatemala.

While Paul was with us, he introduced us to a man he had met at a home group who actually lived in Chicago but was working temporarily for the Duval County School District upgrading their computer systems. This fellow needed a place to stay during the week, but then went home each weekend. The first time we met him he commented that our home was just like his grandma's place! It was a good fit for all of us for him to use our second guest room. He was extremely generous with his rent payment and we hardly ever saw him. Surprisingly, even after the project was completed and he had moved back to Chicago, the rent funds continued. We tried multiple ways to contact him, thinking he didn't remember he had set up an automatic payment from his checking account to ours. It took a long time to get the money flow stopped! In God's providence those funds came at a time when we were really struggling financially, and we often wondered if he was an angel sent to help us.

Do not neglect to show hospitality to strangers, for by this some have entertained angels without knowing it.
Hebrews 13:2

Hospitality on the Mission Field

Besides our missionary colleagues, most often our guests in the countryside of Ethiopia were the pilots from Mission Aviation Fellowship. Where we lived in southern Sudan, there were no motels or service stations. We were tested and stretched as many travelers, including government officials, came to our home in Mundri needing a jerry can of petrol, food to eat, and a place to spend the night.

George wrote in November 1980:

> This month has been especially strenuous as we have
> hosted several delegations of visitors and held several
> special meetings requiring food and lodging. We
> were just figuring up that Janet has served more than
> 200 guest meals during the month. She enjoys being
> a hostess, but a hospitality ministry is much more
> difficult here with limited supplies and resources.
> Our stove has not been working properly so she has
> done much of the cooking on a small charcoal burner
> outside.

On another occasion I wrote to my mother:

> Last night in the midst of our packing for the next trip
> we had three houseguests. The wife of an Egyptian
> doctor from Rumbek had car trouble near Jambo.
> Our lorry on the way to Thiet picked her and her
> two children up and they arrived in Mundri mid-
> afternoon. The driver wanted to spend the night here
> and proceed with his trip tomorrow. The guesthouse
> was full of people from the lorry, so we agreed to
> take the lady and her children, ages nine and two, for
> the night. It was challenging since she only knew a
> few words of English and I only know a few words of
> Arabic, but just knowing my own requirements when
> I travel and multiplying it by having a couple children
> to care for, I was able to anticipate her needs and we
> got along okay.

Hospitality must be very important to our Father – it is one of the
qualifications listed for elders:

It is a trustworthy statement; if any man aspires to the office of overseer, it is a fine work he desires to do. An overseer, then, must be above reproach...hospitable, able to teach... I Timothy 3:1-2:

And Jesus said:

For I was hungry, and you gave Me something to eat; I was thirsty, and you gave Me drink; I was a stranger and you invited Me in... Matt. 25:35-36

Kathy Chapman Sharp wrote:

Take heart, practicing Christian hospitality isn't about glamorous table settings or platters of picture-perfect food; it's about practicing servanthood right in the middle of your practical Christianity. More important, it's about loving others through Christ and making people feel special. While the art of hospitality may come easy for some, it may be quite difficult for others. After all, it's not always easy to give of yourself, much less your hard-earned gains. And like most things in life, hospitality isn't done perfectly the first time. Whether we have the spiritual gift of hospitality or not, it can be a part of our way of life. The New Testament teaches us that Christianity is the religion of open hands, open hearts, and open doors. When we open our hearts as well as our homes, we're practicing Christian hospitality.

In The Message Bible, Peter wrote:

Most of all, love each other as if your life depended on it. Love makes up for practically anything. Be quick to give a meal to the hungry, a bed to the homeless – cheerfully. Be generous with the different things God gave you. I Peter 4:8-11

The Book of 1ˢᵗ John makes it plain that when we love others, we are showing our love for God. He loves us completely and unconditionally and when we love and serve others in the community through hospitality, we are also serving Him. I continue to get great satisfaction from offering hospitality to family, friends, and strangers!

CHAPTER 26
Faithful Stewards

*G*randdad's Money Camp, the manual George wrote in 2007 as a training tool for our grandchildren and others, emphasized True Wealth, which he described in a nutshell as "having enough to give to God's purposes; to provide for the needs of one's own family, and to have more than enough left over to provide for long-term needs and special projects to help others."

There is one place in the Bible where our Father invites us to put Him to the test:

> *Bring the whole tithe into the storehouse, so that there may be food in My house, and test Me now in this,"* *says the Lord of hosts, "if I will not open for you the windows of heaven, and pour out for you a blessing until there is no more need."* Malachi 3:10

He promised to rebuke the devourer on our behalf and to give us the power to create wealth.

> *But you shall remember the Lord your God, for it is He who is giving you the power to make wealth, that He may confirm His covenant which He swore to your fathers, as it is this day.* Deut. 8:18

The first financial decision George and I made, even before we were married, was to tithe from our income. We recognize that it is that commitment faithfully lived out over our lifetime that has caused us to prosper and enjoy True Wealth.

> *For where your treasure is, there will your heart be also.* Matthew 6:21

Faith Vision

We were trainers for the Married for Life course through Marriage Ministries International, both in Florida and in Oregon. The ministry is now called 2=1. The website advertises the course with the following comments:

> Is Married for Life a real possibility or just a great concept? Do you know it takes more preparation and testing to get a driver's license than a marriage license? Do you realize that people invest time in preparing for a career, learning a new skill, or developing a talent, yet they often marry believing it will "just come naturally"?

When we taught the lessons, we trained the participants to do homework assignments, also doing them ourselves. One lesson required us to write out our faith vision for each other. This was what George wrote for me:

> Janet is not only a faithful wife but a leader that deposits valuable fruit in the lives of others. She is Godly in all her ways and her children call her blessed. She is a blessing to many people and is hospitable to people in her home. She has a passion for helping people.

She will continue to grow as a Proverbs 31 woman. Because of her commitment, she is known as a leader by example so her words and quiet spirit are a great gain for many people. She will receive special recognition for a reward of being a servant. This recognition will grow from regional to international honor for being effective in transforming marriages and families into God's holy plan for them. She will receive double honor for her faithfulness.

My faith vision for George included concepts from Scriptures in Proverbs, Colossians, and Philippians:

It is a privilege for me to submit to the leadership of my husband who is submitted to Father God and the Lord Jesus Christ. It is my aim to follow his leadership and enjoy the protection of God's plan for the family. George makes it his ambition to lead a quiet life, attending to his own business and working with his hands, heart, mind, soul, and body to provide for his family.

He walks in a manner worthy of the Lord to please Him in all respects, bearing fruit in every good work and increasing in the knowledge of God. He has learned to be content in whatever circumstances – humble means and prosperity. He can do all things through Christ who strengthens him.

George understands the need for a multitude of counsel. He sows righteousness and can expect a true reward. He is generous so can expect prosperity. He is wise and righteous and can expect God's blessing and to be rewarded on earth. He is able to forget what lies

behind and to press on toward the goal for the prize
of the upward call of God in Christ Jesus.

Through the years we were often asked what our secret was for such
a happy, fruitful marriage. We were committed to unselfishly serving
each other using the principle from the Apostle Paul:

> *Do nothing from selfishness or empty conceit, but with*
> *humility of mind let each of you regard one another*
> *as more important than himself; do not merely look*
> *out for your own personal interests, but also for the*
> *interests of others.* Philippians 2:3-4

As we evaluated the blessings and challenges of life on the mission
field, we noted that *togetherness* was at the top of both lists. Not all
couples enjoy the closeness of being together 24/7 and especially
"when does work stop and private life begin?" Relationship with
colleagues is another area that can be a blessing or a challenge. It is a
historical fact that missionaries coming home from the field early cite
relationship issues with colleagues, not nationals, as a major reason
they were not able to adjust.

The Parable of the Talents

In the parable about stewardship of the talents our Master taught in
Matthew 25:14-30, we are admonished to use what He has given us
wisely. The servants in the story were given talents to work with.
The one given five was faithful to make another five talents; the one
given two gained another two; but the one who received only one hid
his talent in the ground. The first two were rewarded by the Master
saying, *"Well done, good and faithful servant."* The one who hid his
was rebuked as a wicked, evil and lazy slave.

George could never be accused of burying his talent in the ground.
He began considering investment opportunities while still in high

school and we did serious financial planning as a couple early in our marriage. We didn't have income beyond our family's needs until after he graduated from college, and then we purchased a one-half interest in two duplexes.

As time went on, we moved up into larger properties, eventually with the purchase, along with two other parties, of an apartment complex in Springfield, Oregon. The economy took a dive shortly after that acquisition, which was a devastating blow to our investment. Our vacancy percentage increased dramatically, and the other partners wanted out. Without them, we could not manage the mortgage payments. The bank we were dealing with was sold to another party who was not willing to work with us. Sadly, we lost the entire value of that investment, but we did not give up on planning and saving for the future.

Years later, George paid for a subscription and studied with *Investools*, a subsidiary of the ThinkOrSwim Group. He made several investments with the limited funds that were at our disposal. Due to situations beyond our control, many of his efforts did not yield the gain he hoped for, but he did not lose heart. He wanted us to be self-sufficient financially in our sunset years and especially was concerned about my financial wellbeing if he should die before I did.

> *Now this I say, he who sows sparingly shall also reap sparingly; and he who sows bountifully shall also reap bountifully...And God is able to make all grace abound to you, that always having all sufficiency in everything, you may have an abundance for every good deed.* 2 Corinthians 9:6,8

Rental Business

We decided to use George's military retirement income for investment purposes and started a real estate rental business in

Junction City and Harrisburg with our son Dan as manager. We began renting out the house on Laurel Street in Junction City that we and several of our family members had lived in at various times. The next acquisition was a duplex on 13th Street in Junction City that was purchased on a 1031 exchange when our house in New Hampshire sold.

At various times over several years we acquired more properties, totaling 18 units at one point. Early in our experience with property managers, we had some theft and embezzlement, which was incredibly disheartening. We discovered that owning duplexes was preferable to multi-unit properties. We owned one low-rent four-plex that gave us all kinds of trouble. One tenant wanted to run a soup kitchen for the needy; another tenant was a drug dealer; and there were multiple domestic violence incidents requiring police intervention. When the police broke down the door to gain access, they had no requirement to do the repairs or pay for them. All too often we had to send repairmen to that problematic four-plex. Dan grew weary of the extra expense and turmoil and we decided to sell it.

Presently we have a wonderful property manager. My move to Harrisburg coincided with a tenant moving out of the duplex I now live in. It was completely renovated before I moved in and I'm very happy with my home and location. With three bedrooms, I am able to use one as an office and one as a guest room, with adequate space for hosting family and friends.

Space A Travel

Thanks to our faithful financial partners, our missionary income was adequate for living and for our travel and mission expenses. Throughout our lives, we were frugal and took advantage of every opportunity to save. George's military service helped us in many ways. After his retirement from the Army, one perk was the opportunity to fly on Space A (short for Available) flights for some wonderful visits with our families and support partners on the West Coast.

One memorable Space A flight was in September 1998, when we traveled from Jacksonville to Los Angeles for a visit with our daughter Jennie and her family. As part of her husband Mark's work on the music staff at Grace Community Church, his masterful skill as a pianist was requested for a cruise conference on the St. Lawrence Seaway and Eastern Seaboard. Jennie had been invited to join him, but she had to first arrange for someone to stay with their children. That is where I came in. She called and told me about the opportunity to go with Mark, and I volunteered for "grandmother duty."

While George headed out on a ministry assignment in Central America, I stayed with our grandchildren while their parents were away for two weeks. Amy (15), Allison (13) and Austin (10) had assignments for their homeschool studies, and I cared for little April, 16 months old. Whenever she hurt herself or had an emotional moment of missing her mother, one of her siblings or I could wipe the tears away by showing the "goatherd scene," her favorite part of the movie *Sound of Music*. One evening I suggested we watch the whole movie. When we came to the scene where the star, Maria, played by Julie Andrews, was ready to walk down the aisle in her beautiful wedding gown to be married to Georg, April exclaimed, "Ma-ma! Ma-ma!" I could hardly wait to tell Jennie that she had been mistaken for Julie Andrews.

Some Easy, Some Difficult Trips

When my dad's cousin Orin Stager turned 100 years old in 2012, we caught a Space A flight from Jacksonville to Whidbey Island, took a shuttle to Sea-Tac airport and were picked up by a family member to join in the special birthday party in Puyallup, Washington. It all went like clockwork and was a great blessing for us and the Stager family.

One time we had a flight on a new Boeing 737 when there were only three passengers besides us from Jacksonville to a military base in California. Another time we flew from Whidbey Island across the U.S. on an Air Force C-5, strapped into harnesses on the side of the cargo plane. On that occasion, the heater wasn't working and we nearly froze. We landed for a fuel stop at Fort Worth, Texas, where the temperature was well above 100 degrees. It felt really good for about ten minutes to get us thawed out, and then we started to suffer from the extreme temperature change.

Not all of our flights were dependable, which led to some challenging adventures together. The Space A website states that though flying on U.S. military aircraft is usually without cost, it is not a reliable means of travel. Unlike a commercial airline, there are usually no backup flights if the plane is diverted or if there are not enough seats. Although we had many great flights, we did have one of those unreliable scenarios described on the website. It happened during a time when some military families were on spring break. We came close to getting on a flight from Whidbey Island to Jacksonville, but just when we were ready to board, an active-duty military family with several children came in and took those seats. A huge disappointment sending us back to the drawing board!

We did some research to find another way home to Jacksonville. Although it was not our destination, we were able to get a flight to the Naval Base at Coronado in California that held some promise for a flight east from there. We spent the night, and the next morning caught a flight to Dover Air Force Base in Delaware, with the hope of getting on the scheduled flight from there to Jacksonville. Arriving in Dover late at night, we explored options for lodging but were dismayed to learn there was an event going on in the city that had taken all of the motel rooms. We sat up all night at the airport, only to learn the next morning that the flight we hoped to get on was canceled! George had a deadline of being back at the office for an important meeting, so we rented a car and drove the 800 miles to Jacksonville in two days, spending the night in a motel halfway.

Most of our Space A excursions were incredible blessings, so we didn't let that disappointing trip ruin our appreciation for this financial benefit from George's military service.

CHAPTER 27
Holding Possessions Loosely

B oth George and I were especially committed to preserving godly family values. We taught them to our own children and grandchildren and encouraged others to follow our example. This quote came from a teaching George gave to a group of men:

> The consequences of the husband's influence upon the spiritual life of his family cannot be measured. There is no one with more power to encourage or to hinder the family's growth in the Lord than the husband and father. Husbands, consider your wife as a treasure given to you by a loving God. The husband should never think of the authority entrusted to him without remembering the responsibility that goes with it. I exhort you to hold family relationships *tightly* and things and money *loosely*.

We have had several opportunities to test our resolve on that issue. One time when we were traveling in Oregon, we decided to stop at the scenic landmark Multnomah Falls. The parking area is several blocks from the falls and the lodge. I had a cloth bag similar to a diaper bag that I used for personal items and cosmetics. When we locked and left the car, I took my purse but not that bag.

When we returned, we discovered that thieves had entered our car by some means other than breaking a window. They must have had a key that matched the lock. The only thing missing was that bag, which might have looked like an oversized purse to them. Among the items in it were several birthday cards ready to be mailed. Upon questioning the card recipients later, to our amazement they all reported they had received their cards. The thieves were surely disappointed with the contents of the bag, with no money or valuables, but to my surprise they had mailed the cards!

Disheartening Losses

I shared in George's life story Ruth Graham's account of an incident that happened when we were in Hawaii checking out a possible mission opportunity, but I'll share it again here. Frank and Ruth had invited us to join them for a hike to Manoa Falls on Sunday afternoon just before we were leaving to return to the mainland after a month in that beautiful location. Since we had embarked on the trip right after church, we had everything we had taken to the Island with us; our clothes, our suitcases, and our airline tickets. After lunch, we all changed into hiking clothes and we put our church clothes, shoes, purses and wallets into the trunk of their car.

The hike with these friends was delightful, but alas on our return, we discovered that thieves had bashed a hole in the trunk of their car, tripped the lock and taken all of our belongings! It was a blow to the Grahams and to us! We were particularly disappointed to lose our Bibles, highlighted for ease in teaching and sharing.

When we moved from New Hampshire to Brunswick, Georgia, two of George's hunting rifles were stolen from the moving van. We later realized that we should have packed the guns with bedding or goods that would have concealed them, and not in a box that was obviously gun-shaped. We are quite sure that one of the drivers was the thief, but the moving company had insurance and we were paid for the value of the rifles. It was a very disappointing loss for George. Once again, we were reminded that our material possessions are just tools to be used and not to let ourselves get too attached to our belongings.

Unfortunate Incidents

In our travels we liked to stay in guesthouses when possible. In Nairobi, there were two that we especially liked: the Mennonite Guest House and the Methodist Guest House. Even though not pre-arranged, we were often blessed to meet up with old friends, and we always made new acquaintances. One time we had the disappointing experience of losing many of our dressy clothes while staying at the Methodist Guest House. I washed some clothes and hung them on a clothesline outside to dry, but someone stole them when I wasn't looking. It was very frustrating because they were not our everyday clothes, but the better ones that we saved to wear in town.

When traveling to Sudan from Nairobi, we transported our goods in barrels. After we arrived at our destination, the first barrel we opened had been broken into. Several things were broken or missing, and we discovered a sweater, dress, and sweatshirt that were not ours. Undoubtedly this exchange occurred at the customs office. Among the things missing were two tablecloths and some bed sheets that I had bought from a missionary family leaving Kenya. The customs people must have helped themselves to the linens I had purchased. We decided that the officials who evaluated the contents couldn't get everything back into the barrel easily, and just jumped on it to get it closed, causing the breakage.

Attempted Burglary

The first time we returned to Guatemala without the security of having someone living in our house, our home was broken into in broad daylight. Our neighbor on the street behind us just happened to be looking out her kitchen window that morning about 11:30. She saw three men jump the fence into our backyard, break the glass on the back door with a crowbar and enter the Florida room we used as an office. She called 9-1-1 and several police cars quickly came to the scene.

Later we learned that one man stayed outside as a watchman while the other two men ransacked the house, especially our bedroom, apparently looking for money, guns, and jewelry. They gathered their stash near the front door, ready to load into the stolen van in the driveway with the engine still running. A police car pulled in front of the van to block their departure. When the watchman alerted the men inside, they ran out the back door, dropping some of the goods as they jumped the six-foot fence. One of the items found in the yard by the police was a pistol.

Our office in Guatemala got a call from the police asking George to call them to answer their questions about several things, particularly whether he had a pistol. He did have a rifle, but no pistol. After the perpetrators of the crime were apprehended by police with dogs, they were charged with armed robbery. The police were very pleased to capture those guys who had robbed others in our neighborhood. Even though the men were in their early twenties, they already had long rap sheets. That incident had a good ending since the burglary was disrupted, but we realized we could not leave our home for extended periods without protection. And what if I had been home working at my computer in the office?

Taking Inventory

George wrote in 2008:

> The store where we buy groceries is closed several days this week for inventory. As a new year begins, it is common for people to evaluate where they have been and where they are going. We need to pursue

excellence in all aspects of life; our relationship with God and with the important people in our life, husbands and wives, children, and friends.

Be careful how you walk, not as unwise men, but wise, making the most of your time because the days are evil. So then do not be foolish, but understand what the will of the Lord is. Eph. 5:15-17

Most of us recognize our weaknesses and areas we need to improve. If we seek Him, God will help us manage our time and priorities and show us what is good, better and best. Each day we need to make a prayer of commitment, presenting ourselves to God for His will and purposes by a fresh and renewed commitment. We need to agree to cooperate with God as He is leading us to become the person He created us to be.

Does your situation in life suit you? Are you learning the lessons God wants you to learn in the place where you are now? Life's greatest purpose is to do the will of God. For with every trial, God gives the grace to overcome.

Therefore let him who thinks he stands take heed lest he fall. No temptation has overtaken you but such as is common to man; and God is faithful, who will not allow you to be tempted beyond what you are able, but with the temptation will provide the way of escape also, that you may be able to endure it. I Corinthians 10:12-13

Blueprint for Prosperity

Excerpts from an article George wrote in June 2006:

My blueprint for prosperity stems from my value system, *integrity* driven by biblical *knowledge*. The combination of those two qualities leads to *True Wealth*. This type of wealth is the positive virtue of not what I possess, but what possesses me. True Wealth comes from a vision of my birthright. I am of the lineage of Abraham, Isaac, and Jacob; I'm in covenant and have inherited the promised blessings. I progressively create a vision – what I can conceive, I can achieve.

Together with my wife and children we pray, dream, create and plan a shared vision. From this multi-generational vision, strategies flow for *Total Wellbeing – True Wealth*. This leads to multiplying multi-generational prosperity for future generations, the manifestation of the benefits of the Kingdom and *Shalom* of God.

True Wealth envisions, empowers and equips the successive generations of my family with *wisdom*. Therefore, each generation has the capacity to learn, earn, give, serve, invest and receive an abundance of grace to obtain and pass on, increasing True Wealth. Through wisdom and the application of it to life's situations, we encourage and empower members of our multiplying family and do not destroy initiative or motivation through dependency. Individual initiative and creativity are rewarded with the opportunity to learn more about life, its responsibilities and the blessings received from faithfulness.

The principle is that of "the Lock, the Key and the Hand that turns it." Laid out before each of us is a measured number of days of life. Wisdom is the key to unlock the treasures of life and eternity. It is our own hand that will determine our destiny by daring to turn the key that unlocks a future of opportunity based on our individual faithfulness and employment of eternal laws and principles.

This *blueprint for prosperity* is capable of expanding to accommodate our growing capacity to receive; to bring clarity to the processes of True Wealth accumulation; to increase our capacity for philanthropy; and to maintain our lives together on life's journey in handling misfortune and rejoicing in success. In the transition from this life to the life which is to come, we can all truly rejoice that the Holy Spirit is our Helper. Our Father is the One who gives us the power to obtain wealth and we are secure in Him.

CHAPTER 28
Ministries We Served

C MF, FMI, ACROSS, MAP, CI, GTN, GLODEV: This alphabet soup represents the Christian ministries that George and I served together during our 40 plus years of international missionary service. My intent in this chapter is to summarize our work with special emphasis on my part.

Christian Missionary Fellowship (CMF)

When our family decided to join the mission team in Ethiopia, I left the prestigious position and good salary at Good Samaritan Hospital to give my life to mission service. Enclosed with a gift at my going away party at the hospital on May 31, 1972, was a handwritten note from James R. Mol, the hospital administrator.

> Enclosed is a small expression of faith in what you are doing. In all honesty, I must add that it's also a small expression of appreciation for your help to me and the Hospital, Janet. I'm going to miss you! I'm just glad I'm losing you to such a good cause...I hope we'll hear from you when you're in Ethiopia. God be with you all!

When we joined CMF in 1972, there were only two options for places to go – Ethiopia and Brazil. Ethiopia had been selected as a field of missionary endeavor by the Fellowship on the basis of governmental stability, openness to Western missionaries and evidence of winnable people. Our interest was in Ethiopia because of our connection with Doug and Marge Priest, who recruited us to join them.

Kiramu, the station where we lived, was established in 1965. In good weather the trip to Addis Ababa by Land Rover took 15-18 hours; by MAF plane only one hour and 15 minutes. Mission Aviation Fellowship provided planes and missionary pilots at about one-half the commercial cost to mission groups such as CMF. Each station was equipped with a two-way radio for daily communication with Addis Ababa and the other stations.

Methods used to reach the people were many and varied according to prevailing conditions and changing situations. The agreement reached with the government required the missionaries to help with education and medical clinics. Acquisition of the national language, Amharic, was also required, but the mission leaders decided that some of the wives should study Gallinya (Oromo) to be able to communicate with the women.

My Role

While visiting with families and church groups in America before going to Ethiopia, I was frequently asked, "What will *you* do in Ethiopia?" I could only guess at my role, but after being there George responded:

> To answer that question, Janet could only suggest some possibilities, but I want to assure you that she has really been kept busy. She keeps up with correspondence with our family and support partners, maintains clinic records and funds, prepares drug

orders, participates in ladies meetings, and does my secretarial work. This is all in addition to the necessary household tasks of cooking, cleaning, and laundry. It takes a special kind of woman to be a missionary wife and Janet has been very faithful in her role. She is a real companion to me in this isolated place. We have become like the proverbial "grandmother and grandfather" as we spend long evenings in front of the fireplace watching each other grow old.

Our time of service with CMF in Ethiopia from 1973 to 1976 is well documented in the book, *George H. Meyers, His Remarkable Life Story.* We left as a result of a Marxist takeover and political instability in the country. We have remained in contact with former colleagues and greatly admire the continuing work of CMF International in many locations in the world.

Frontier Ministries International (FMI)

When it became certain that we would not be able to return to Ethiopia, we actively pursued affiliation with other mission agencies and had some invitations to consider. As we projected our future ministry, we desired to also see many others enter into mission service. In many countries, the only way the message of Christ could get in was by professional people: doctors, nurses, agriculturalists, engineers, etc.

George spent quality time in research to establish Frontier Ministries International (FMI), a tax-exempt organization with a vision for sending professional people as missionaries to unreached people groups. Our son Dan had an important role in qualifying applicants for service and overseeing the financial matters of FMI.

ACROSS (Association of Christian Resource Organizations Serving Sudan)

We were granted permission to enter Sudan with ACROSS in 1980. It was a cooperative effort of churches and the Sudanese government to restore a land ravaged by civil war. Intense fighting and guerrilla warfare from 1955 until 1972 had left southern Sudan devastated. Immense problems of rehabilitation and restoration presented a challenge to international service agencies and mission groups. George's work required extensive correspondence with government officials, for which he depended upon my secretarial skills.

Our time in Sudan was cut short by the start of the second civil war. We learned that George was on an assassination list. Our subsequent escape from Tonj District, and our final weeks in the country are documented in the chapter *The Incredible Journey.*

MAP International (Medical Assistance Program)

We explored possibilities with *Intercristo*, an organization in the Seattle area that matched openings with qualified applicants. After submitting our credentials and reviewing many opportunities, George was hired as Vice President of Program for MAP International, based in Brunswick, Georgia. MAP's mission is to advance the total health of people living in the world's poorest communities. George enjoyed his work of supervising an international staff of about 70 people, including doctors, health professionals, trainers in international development, and national workers. Though George's job there only lasted two years, his work had lasting influence in the areas where he served.

Calvary International/Go To Nations

Of the more than seven billion people living in the world today, approximately 41% remain unreached. In global partnership with

252

the body of Christ, Calvary International missionaries train leaders to change nations, ignite the fires of evangelism, bring hope to the hurting, and plant strong national churches. This is accomplished by envisioning, mobilizing, training, and serving the church worldwide to conduct cross-cultural missions ministry.

Go To Nations' missionaries and national staff work in East, South, and West Africa, Asia Pacific, Eurasia, and Central, Latin, and North America. The ministry includes Bible Schools, Business as Mission, Discipleship, Children's Ministry, Church Planting, and Community Transformation. Other aspects are Education, English as a Second Language, Equipping Churches and Nationals for Cross-Cultural Missions, Evangelism, Leadership Development, Literacy, Orphanages, Relief and Development, Youth Ministry, and Ministry to Victims of Human Trafficking.

Go To Nations has seen a shift in ministry focus since 2012, bringing four distinct areas of ministry to the forefront:

- Ministry to children, youth and young women, most of whom are considered vulnerable and at-risk.
- Ministry to the poor through community transformation.
- Ministry to mobilize national missionaries into the harvest as co-laborers.
- Ministry to help missionaries lead confidently, with clarity, focus, and direction through fresh impartation, individual coaching and team ministry.

The fruit of the righteous is a tree of life, And he who is wise wins souls. Proverbs 11:30

George and I served with Calvary International dba Go To Nations from 1993 until his death in 2013. Their mission is to Go To Nations with the Gospel of Jesus Christ until every tribe, every tongue, every nation has heard. A major focus is to help the nations discover their own need to participate in reaching the world for Christ. Part of the discipling process is to train the believers to reach out beyond their own families, villages, cities, nations and into the uttermost part of the earth.

GloDev, Inc.

I am pleased to serve on the board of directors for GloDev (short for Global Development), the relief and development arm of Go To Nations. Tim Lovelace, the founder of GloDev, stated that the life message of Dr. George Meyers changed his thinking about how to serve as a missionary. Dr. George had written, "When proclaimed and implemented holistically, the gospel is Good News, a new and better way in every measurement." It was that influence that prompted Tim to start GloDev as a means of showing the love of Christ through community development projects that alleviate poverty and restore hope and dignity to the disadvantaged.

My Beloved Family

"That the generation to come might know, even the children yet to be born, that they may arise and tell them to their children, that they should put their confidence in God, and not forget the works of God, but keep His commandments."

Psalm 78:6-7

CHAPTER 29
Remembering Daddy and Mama

My Father

I have already shared quite a lot about my parents in previous stories, but I want to highlight some other happenings that I recall or heard about. When Daddy was in his teens working on the family farm, he was kicked in the head by a horse. Medical options were sparse, but he had surgery and the doctor told the family that he died twice on the operating table. Somehow, they brought him through and he recovered. He had an indentation in his forehead between his eyes, the only evidence of the dreadful accident except for regular headaches requiring Anacin, his favorite remedy.

I remember him being a hard worker and a good family man. He relished Mama's good cooking. I can picture him eating a summer supper of meat, potatoes, and gravy, sliced tomatoes and sweet corn with a towel nearby to wipe the sweat off his brow as the butter dripped off his corn. He loved pies and cakes and Mama was well-known for her baked goods.

Daddy worked in the timber industry as a sawyer in the years that I was still at home. In 1955 he got a job at Houser Lumber Company in Newberg, where he worked as a salesman and truck driver for 19 years. Although his formal education was limited to the 10th grade, he had extraordinary skill in figuring out math problems in his head, which was a valuable talent in calculating lumber orders.

I never understood the logic for the system my parents had for buying groceries. Perhaps they discussed the menu ahead of time, but most everyday Daddy would go to the nearby grocery store to purchase the meat and perhaps other items that would be served for supper that night. Places I have lived required me to plan way in advance for meal preparation. In fact, when we lived in Ethiopia, we purchased groceries for a year from Addis Ababa and packed them in barrels to be transported by a lorry to our village in Kiramu, when the road was passable. We supplemented with vegetables available in season in the local market and raised our own chickens and beef animals.

Daddy had a very generous heart and served the Lord faithfully. He was jovial, fun to be with and enjoyed people. He was an active member of the Newberg Christian Church for 37 years, serving as a Sunday school teacher, elder, and chairman of the board. He was the elder who regularly took communion to the shut-ins on Sunday afternoons. That sense of duty caused tension with my mother because he often wasn't available to participate in family events. He liked doing practical things to bless people, and I remember him buying a set of tires for several pastors.

My Mother

In the chapter "The Olden Days" are Mama's memories of her life growing up. Her teaching career brought her joy and satisfaction. I described earlier her teaching in a one-room school with all eight grades. In her later years of teaching in Oregon, she was assigned to only one grade or maybe a combination of two grades. She especially liked to teach the 4th grade. In her words, "Fourth graders are eager to learn and already know a lot, but they don't yet think they know everything!"

In 1963 she got a teaching job at Hebo Elementary School on the Oregon Coast. It was too far to drive from Newberg every day, so Daddy bought a cottage in the Wi-Ne-Ma Town Site, 11 miles south of Hebo, for Mama to stay in during the week. It was a great idea that was to have far-reaching benefits for our family. But alas, Mama was fearful of staying there alone because of the thunder-like sound and perceived threat of the ocean. She tried putting the posts of her bed up on blackboard erasers to lessen the vibration from the breakers crashing on the beach, but it must not have helped enough. After a short time, she moved to a rented apartment across from the Hebo School.

After 29 years of teaching, she decided to retire in May of 1973. An incident occurred earlier in the spring that speeded up that date. While she was on duty on the playground at Dayton Elementary School, a child chasing a ball accidentally knocked her down, resulting in a broken hip that ended her teaching career. It was a blow to her skeletal system which was already invaded by arthritis and she experienced serious decline in her mobility.

Grandmother Support

Thinking of significant times in Mama's life brings back memories of her wonderful help to us each time we had a new baby. Her specialty when visiting us was folding clothes. I think she thought we took in laundry from the neighborhood! She loved all her grandchildren and great-grandchildren as they were added to our family circle. She remembered their birthdays and faithfully sent greeting cards.

The entire extended family marveled at her memory of dates and happenings in the family. We might be able to remember the year something happened, but Mama would remember the specifics. She kept her mind keen by reading the newspaper, looking up things she didn't know in the encyclopedia, and working the Jumble puzzle in the newspaper.

Long Distance Separation

When we first shared with my parents in 1972 that we were considering missionary service in a remote area of Ethiopia, and that our children would be students in a boarding school, their reaction was understandably one of concern. They said that it was okay for us to go, but we would need to leave the children with them! Of course, that was out of the question, and gradually as we developed our plans, they became more understanding and supportive. They came to visit us in Ethiopia in 1974 and later visited us in southern Sudan. Mama enjoyed their travels to Europe and Israel with a tour company, but the primitive situations in Africa were almost more adventure than she could tolerate.

While we were overseas in mission service, I wrote a letter every week to my parents and George's mother, who was then a widow. I knew that as I shared stories of our life on the field it would help them feel less apprehensive about our well-being and the thousands of miles that separated us. MAF flights with mailbags were often five or six weeks apart, so the outgoing aerograms piled up and several would get sent at one time. They treasured the letters and at my request they saved them. Those letters constitute my journal for our missionary career.

The Apron Story

Mama's baking skills were a blessing to our family. Whenever we were planning a family get-together, our children always said, "Be sure Grandma brings custard pies!" My folks were famous for homemade doughnuts. Daddy would say to Mama, "Baby, if you will stir up a batch of doughnuts, I'll fry them." That was a very common occurrence and they loved sharing the doughnuts with friends and family.

One Christmas much later I decided to make matching aprons for Mama and Daddy with felt letters on the front that stated, "World's Best Doughnut Maker" and "World's Best Doughnut Fryer." Unbeknownst to me, my brother Lyle's wife Melodie had the same idea. The aprons she made were very similar with only a slight variation in the wording. We were overseas when the folks opened their Christmas gifts that year, so we missed their reaction to the funny coincidence.

Dearly Loved Aunts

Some of the siblings of my parents were a significant part of my life. Most of them lived far away, but two, Aunt Irene (Daddy's sister) and Aunt Theresa (Mama's sister), lived close to us. I want to share some stories of times with them that are precious memories.

After our family moved to Oregon, we became very close to Aunt Irene, Uncle Luke and my cousin Douglas. Aunt Irene was a very special confidante for me as a teenager, then as a young wife and mother. Things I didn't feel free to talk about with my mother I would share with her, knowing that I would have her listening ear and loving acceptance.

Douglas was four years older than my brother Lyle and was kind of like a brother to Marilyn and me. Nearly every Sunday we would all get together for a meal and perhaps a drive in the country to see some new scenery. We spent all of the holidays with them.

A funny incident that happened one Halloween has become part of family lore. We had a filbert orchard and Daddy had a small business of selling filberts and walnuts to family and friends in the fall. He had purchased a set of horn-rimmed glasses and large bulbous nose that was his Halloween "costume." Our family went to visit the Weilers in Portland and Daddy took along a large sack of walnuts for Aunt Irene. When he went to the door wearing his costume, he disguised his voice and asked if she would like to buy some walnuts. Her reply was hilarious! "No thanks, I get my walnuts from my brother in Newberg."

My mother's oldest sister, Theresa Rickett, and her daughter Ann moved to Portland a few years after we had relocated to Oregon. I remember Mama getting a letter from Aunt Theresa saying that she was getting "unmarried" from Harold Rickett, her husband of 35 years. Marilyn and I didn't know Uncle Rikki well because we had never lived near them. The news was a shock to Mama and this was the first time I had ever known anyone who was divorced. Their family had lived in Portland in an earlier period of their lives when Ann was four years old. Their close friend Margaret Parker had a son Tom who was 12. Tom fell in love with Ann way back then and waited for her to grow up and then they were married.

Aunt Theresa didn't own a car and did all her travel by public transportation. She and Ann were very grateful to go with my family whenever we went sight-seeing or to any events. Aunt Theresa loved classical music and invited our family to go to the symphony with her several times. Little Lyle didn't enjoy those events, and whenever he heard that one was coming up, he pitifully complained, "We'll just have to sit through it and when we get home the house will be dark and cold!"

One time after George and I were married, and Ann was married and had moved to Arizona, Aunt Theresa rode with us on a family trip to Grand Canyon and on to visit Ann and Tom. Evidently, up until then, she had never noticed our children quarreling with each other. After a disturbance in the back seat that required some stern correction from George, she later told us that she was glad to know that our kids were normal.

Catlin-Gabel, a private school in Portland where Aunt Theresa taught, had an annual rummage sale. We were recipients of wonderful treasures that she purchased in the teachers' pre-sale. Jennie remembers receiving gifts of special books and credits her love of good literature to that collection.

More Aunts and Uncles

After I was married, we only had a few chances to visit Mama's family in Wisconsin. I wanted George to get to know the family, plus I wanted him to experience some of the extreme weather I remembered from my childhood. One memorable time, my parents traveled with us for a planned stopover in Wisconsin when we were driving across country to an army assignment in Fort Benning, Georgia. It was winter, and as we left Oregon, we heard on the radio that a snowstorm was coming that had the potential of delaying us and causing us to be late for George's military assignment in Georgia. We had a heavily loaded station wagon, and before we had gone very far we had a flat front tire. While we were having the tire fixed, Daddy bought new snow tires for the rear to prevent more tire trouble on the rest of the trip – an incredible blessing for us.

Since Daddy was able to help George with the driving, we kept going night and day to try to reach our destination before the storm arrived. It caught up with us in Iowa while we were visiting George's sister Emily, a good place to wait for better weather. The delay was not long and we felt we could still meet George's check-in time if we hurried.

After we arrived at Aunt Caroline's in Woodford, Wisconsin, the temperature dipped down to 32° below zero. Uncle Willard had to pull our car with his tractor to get it started when we resumed our journey to Fort Benning. My parents planned to have a longer visit and return to Oregon by train.

Another time when we visited family in Wisconsin in the summer on our way to Fort Benning, George and the kids got to experience a typical electrical storm; thunder and lightning with the sky opening up, dropping 6.25 inches of rain in two hours. That time we had to take a circuitous route to continue on our way because much of the county was under water. George had now experienced both extreme Wisconsin weather conditions I had told him about.

Mama had five siblings. Theresa lived in Oregon; Earl and his wife Florence had a dairy farm in Rudolph, Wisconsin, where my mother grew up; Caroline and her husband Willard lived on a farm in Wisconsin and in Arizona in their retirement; and Helen and her husband Glennon had a supper club in Wisconsin Rapids. Though we had very few opportunities to visit some of those relatives, we always enjoyed their company. Mama's brother Matthias, called Mack, died at age 21 from complications of diabetes.

I remember visits with Uncle Leonard Joslin, a brother of Grandma Peck. He and his wife, Aunt Racie, had no children of their own so Grandpa and Grandma loaned them their daughter Irene, which was not uncommon in those days. Aunt Racie's unmarried sister, Aunt Puss, was also part of that family. After Aunt Racie passed away, Uncle Len married Aunt Lucia and they moved to Arcadia, California. Now decades later, my granddaughter Allison Leung and her family live in Arcadia, near the Santa Anita racetrack.

Daddy's Other Sisters

Besides Irene, Daddy had two other sisters, Camille and Etta. Sadly, Etta died from diabetes when she was a young mother. My only memories of her are from pictures and stories. My family did not have many chances to visit Aunt Camille and Uncle Louis Hamel in Wisconsin or after they moved to Michigan, but whenever we were in the vicinity, we made a point to include them in our itinerary. They had five sons before their daughter Kay was born. As a young adult, Kay had twins named George and Georgia, and another daughter named Alicia. When her children were very young, Kay was killed in an automobile accident and Aunt Camille and Uncle Louis raised those grandchildren. Tragically, they also had the misfortune of losing their two oldest sons in untimely deaths: Harry, my age, died from cancer, and Louis Jr. (called Ossie) died from a heart attack.

I loved Aunt Irene and Aunt Camille and kept in touch with them by phone and letters, even when we were overseas.

An Eternal Perspective

A few months before our planned departure from Ethiopia in 1976, Daddy had a debilitating seizure and was hospitalized. The doctors were never able to determine the cause of that incident, but while he was undergoing testing he was diagnosed with prostate cancer. He lived ten more years before he became incapacitated. He had some serious health issues at the time George was working for the Holstein Association and we were living in New Hampshire. I was able to fly to Oregon to spend some time with him just prior to his death in 1986 at age 78 years.

In 1990, we returned to Oregon for George's work at Smucker Manufacturing, Inc., in Harrisburg. I was able to take care of my mother in our home in Junction City following her hip replacement operation in 1991. Through the years Mama had expressed great concern and worry that she might someday have a stroke. We were disappointed that during her hip surgery, the surgeon accidentally severed a nerve which caused her to have drop foot and walk like a stroke victim. Though she worked hard in physical therapy to overcome that setback, we could not convince her to have the other hip replaced as had been planned, and her gait was compromised during the last years of her life.

Mama passed away in 2003 at the age of 91 after a short hospitalization in Hood River. At that time George and I were serving in the jungle region of northern Guatemala. I was able to get a special Air Force flight from our remote area to Guatemala City; and the next day I traveled on a commercial flight and arrived in time to speak at her memorial service in Newberg, Oregon.

As believers, we know that our separation is not forever and that we will be together again for all eternity. What a wonderful promise and assurance!

CHAPTER 30
My Sister and Brothers

Marilyn Mae Wilson

My sister Marilyn is just 13 months younger than I. We worked and played together through the years until I was married and moved away from the family home. Now we love to get together to look at pictures and reminisce about happenings in our lives in Wisconsin and Oregon. She visited us often and helped at various times with our little ones. She was a fun aunt, always taking time to play with them.

When we lived in Corvallis when George was at Oregon State, Marilyn came to live with us. Our parents provided her with a small travel trailer which she used for sleeping and studying, but she had her meals and companionship with us. She loved our kids and they adored her! She commented that she learned a lot from George as they traveled together to and from OSU.

Mark Wilson came into her life while she was teaching physical education at the high school in The Dalles. Mark was on the board of directors of the school and owned a large orchard near Mosier, growing mostly cherries and some apples and peaches. They were married and had two children, Brian and Nancy. Marilyn was very fulfilled as a mother and in helping with the management of the farming enterprise.

Sad Family Time

In September 1984, at the same time as our son Dan and Laurie were expecting a new baby, a tragic plane crash near The Dalles took the lives of Marilyn's husband and their son. Mark and 12-year-old Brian had gone to the hangar nearby where the annual inspection had taken place, so they could fly the plane back to the farm. At the same time that Mark's plane took off, a plane with four businessmen took off from the airport. Air Traffic Control did not foresee the tragedy about to occur. The two planes crashed mid-air and those four men and Mark and Brian were all instantly killed. The whole community was in shock and profound grief, and our family was devastated!

We were living in New Hampshire at that time, but as soon as I heard the news I booked a flight from Hartford, Connecticut, the nearest airport to our home, to travel to Oregon. I was able to spend time consoling Marilyn, attend the memorial service, and help her with end-of-life issues. Although losing them both was extremely painful for her, Marilyn recognized that they were so close as father and son that she would not have been able to comfort either of them if they hadn't died together. Their daughter Nancy was nine years old at that time.

September 6, 1984, the day after the funeral service for Mark and Brian, was the birth date of our first grandson, Joel Daniel, Dan and Laurie's second child. We were thankful for the baby's safe arrival but incredibly saddened by the loss of Marilyn's husband and son. The full gamut of emotions – death and new life in the same week!

Marilyn has since sold the orchard and lives in Hood River. She has been very supportive as a grandmother to Shaiyan, Ciena, Hunter and Oakley, Nancy's children, as they have grown up. And now she helps with her great-grandson Matthew. Nancy and her husband Aron and their family live close by, and Marilyn enjoys attending the boys' sporting events. I live about three hours away from her extended family, and I'm happy to see them as often as they can join us for family events. Our kids have greatly appreciated their Aunt Marilyn's loving support through the years.

Lyle Gordon Peck

I was 11 when Lyle was born and I have many wonderful memories of his growing up years. He was a cute little redhead and much loved by our whole family. When George began courting me and sitting with me in church, Lyle would often sit on his lap. He was six years old when we got married. He and George's youngest brother Jack had important roles in the ceremony.

After I was married and we moved to Eastern Oregon, I didn't have close touch with Lyle, except for family visits. I have a mental picture of him as a pre-teen, with Mama's homemade doughnuts stacked on the fingers of one hand and a tall glass of milk in the other hand. When he was 11, he came with Mama to help with our little boys when Jennie was born.

According to Lyle, it was love at first sight when he met Melodie Reese while picking strawberries in the summer of 1964. We first became acquainted with her when she presented him with a special box at Christmastime that she had crafted and filled with elaborately decorated homemade cookies. She had obviously heard that the way to a man's heart is through his stomach, and she surely did win his heart!

Lyle lived with us in Corvallis for two years beginning in 1968, his first year at Oregon State, where he majored in mechanical engineering. He entered the Air Force Reserve Officer Training Corps and moved up in the ranks. He was selected as Group Commander in his senior year, the highest cadet position at Oregon State ROTC.

Before Lyle and Melodie were married, I helped her get a good position in the medical records department at Good Samaritan Hospital, where I worked. She lived in an apartment a couple blocks from our house, and our kids loved to be able to stay with her sometimes when they got home from school and George and I weren't yet home from work.

Lyle and Melodie were married September 6, 1969, and Lyle moved into her apartment down the street. Their first child, Clinton Scott, was born in 1972. We enjoyed the close association with them and were glad that we lived near enough to get together often during the years we all lived in Oregon. Their family was blessed with a daughter, Tracy Elizabeth, in 1974.

Lyle entered the United States Air Force in September 1973 and served in multiple strategic missions at various places throughout his military career. He distinguished himself in various assignments, some so secret that he was not able to tell us about them.

George and Lyle had many interesting military conversations, both having attained the rank of Lieutenant Colonel in their chosen branch of service. Lyle's last position before retiring was at Eglin AFB in the panhandle of Florida. We were also living in Florida then and were able to see them several times. In 2014 they moved to Winchester, Tennessee, where they live now. I had a lovely visit with them once at their home there on my way home to Oregon from my work in Jacksonville.

Clint followed his dad's military path, joined the Air Force and was stationed in Alaska, where he met his wife Katrina. Later he transitioned to a career with the Anchorage Police Department. He and Katrina have three children. In 2018 they moved to Post Falls, Idaho. Tracy is a nurse practitioner and is married to Bob Jackson, an orthopedic surgeon. They live in northern Indiana and have two college-age children.

Robert Earl Grunewald

About the year 2000, I felt prompted that I should visit my dad's sister, Aunt Camille, who lived in Nekoosa, Wisconsin. She was in her mid-90s and we had not been able to visit her often. I mentioned it to George and he urged me to find a way to schedule a visit. Soon after that, we had a ministry trip that required us to pass through Chicago and we scheduled a couple days to visit family in Wisconsin. We rode the bus from O'Hare Airport to the town of Nekoosa for a welcomed visit with Aunt Camille.

While we were chatting, she brought out a box of old snapshots for me to look through. Since she was nearly blind and not able to identify pictures anymore, she told me to take any pictures I wanted. It was a joy for me to find some pictures of my dad as a little boy and several other pictures I had never seen of other family members.

While I was looking through the pictures, Aunt Camille said, "You know about Bob." I couldn't think of a Bob in our family and she followed up by saying, "You have a brother named Bob." I was surprised to learn that Bob had been born to my dad and his first wife, Isabelle, in an earlier time period. The marriage only lasted a short time, but Aunt Camille and Uncle Louis were neighbors to Isabelle and her second husband, Bill Grunewald, who adopted Bob when he was five years old.

Aunt Camille told me that Bob lived just down the road from them and she had known him all his life. I said, "If you know him, I want to know him too." She went to her special phone on the wall, made especially for sight-impaired people. She called Bob and within five minutes he came walking up the driveway. His resemblance to my dad was profound, and I held out my arms to welcome him. We hugged and kissed and cried!

Aunt Camille had kept the secret through the decades but didn't want to die without sharing it with me. Bob didn't realize that we had never been told about him so thought we didn't want to know him. That period of history was evidently very painful to my folks and they chose not to tell the rest of the family about the previous marriage or Bob, so sadly we missed having him in our lives as we were growing up. The next step was to introduce him to Marilyn and Lyle.

It was a great blessing to Bob to know that George and I readily accepted him as part of our family. He had many mannerisms in common with Daddy, and we quickly came to love him and his wife Catherine and their children. In the next few years, we visited them several times at their place in Wisconsin, and they came to see us in Florida. Even though we lived far away from each other, we got together as often as possible to make up for lost time! We were pleased to learn that Bob was active in his church and community. He was great fun to be around and we enjoyed some great fellowship. While on some business trips in the Midwest, our son Dan fitted in some Wisconsin visits and twice was able to join Bob and the men in his family on a hunting trip in northern Wisconsin.

Bob experienced some serious health challenges in his later years and he passed away while George and I were serving in Guatemala. We felt sad that two of our children, Steve and Jennie, never had the chance to meet him. After his death, one time when Dan was planning to be in that part of the country on a business trip, he encouraged me to fly into Minneapolis so we could drive together to visit the Grunewalds and Aunt Camille's family. In August of 2017, Catherine and their son Tim and his wife Renee were able to join us on the Oregon Coast for our family reunion.

CHAPTER 31
Special Family Times

T hrough the years we have had many enjoyable family get-togethers. I am highlighting just a few that bring back precious memories.

We had many wonderful times with the Weilers as I was growing up. Aunt Irene was well known by family and friends for her hospitality and delicious meals, but she was truly famous for her special baked beans recipe. Years later, when we lived farther away and saw Uncle Luke and Aunt Irene less frequently, our son Steve, with his humorous bent, referred to her as Aunt I-bean!

Aunt Irene had met Uncle Luke when they both worked at the "San," a TB sanatorium in Wisconsin. Later in her own home, before serving food she always pre-warmed the dishes by pouring hot water on them for a few minutes to preserve the heat, a skill she had acquired while working at the San in the kitchen. In those days there were no special covers to keep food warm during delivery to the patients. Continuing that pattern of pre-heating the dishes with hot water was her trademark way of serving delicious hot food.

1959

We lived on the ranch at Double M Herefords when Danny was a toddler. We encountered a unique predicament when we hosted my parents and siblings, plus Grandpa Peck, Aunt Irene, Uncle Luke and Douglas for Thanksgiving in 1959. While we were enjoying our visit, someone reported that the toilet wasn't flushing. George evaluated the situation and discovered that when he used the plunger it would flush, but the dilemma kept recurring.

Plumbing problems are never pleasant, but all the more exasperating with a house full of people and only one bathroom. By afternoon it was necessary for George to remove the toilet to thoroughly assess the problem and do whatever it took to fix it. The offender turned out to be a jar lid. Little Danny had plenty of toys, but he loved to play with kitchen utensils such as measuring cups and jar rings. We had not realized that when he had put a bunch of jar rings and lids in the toilet, one lid disappeared out of sight. That jar lid exactly covered the opening, totally blocking the passage after each episode of plunging.

1961

When Jennie was born in August 1961, we were living in the house across the street from the post office in Adams. That Thanksgiving we traveled to Newberg to spend the holiday with my parents and the Weiler family. After our family dinner when I was washing dishes, Aunt Irene noticed a protrusion on my back between my shoulder blade and my waist, about the size of an egg. Neither George nor I had noticed it before then, and of course we were concerned.

As soon as we got home, I tried to make an appointment with my doctor in Pendleton. Alas, he was on vacation for two weeks. In that much waiting time, my imagination created a very negative scenario. I was sure it was cancer and I pictured my three little children without a mother. The day I finally did get in to see the doctor, he seemed concerned also and scheduled me for surgery the next day. The surgical team decided to do the operation under local anesthesia, a decision they regretted. The growth was about the size of an inch-thick pancake with tentacles wrapped around several of my ribs, nerves, and ligaments. Extracting the tumor in surgery required more and more injections of anesthetic. I was awake for the whole unpleasant experience. Following the operation, the pathologist diagnosed it as a benign lipoma. Because the location was in the area where the cultivator had hooked into my back during the tractor accident when I was young, we thought the tumor might have been growing for many years and just become visible when I was in my early twenties. A frightful story with a happy ending!

1970

For our family vacation the summer of 1970, we pulled our 16-foot travel trailer on a scenic tour through Alberta, Canada, with stops at Glacier Park, Waterton Lakes, Lake Louise, Banff and Jasper. George's sister Dot and her family and his brother Jack from Alaska met up with us for the trip, which included a snowmobile tour of Athabasca Glacier. George's mother wasn't able to travel with us, but she treated us all with tickets to the Calgary Stampede, which everyone enjoyed very much, especially the chuckwagon races.

1981

Our son Steve came to visit us for five weeks in Sudan in July 1981. We met him in Nairobi and had about 10 days together in Kenya. Our time away from Sudan was refreshing to our bodies and spirits. We returned to Sudan on a charter plane that stopped in Juba for a short time then continued on to Mundri. We were blessed by a cool, cloudy day to give us all a chance to become adjusted to the intense heat more gradually.

Steve was feeling quite confused after making contact with many of our Sudanese workers and friends. They all looked the same to him at first, dark complexion with black curly hair, but after a few days they became separate people to him. It is interesting to me that many of the black people we have worked with have commented that all white people look alike! It was great to have that time together and Steve was a great help to us. We were sorry that Jennie and Dan were never able to visit us during the three years we were in Sudan.

1984

The highlight of our summer in 1984 was a reunion with our family in Hinsdale, New Hampshire. Dan, Laurie, and little Anna were on their way back to Oregon after their mission assignment with YWAM in Mombasa. When we learned that they could visit us, we organized a family reunion during the Fourth of July holiday that included my folks, Alice and Earl Peck, our daughter Jennie, her husband Mark and Baby Amy, plus our son Steve.

After moving to Vermont for George's job at the Holstein Association, we had rented an apartment for the winter, and then in the spring we purchased a large farmhouse in the New Hampshire countryside, across the Connecticut River from Brattleboro, Vermont. It had been built in 1825 and some improvements had been done through the years, but it was a genuine fixer-upper when we got it. That summer, with help from our children, we gave the house a much-needed coat of exterior paint.

We had not been together with all of our children since December 1979, so we all considered it a very special time. During the family visit the above-ground pool got a lot of use, but previously even when it was warm enough, George and I had not had much time to enjoy it. We scheduled some family pictures while we were together. Trying to get our granddaughters, Anna (age 2) and Amy (age 1), to look happy was a challenge. At that age, they didn't have much appreciation for each other, and it showed in the pictures, but as they grew up they became good friends. Dan's wife Laurie was pregnant with Joel at that time, but we had to wait a couple months for him to make his appearance.

1985

Our summer vacation in 1985 was a very special time for us. We flew to Los Angeles and had a few days with Mark and Jennie in Mission Hills and my brother Lyle's family near San Bernardino. Lyle loaned us their van to drive to Oregon so we would have room to take Mark, Jennie, and Amy, plus some furniture for our Wi-Ne-Ma cottage. The highlight of our trip was five days there on the Pacific Coast with all our children and grandchildren, as well as visits from our folks. Among the special events was a wonderful picnic in Newberg with 60 or more family members and friends.

1987

It was delightful in the fall of 1987 to have two of our children and their families with us in New Hampshire. Jennie, Amy (4½) and Allison (2) came for two weeks in September. We went on a sight-seeing outing on a very chilly day. Little Allison, being pushed in a stroller, told us in a pitiful whimper that she was "freeeezing." Steve, Leslie, and Lauren (11 months) arrived later in the month for the annual sport of "leaf peeping," enjoying the brilliance of the colored leaves. George's mother visited us there also, but at a separate time.

For our last week of vacation that year we traveled to Oregon for the week between Christmas and New Year's Day. Our California children were planning to visit their families in Oregon, so we couldn't pass up the chance to have all of our immediate family together for a few days. We had not seen Dan and Laurie, Anna (5) and Joel (3) for two years, and we also visited our mothers and brothers and sisters.

1990

In 1990 when we were living in Brunswick, Georgia, we were blessed by a visit from Steve, Leslie, Lauren (4) and Stephanie (two months old), along with Jennie and Austin (2), who joined us for that wonderful family time. We have some cute pictures of the little kids at the Okefenokee Swamp on one of our outings. We carefully avoided the sluggish alligators lying around, not trusting them to remain lethargic.

1994

We were separated from our grandchildren much of the time in their growing up years, so it was a great blessing when our schedule allowed us to get together with them. In 1994 we were able to join our children and grandchildren who were together for the holidays at Steve and Leslie's lovely home in the San Francisco Bay area, about halfway between Harrisburg, Oregon, where Dan's family lived, and the Los Angeles area where Jennie's family lived. My mother loved to be with us and wanted to join us. She didn't want to travel alone, so we made it possible for our granddaughter Anna (age 12) to accompany her on the train from Eugene, Oregon. MaaMaa (the grandchildren's special name for George's mother) was also able to come and we are glad we had a family photo taken to record the occasion.

1996

Our 40th wedding anniversary was celebrated with a picnic at Orchard Point Park at Fern Ridge Reservoir, near Eugene, Oregon. It was wonderful to see so many family members, friends, and support partners. We received treasured greetings and expressions of love from those who attended and some who were not able to come. As a representative of our children, our daughter Jennie put together a masterpiece photo album, entitled "Memories of Their Life

Together – 1956 – 1996." We had a new picture taken of the two of us for that occasion, which we made available as a prayer reminder for our prayer and financial partners.

2000

Steve and Jennie's families joined Dan's family in Harrisburg for a late Christmas in 2000. Although George was traveling as part of his work for Calvary International, he gave me the gift of a ticket to Oregon, so I could take advantage of the opportunity to be with all my children and grandchildren who were gathered together in Oregon for the holidays.

Our Golden Anniversary – June 2, 2006

Our 50th wedding anniversary was truly a special celebration with about 120 friends and relatives gathered in Dan and Laurie's beautiful backyard in Harrisburg. Our children and grandchildren planned for a year in advance and all their hard work produced a wonderful event to honor us and give thanks to the Lord for the blessings He has given our family. Our grandchildren sang "I Love You a Bushel and a Peck," famous in my family because we were four Pecks (a bushel measure) until Lyle was born. Doris Day recorded the song in September of 1950 when Lyle was nine months old.

Celebrating 70 Years of Life

After George's 70th birthday was celebrated in March 2007, he insisted that a similar celebration be planned two years later for my 70th birthday April 23, 2009. Our children, Dan, Steve, and Jennie, plus my sister Marilyn, my brother Lyle and several cousins from far away came to Jacksonville for the weekend to honor me. Ninety-four guests signed the register at the open house celebration at Calvary International. What a special event!

2010

Our trips to the West Coast from Florida were always multi-purpose. In June 2010 we surprised my sister Marilyn with a party to celebrate her 70th birthday. After that event, we hosted some support partners at our cottage on the coast and completed some maintenance projects. The finale was a tent camping trip with all of our children and grandchildren at Lake Shasta, California, on Labor Day weekend. Water sports were the main entertainment and we were persuaded to ride in the donuts pulled behind the boat. More memories to treasure!

Graduations and Weddings

We seldom got to attend the graduation ceremonies for our grandchildren, but we acknowledged their achievements with pride. We were thankful to be able to participate in joyful wedding celebrations in California in 2011 and 2012. Three of our grandchildren's weddings came in close succession: Austin and Hannah Rice, November 5, 2011; Joel and Kristen Meyers, December 18, 2011; and Tony and Stephanie Cozzolino, April 6, 2012.

Dr. Ron Cottle, the founder of Christian Life School of Theology based in Columbus, Georgia, had asked George to prepare lessons from his books, *Granddad's Money Camp* and *Kingdom Business Leadership,* to be recorded and made available on DVD at CLST. After the November wedding, while we waited for the December wedding, we stayed at Wi-Ne-Ma, working hard to complete the required question and answer sheets for the lessons.

Later at the CLST headquarters in Georgia, George was filmed teaching the chapters of each book, which are now available on DVD to students all over the world. Shortly after that, we returned to the West Coast for Stephanie and Tony's wedding at a picturesque venue in Pleasanton, California.

Wi-Ne-Ma Family Reunions

On the Fourth of July weekend in 2011, we gathered at our beloved cottage on the coast for a joyful get-together of the family. We rented two extra houses to accommodate our large family. The next reunion was when everyone gathered there in September 2013 to attend the graveside service after George's death. Although it was a profoundly sad time for me, it was comforting to have my entire family with me.

August 2017 was a grand reunion of all of my children, grandchildren, and great-grandchildren as we dedicated the renovation of the cottage and the special memorial wall in George's honor. I'm looking forward to a similar event during the summer of 2019.

CHAPTER 32
Our Marriage and Family

Agreement in Marriage

We had lots of experience in learning to come into agreement about important issues of life. The Married for Life course that we taught had great training tools and especially encouraged the participants to be faithful to study the Word of God, our Creator's instruction manual for life on earth. We were admonished to take our separate instruments and fine tune them under the hand of the Master Conductor. If we did not walk in agreement, there would be a lack of peace in our home.

> *Again I tell you, if two of you on earth agree (harmonize together, make a symphony together), about whatever [anything and everything] they may ask, it will come to pass and be done for them by My Father in heaven.*
> Matthew 18:19 Amplified Bible

I particularly remember one admonition: *The time it takes to come into agreement is far less than the time it takes to unravel a wrong decision.* We can't always see what is ahead, around the corner. For example, the workers on the deck of a riverboat often can't see the way ahead because of the fog, and they are unsure of the safety of the course; whereas the captain up on the bridge can see the way above the fog and knows the route is clear. Our dairy farm venture was an example of us being in agreement as a family, but not aware of the adverse circumstances we would face when the owner began acting irrationally.

When we taught the Marriage Ministries lesson on agreement, George and I ran into the room with our legs tied together. Our point was to show to the trainees that even though it is challenging at times, it is possible to run the race of life together in agreement. We remember the story of Ananias and Sapphira in Acts Chapter 5. They were apparently in agreement with each other about the proceeds from the sale of their property, though they were deceiving God, which cost them their lives.

One time when we lived in New Hampshire on an eight-acre property, George wanted to get a pickup for jobs such as hauling feed for our two steers. We talked it over, evaluated our cash position, and agreed that we didn't want to go into debt for this purchase. We determined that he could spend $2,000 for a pickup. Sometime later when he was on an errand in Keene, he saw a pickup at a dealership that he said was a "honey" and just what he wanted. He put earnest money down and drove it home to show me. Of course, I asked how much it cost, and he sheepishly told me $3,000. I said, "We agreed that you would only spend $2,000," and he guiltily admitted that I was correct. The next day he drove the pickup back to the dealership and told the salesman he wasn't able to follow through with the sale because of our agreement as a couple. The man was shocked at his faithfulness to his commitment with me, and although it was against company policy, he returned the down payment.

What Makes a Marriage Last...

This poem from a greeting card was taped on the back of the door in the bathroom where both of us saw it every day. The author is unknown.

To do what is best for your partner in life,
To respect the commitment of husband and wife,
To be still and just listen – not have to be heard,
To forgive and forget and not need the last word,
To admit you're not perfect – you'll both make mistakes,
To support the decisions that each of you makes,
To be willing to laugh when the day has been rough,
To divide up the burdens when life becomes tough,
To support one another when things are too hurried,
To comfort each other when stress keeps you worried,
To be willing to cherish your true love and friend
With a joy and compassion that never could end.

Teaching by Example

The ultimate blessing of raising children in righteousness is observing that they have patterned their lives after the training and positive examples of our lives. Now our children are not only parents themselves but have also entered the wonderful world of grandparenting. Their goal is to live before their children and grandchildren in such a way that they learn to make good choices in life and are spared the consequences of poor decisions.

The truth about children walking in the footsteps of their parents was quickened to us by recalling an incident during George's childhood. His father chewed tobacco and had to spit frequently. On their family car, the back doors opened in the opposite direction of the front doors. One time when they were driving, Pap opened his driver side door to spit. Three-year-old George opened his door to spit, too. He was holding on to the door handle and when the wind caught the door, he was thrown out, causing him to roll in the gravel along the ditch. Miraculously, he wasn't seriously hurt. He just "got rocks in his head," according to his older sisters. His guardian angel was evidently on full alert!

Future Generations

I want to share an update on the status of my three married children, 13 grandchildren and nine great-grandchildren, as of this writing.

Our Firstborn, Dan

Dan and his wife Laurie live a half mile from me in Harrisburg on a mini-farm. Dan worked as a CPA in public accounting for 11 years and now has worked for Industrial Finishes & Systems, Inc., in Eugene for 21 years. He is currently the Vice President of Finance. Laurie homeschooled their children and has a home-based medical transcription business, but the current love of her life is "grandmothering." They have four daughters, one son and six grandchildren, four in the Portland area and two in Houston.

Together they served three years with Youth With A Mission in Mombasa, Kenya, and they have enjoyed subsequent travels abroad. Laurie especially appreciated the chance to take all their children to Ethiopia to visit her missionary parents and to see where she grew up. Dan has been on ministry trips to Guatemala, Mexico, Cuba, and India. They celebrated their 40th wedding anniversary on a cruise to Alaska and have been to Hawaii twice together. He inherited his father's passion for hunting and fishing and looks forward to several trips each fall to the Blue Mountains of northeast Oregon. Green Peter Reservoir provides delicious kokanee (land-locked salmon) as well as water sports for the family in the summer. In 2016 after trying for 16 years, he drew the trophy bull elk tag for the Walla Walla unit and bagged a giant elk, whose impressive antlers hang above the piano in their living room.

Their one-acre property includes extensive garden areas. Laurie has beautiful flower gardens and Dan raises five varieties of table grapes as well as blueberries, blackberries, marionberries, raspberries and various fruit trees, which they generously share. He and their daughter

Christine have had several weekend adventures hiking through Oregon on the famous Pacific Crest Trail. They have completed 350 of the 450 miles and hope to finish the last 100 miles in 2019.

Dan and Laurie's Children

Anna and Brett Smith are far away in Houston, Texas. Brett is an executive with M.D. Anderson Cancer Center. Anna has retired from her commercial real estate career to be home with their cute munchkins, Coleson Robert Daniel (November 2012) and Evelyn Beth Anne (April 2015). Houston is not far from the beach at Galveston, which they visit quite regularly. They are always happy when Grammy comes to visit them in Houston or they get to come to Oregon.

Joel and Kristen Meyers live in Tigard, where Joel works as a manager with Huron Consulting, leading teams that provide support and consulting services to U.S. healthcare provider systems that use Huron's software products. Kristen, an elementary school teacher, is now focused on homemaking and their children, Joshua Joel (April 2015), Elliott David (June 2017), and Isaac Jameson (February 2019).

Marie and Ryan Kirkpatrick live in Vancouver, Washington, where she works as a Physician Assistant at Peace Health Family Medicine. Ryan commutes to Swan Island in Portland for his work with Daimler Trucks North America as a senior pricing analyst. Their daughter Rachel Marie's (December 2017) expressive personality has given the extended family lots of joy.

Christine and Aaron Kost tied the knot on November 3, 2018, at Life Bible Church in Harrisburg, where Christine is a part-time pastor for the junior high kids. She works as a registered nurse at Good Samaritan Hospital in Corvallis, specializing in Intravenous Therapy. Aaron is a salesman at Verizon in Eugene, plays the guitar on the worship team, and helps Christine with the youth activities. I am so happy that they live across the street from me.

Sarah is a senior nursing student at the Klamath Falls branch of Oregon Health Sciences University and a CNA at Sky Lakes Medical Center. Her husband, Avery McMillan, is a student in the Oregon Institute of Technology mechanical engineering program and an engineering intern at Jeld-Wen Windows & Doors. They live in Klamath Falls and are looking forward to finishing their education and pursuing their careers.

Second Son, Steve

Steve and his wife Leslie met in 1985 while working on a computer systems project together at the Concord, California, offices of Chevron. Steve continues as Manager International Tax Compliance; Leslie retired from Chevron and volunteers a few hours each week at various charities, as well as pursuing an active lifestyle. They have two daughters and one son.

Both Steve and Leslie have had numerous international trips for work, Steve in Nigeria and Kazakhstan and Leslie in South Africa and the Philippines. They have enjoyed bicycle touring trips in Italy, France, Germany, and Austria, including a side trip to Switzerland. In 2016 they circumnavigated the island of Taiwan (550 miles) on bikes, which required their most authentic eating experience of solely Asian food using chopsticks. They have climbed eight 14,000-foot peaks in Colorado. In 2018 they had a very arduous 12-day trek to the Everest Base Camp in Nepal, reaching 17,500 feet. They regularly cycle with close friends near their beautiful home in Danville, California.

Steve and Leslie's Children

Lauren was married to Rolando Zegarra in a beautiful ceremony on October 13, 2018, in Malibu, California. They met when they were both working in the same company in the movie industry. Lauren is a creative development coordinator at MGM Studios, and Rolando is an international marketing coordinator at Sony Pictures Entertainment. They live in Los Angeles and enjoy traveling.

Stephanie and her husband, Anthony Cozzolino, met in biology class at San Francisco State College. They live on a farm in Half Moon Bay, near San Francisco, where they raise flowers, pumpkins, and decorative gourds, which they sell at farmers' markets and their own produce stand. In addition, they have six hundred cage-free chickens and sell eggs at a premium price year-round, and in December they operate a Christmas tree lot. Except during the intense fall marketing time, Stephanie also works as a customer service representative at a Farmers' Insurance office.

Steve and Leslie's son Eric is fulfilling a dream of working for the railroad industry. His training helped him get a job in Shreveport, Louisiana, where he works as a freight conductor for Union Pacific Railroad. When he lived in California, he loved to go duck hunting with his brother-in-law Tony. Although his work is demanding, he is an avid fisherman when he gets the chance.

Our Daughter, Jennie

Jennie and her husband, Mark Rice, recently moved from Quartz Hill to Canyon Country, California, much closer to Mark's work in the music department at Grace Community Church. She and Mark have appreciated opportunities to travel together as Mark has played the piano for Christian conferences on several cruises to New England and Alaska. Their most recent trip took them to Wittenberg, Germany, for a conference celebrating the 500th anniversary of the Protestant Reformation.

After Jennie's 27 years of homeschooling their five children, their youngest two are now in college. She has enjoyed working with children of all ages through the years, whether teaching Sunday school or leading music for elementary age students, or teaching English or history in homeschool co-ops. She continues to do medical transcription from their home and thoroughly enjoys their three grandchildren, who are welcomed to their house by a porch sign that reads: *Grammy and Grampa's House...where memories are made!*

Jennie and Mark's Children

Amy lives in Portland and loves her job as a manager with Huron Consulting. In her spare time she runs, cooks, travels and wrangles her two cats. She enjoys playing the piano and writing music and loves being "Aunt Mim" to her nephews and niece.

Allison and Thomas Leung have two children, Marcus Alan (November 2014) and Olive Vivienne (November 2016), who share the same birthday. Besides her work as a wife and mother, Allison's art degree is utilized in her part-time work for Kenton Nelson Studio in Pasadena and in projects on the side using her creative skills. Thomas puts his expertise in cooking and the restaurant industry to good use in his sales job at *Chef's Toys,* a food service equipment company.

Austin and his wife Hannah moved from Lancaster to Orange County, California, in May 2018. Austin is a CPA working as a senior accountant for Haskell & White. Hannah is a stay-at-home mom caring for their son Shadrach Joseph (June 2017), and also works part-time as a trainer at 24Hour Fitness. Both Hannah and Allison are involved in leadership of their respective MOPS groups (Mothers of Preschoolers).

April received her Associate degree from College of the Canyons in Canyon Country in June 2018 and then moved to Camarillo to attend California State University Channel Islands, majoring in communications with an emphasis on health communications. Along with working at a restaurant to earn money for college, she loves working with kids and has been a valuable asset to her church nursery.

Alec is in his second year at College of the Canyons, working toward a degree in mechanical engineering. He is a manager at a large McDonald's near the campus and his hobby is music, following in his dad's footsteps by playing the piano beautifully.

Close Family Ties

Although our family is spread out geographically, it is always a joy for us to be together. I am thankful that my children make it a priority to support each other's families by attending weddings and special occasions. We all log a lot of miles by air and by road to stay connected. I cherish the times that I can participate in the family gatherings.

Fulfilling My Destiny

"Older women are to be reverent in their behavior...teaching what is good, that they may encourage the young women to love their own husbands, that the Word of God may not be dishonored."

Titus 2:3-4

CHAPTER 33
My Testimony

I have been faithful in my walk with the risen Christ for nearly 70 years and have been blessed abundantly in my family relationships and quality of life. In the early years, I didn't realize that the Holy Spirit wanted to be involved in the intimate affairs of my life as well as major family decisions, so I'm especially grateful for His direction for our family even when I didn't know to ask specifically. As I became more enlightened, I determined to acknowledge the Holy Spirit as the Blessed Controller of all things.

I recognize that *"to whom much is given, much is required"* (Luke 12:48) and I desire to be used by my Father as His vessel to point people toward the Savior and to be a blessing to the people I'm in contact with on a daily basis. In my regular time of fellowship with the Lord, I am growing in discipline and ability to hear His voice and to be willing to obey. Thank you, Holy Spirit, for helping me not take more responsibility than my Father intends me to have, but to do what I am assigned with grace.

> *Do nothing from selfishness or empty conceit, but with humility of mind let each of you regard one another as more important than himself; do not merely look out for your own personal interests, but also for the interests of others.* Philippians 2:3-4

The Sabbath Rest

After George's heart attack and subsequent open-heart surgery in 1999, we repented of our neglect of keeping the Sabbath. We had observed the Sabbath off and on for decades, and when his health was in jeopardy, we recommitted to faithfully celebrate that anointed rest day.

We knew that the Sabbath rest is a gift from our Creator, but also realized that of all the Ten Commandments, observing the Sabbath is the least understood and most disobeyed. A hazard for us was having a well-equipped office in our home, which made it too easy to continue working on into the evening and on weekends. After his heart attack we determined to avoid night meetings. George's comment was, "Let's let someone else work the night shift."

Isaiah 58:13 was quickened to us:

> *If because of the Sabbath you turn your foot from doing your own pleasure on My holy day, and call the Sabbath a delight, the holy day of the Lord honorable, And shall honor it, desisting from your own ways and seeking your own pleasure, And speaking your own word, Then you will take delight in the Lord And I will make you ride on the heights of the earth; and I will feed you with the heritage of Jacob your father, For the mouth of the Lord has spoken.*

Teaching the Principle of the Sabbath

I was invited to teach missionaries in the Leadership Development Forum at Go To Nations on the Sabbath rest. We are all subject to burnout physically, mentally, emotionally and spiritually when we don't take time to rest. We will never be able to enter into natural rest until we first learn to enter into spiritual rest. When we believe the

Word of God and mix faith with it, we enter into spiritual rest. From the beginning, our Father set a pattern for His creation to follow. He created the world and all that is in it in six days and on the seventh day He rested. He modeled the plan for His creation to pause and remember that life and meaning for living are found only in Him – our Creator.

Learning from Others

Quoting from an article in the book *Mentoring for an Audience of One*, by Charles G. Oakes:

> God rested. He didn't need to rest. He is God, and His energy and energy reserves are beyond measure. He came to the end of His week of creation and said it was good. He was satisfied with what He had accomplished, and He now was preparing to fellowship with man and to guide man as He oversaw the creation. The Sabbath is not so much a day of rest from what lies behind as much as it is a preparation for what lies ahead. It is a day or period of time when work is laid aside; acknowledging that work should not control man and man truly can be a steward over work.

The book *24/6, a prescription for a healthier, happier life* by Matthew Sleeth, M.D., gives some excellent recommendations for keeping the Sabbath. Eugene H. Peterson, the author of The Message Bible, wrote in the Foreword:

> The subject of Sabbath keeping is in the air these days. Dr. Sleeth's credentials are impressive. His years of experience as an ER physician in hospitals qualify him as a veteran in a culture of demanding overwork. His entry into the Christian faith ten years

ago provides a total reorientation of his imagination in the Hebrew/Christian culture of Sabbath keeping.

And most impressive of all he explores the many details of what is involved in practicing Sabbath in a world that is unrelenting in its distractions and pressures to work longer and harder. He does it not as an impersonal "expert" but firmly in the context of marriage and family, with all the domestic and relational details involved in doing nothing where doing nothing always requires constant coordination and relationship.

We all know people who have simply burned out and compromised their health by not taking time to rest from their labors. Truly, obedience to Sabbath rest is better than sacrifice. It requires discipline to set aside time for personal and corporate worship and to make time to read, reflect and respond to the Word of the Lord. It is the quiet place of internal stillness and rest where we learn to listen and hear God above all the other demands for our time.

As stated by Jack Hayford, former senior pastor of The Church on the Way in Van Nuys, CA, and Chancellor Emeritus of The King's University:

To try to live any other way is to presume I can serve the Lord on my own terms and in my own strength. Over the years, I've come to learn that when I don't observe the Sabbath, my other days are not as productive. When I do observe it, He blesses the rest of my days. It's like tithing. You give a tenth to the Lord, and He multiplies the rest beyond what it would be if the tenth was included. When you observe the one day in seven, He'll bless you with more wholeness and productivity than you could possibly attain by NOT taking a day of rest.

It is the conviction of many Messianic and Christian leaders that revival and restoration of the Church in these last days will include a much greater embracing of the knowledge and celebration of the Sabbath. Our modern cultural practice has replaced the Sabbath with a day off or weekend, but we have missed our Father's intent. The culturally established Christian Sabbath (Sunday) is often the most hectic day of the week, especially for people in ministry. The practice of keeping the Sabbath day holy is a powerful witness that the Kingdom of God has come into our lives.

Applying Scriptural Principles

We moved to Brunswick, Georgia, for George's position with MAP International in 1989, the year I turned 50 years old. We had many wonderful opportunities there, including one time when we toured the ship *Anastasis* and hosted the founders of *Mercy Ships*, Don and Deyon Stephens, in our home.

I was privileged to travel with George to East Africa that fall. An excerpt from my diary on Sept. 25, 1989:

> Dear Father, I come to You this day with my heart overflowing with gratitude for the privilege of being in East Africa with George sharing in the special times of meeting old friends and getting better acquainted with the MAP families. It is a joy to be in Your presence being built up by the study of Your Word and gaining inspiration for the times in the near future when I'll be sharing with others from the overflow in my heart. I desire to be edified in my spirit by communion with You through the Holy Spirit. Fill me with a greater sense of purpose in my

life. I desire opportunities to have a significant role in reaching people to introduce them to our loving Savior and His purpose for their lives. I recognize the fulfillment in my life of Your promise:

For I know the plans I have for you, declares the Lord, plans to prosper you and not to harm you, plans to give you hope and a future. Jeremiah 29:11

Priorities

On December 2, 1989, I wrote, "Thank you for the wonderful husband George is to me. I appreciate his masculine strength and abilities, but most of all his spiritual strength and leadership skills, which are a direct result of his relationship with You, dear Father. Thank you for such a wonderful friend and lover as my life partner. May I have your grace and wisdom as I serve as his helpmate."

I benefitted greatly from reading the book *Ordering My Private World*, by Gordon MacDonald. It helped me put on paper the priorities I had been trying to follow for years:

1. My relationship with the Lord
2. My relationship with George
3. My relationship with our children and grandchildren
4. Faithfulness to my job
5. Ministry to others

The hard one for me was how to fit my job into my priorities when it took so much of my time and energy. I prayed that the Lord would multiply the remaining time to accomplish the things He was calling me to do.

George and I were led to pray that our grandchildren would love the Lord from an early age and never rebel against Him or their parents.

We prayed that their spouses would be prepared by their parents and be identified at just the right time. At the time that George wrote *Granddad's Money Camp* to help our children and other families establish a solid foundation for their financial future, I was inspired to write a correlating statement. "True wealth is genuine prosperity in spirit, soul, body, education, culture, economy, marriage and family. Money is only one aspect of the issues in studying true wealth. Youth should be challenged to create *true wealth* as they progress through life. Money can rapidly fly away, but true wealth is anchored in the soul."

Overcoming Generational Beliefs

In my family there had been many pagan concepts passed down from previous generations. Especially on my mother's side of the family, there were many dubious superstitions. For example: 1) avoid a black cat crossing your path, 2) don't break a mirror or you will get seven years of bad luck, 3) don't walk under a ladder, 4) if you drop the dishcloth, you must throw salt over your left shoulder, 5) avoid the number 13, and 6) beware of bad luck on Friday the 13th.

Another common practice: When the wishbone of the turkey had dried, someone pulled on each side until it broke. The one who got the larger piece should expect to have good luck. Our entire culture is steeped in countless pagan beliefs. For example, you seldom see a row 13 on a plane or a floor number 13 in a tall building.

George and I prayed for discernment and for this generational curse to be cut off from our lives and from our descendants. Thankfully, our children or grandchildren are not affected by these superstitions, and our family is free from the curse.

Useful Instruction

Dr. Jerry Williamson, the president of Go To Nations, the ministry I serve, often sends inspirational messages to all of the missionaries. He wrote that the Holy Spirit quickened Psalm 90:17 in his spirit as a declaration of faith as he was hearing a minister speak.

> *May the favor of the Lord our God rest upon us; establish the work of our hands for us – yes, establish the work of our hands.* NIV Psalm 90:17

He encouraged each of us to speak this verse over every project, task, and whatever God-assignments we are addressing. Dr. Jerry wrote:

> Ask the Lord to *"establish the work of your hands for you,"* in the midst of your assignments. The Holy Spirit wants to do more through us when we can operate in a place of rest. He wants to remove blind spots so we can see things we couldn't see before. He wants to get right in the midst of all we are doing and be the *Establisher* of the works of our hands. He wants to release God-ordained miracles through our labors that He has planned since the beginning of the world. As you pray this verse over your God-given domain, I come into agreement with you for the supernatural ability of God to be released on your behalf.

The Feasts of Yahweh

I've come to a much greater appreciation for the High Holy Days, our Creator's Appointed Days, usually thought of only as Jewish Festivals. In my study, I've learned that Yeshua our Messiah fulfilled the Spring Feasts of Yahweh at his first coming, from his crucifixion at Passover to his resurrection on the Day of First Fruits and giving of the Holy Spirit at Pentecost (*Shavuot*). The Fall Feasts are prophetic shadows of Yeshua's return, the second coming. The divine plan of restoration to true worship involves a renewed appreciation for our true biblical heritage, including The Feasts of Yahweh (Leviticus 23).

For several years, I have joined my Sabbath-keeping friends for *Sukkot*, the Feast of Tabernacles, at Riverbend Campground near Sweet Home, Oregon. A family we had known many years ago have generously allowed me to stay in their cabin next to the picturesque Santiam River for the week of Sukkot each year.

I treasure the teachings from William Bullock, Sr., Attorney at Law, at the Biblical Lifestyle Center in Texarkana, Texas. He is called *The Rabbi's Son* (the Rabbi being Yeshua, the Messiah), and he has helped me understand the Torah as our Creator's instruction manual for life on earth. His teaching ministry began as lessons for his home-schooling family.

I appreciate William Bullock's weekly online Bible study, with emphasis on joining the commandments of Yahweh with the testimony of Yeshua. Several months ago, I sent a message to him to ask about his understanding of the correct pronunciation of the Tetragrammaton YVHV. Is it YAHWEH or YeHoVah or another name? Even though the scope of his ministry includes thousands of believers, to my amazement, I received a personal reply a couple days later, which he simply signed, Bill. He is totally convinced that no one alive today knows the answer to that question and he said he regularly asks the Holy One to forgive us when we innocently mispronounce the Name. "We just do not know how the Holy One Himself pronounced it when He spoke to Moses or any of the other well-known figures in the Bible."

Guidance for Giving

These excerpts from one of Bill Bullock's articles were helpful to me:

He looked up and saw the rich people who were putting their gifts into the treasury. And He saw a certain poor widow casting in two small copper coins. And He said, "Truly I say to you, this poor widow put in more than all of them, for they all out of their surplus put into the offering; but she out of her poverty put in all that she had to live on." Luke 21:1-5

The purpose of Torah-inspired giving is not to bring about some good in the earth or to bring the giver any good thing in this life or the next. Please heed Yeshua's challenge not to "give to get." Be a giver, yes – but not out of a sense of duty, obligation, or guilt. Give, when you give, because the Spirit of God inside you cries out, "This is why I caused this money to pass into your hands! No one is watching – Do It Now!"

Open your eyes and look around you in your neighborhood, the marketplace, or the streets of your town - don't worry about the tax deduction, and you may be surprised at how easy hearing our Divine Bridegroom's voice can be.

CHAPTER 34
Rewarding Accolades

I n February 2013 our three children, Dan, Steve, and Jennie, prepared a special newsletter to send to family, friends and our support partners honoring our 40 years, 1973-2013, in global missions and international development; and 20 years, 1993-2013, with Calvary International (Go To Nations). They called it the 40/20 newsletter and some excerpts follow:

Please join us in celebrating two major milestones in the lives of our parents – George and Janet Meyers. We went as a family to Ethiopia in June of 1973. Our parents were missionaries in Wellega Province and we were boarding students at Good Shepherd School in Addis Ababa. During our school vacations in the summer and at Christmastime, we participated in missionary life.

In the early years of the team's missionary service among the Oromo and Gumuz people, 30 churches were planted with about 4,000 believers before Christian missionaries were forced to leave the country. During the 15 years that Marxism ruled the country, in spite of persecution, those churches multiplied to about 300 churches with 40,000 believers.

After being away from the country for 20 years, our parents were able to make a 5-country trip to Africa in 2002. They went by down-country bus to Kiramu village where we used to live. The whole time we lived in Ethiopia they never made a phone call, but to their amazement, while on the bus they heard a phone ring and watched a lady reach into her dress and pull out a cell phone! About the same time, they passed a field with six yokes of oxen plowing around a cell phone tower in the center of the field!

Our Dad:

Dad was always thinking of new ways to build relationships with the men. His conviction that salvation encompasses more than saving the soul has given him many opportunities to improve the lives of people. His passion for community development was stimulated in the primitive villages of the highlands of Ethiopia where technology, lifestyles, and customs were just like in Bible days. This setting inspired him for fruitful community transformation work in other ministry locations.

Dad has always had a passion for holistic ministry to improve the plight of people living in extreme poverty. On his desk is a plaque with the quotation from Proverbs 19:17, *"He who is gracious to the poor lends to the Lord."* In his travels and living abroad he is always looking for opportunities to help people and to release the Lord's blessing for salvation in all of its forms – spirit, soul, and body.

Our Mom:

Mom loved the medical clinic work at Kiramu in Ethiopia. She ordered the medicines and helped Erketa the clinic worker when he requested. That village clinic served a population of 4,000 people in Wellega Province.

When Ethiopia closed for them, they moved to South Sudan and from 1979-1983 they lived in three different places: Mundri, Yei and Tonj. Missionaries were not permitted to work in Sudan, but Dad's credentials as an agricultural advisor allowed them to work in the country.

In spite of the intense heat, humidity and limited food and grocery supplies, Mom was famous for her gracious hospitality. They served with a team of 70 agricultural, medical, water development, construction, and educational workers from 17 countries and also helped to start an enduring network of churches.

We are very proud of our parents for all they have accomplished over these 40 years. Marveling at their productivity, we give God the glory, acknowledging that he has uniquely gifted them individually and as a couple for the tasks He has called them to. Thank you, everyone, for the many ways you have blessed and encouraged them through this amazing journey. We hope you have enjoyed this stroll down Memory Lane with us.

From Dr. Grady L. Carter, Chairman, Board of Directors, Go to Nations:

> George and Janet's influence was significant in many ways. Their impact on the people they met was not just their salvation, but their involvement and commitment to the cause of Christ. As a team, their innate understanding of where a person was in life and their ability to relate specifically to that person was truly a gift from God. Together they had the ability to captivate any audience around, whether that audience was one or many.
>
> One of my many fond memories of George and Janet was visiting them when they were in town with my then young family. My children who were not that easy to impress were captivated by the many wonderful stories about their time on the mission field.

Janet is a unique figure, a person created in a time that will never be repeated, a woman passionate and dedicated to those things she holds dear, that being people won for Christ and busy in the kingdom work. Janet's true humility and servant's heart always placed her in a position to meet people where they really existed without the pretense and walls so often seen. Janet's disarming demeanor allows an avenue for her keen spiritual insight to get right to the base of a matter. Janet has a gift for seeing what is really present, not just what people want her to see. Behind that kind exterior lies the heart of a tiger for getting to the truth of a matter and seeing it through.

George and Janet as a team left shoes that could never be filled. Their shadow was much larger than the two of them could ever be. God implanted wisdom in them that is rare, in this time or any other. Janet remains a gift and a blessing to those she touches. Thankfully George and Janet had a multigenerational impact. Those whose lives they touched here and around the world are continuing to touch generations of others because of George and Janet's love for people and dedication to their calling.

Lifetime Achievement Award

On April 19, 2013, the staff of Go To Nations hosted 154 people for an evening of celebrating the goodness of God and the fruit of 32 years of ministry to the nations. George had been in the hospital and was discharged that morning. He didn't know that the staff had planned something very special for us.

Quoting from President, Dr. Jerry Williamson:

From time to time, the Executive Team of Go To Nations recognizes individuals that have made a significant impact on the ministry of GTN and through the ministry for the sake of the global harvest. We recognize these distinguished individuals by presenting them with the GTN Lifetime Achievement Award.

In our 32-year history, two couples have received this award. This year, 2013, we want to honor our third recipients, Dr. George and Janet Meyers. If there was anyone that was worthy to receive this honor, it is this precious couple that we have come to love so much. The established criterion for receiving this award falls into four main categories:

1. The recipients have a long-standing relationship with GTN of 20 years or more.
2. The recipients have made a significant impact in GTN through the use of their time, talents and resources.
3. The recipients have brought into GTN significant partners and/or team members from their sphere of influence.
4. The recipients have demonstrated a lifetime of commitment to the fulfillment of the Great Commission.

At this stage of their lives, Dr. George and Janet serve GTN in three distinct and important ways:

- As spiritual parents to all that are a part of GTN.
- As missionary statesmen to the Body of Christ in the area of missions and leadership.
- As special assistants to the President.

George was very weak, and I wasn't sure if he would have the strength to attend the event. The Executive Staff had been praying that Dr. George would be able to come. I determined to take him, but I was prepared to leave early if it was too much for him. As he interacted with the people attending and the award was presented, he supernaturally gained strength and was able to stay through the entire evening.

We wrote a message to our ministry partners in our next newsletter. "Without you, our dear partners, we could not have followed the leading of the Lord in missions ministry for all these years. Thank you for praying for our success! We love and appreciate you! Consider the award we received as partly yours."

Rewarding Comments

I have received dozens of messages from people who have read Dr. George's life story. I am choosing to share a couple recent ones that have especially blessed me.

From Mark Goode, Big Sky, Montana, a Board Member at Go To Nations:

> Your life with George and your approaches to both Kingdom Business and Kingdom Leadership have been a focus in the life of a new friend of mine for almost a year now, and a primary reason that we have connected. I found out his interest in missions literally a day or so after I finished reading your biography of Dr. George and it has been an inspirational guide in talking with my friend. It is because of your message that he has become interested in Go To Nations. Thank you for all you have done for our Lord.

I received a special letter of appreciation from the chaplain of the Board of Directors of Go To Nations, Pastor Wendell Shaw. I had sent him a birthday card on the occasion of his 80th birthday in May 2018. He shared a testimony of the celebration with his family and the following message to me:

> Janet, my respect and appreciation for your (and of course George's) lives and ministry has been an encouragement to me. Humility, dedication, faithfulness, and complete surrender are things named, but actually difficult to find. Your names would be used by me for an example of those distinctions. Bless you for your willingness to serve, attitude of victory and joy that is evident. You are special and again I appreciate your friendship and commitment to Christ and His Kingdom work through Go To Nations.

Another came from friends who used to be in the same homegroup with us when we lived in Brunswick in 1989-90. Somehow, they had been missed in the book distribution in 2016. We reconnected at a special event at Christian Renewal Church and had a lovely visit. It was only then that I discovered they had not received a book and I promptly sent them one when I got home.

From Linda and Tom Walker, Brunswick, Georgia, May 30, 2018:

> Thank you! Thank you! What a tribute to George and to you. Upon receiving your book a few days ago and starting to read it immediately, it's been hard to put down. I kept saying, "Tom, you're going to love this!"
>
> It is a treasure to have and makes me feel very close to you and George. (Janet, no wonder you were always so radiant!) What a legacy of lives well-lived. It is such a joy and privilege to know more about your

lives. The stories and scriptures, the photos and the testimonies are way beyond touching my heart and impacting my life.

Your book and sharing in such a deep and personal way have challenged me and made me laugh and cry and reflect and thank God. The importance of friendship and family was and is vital.

In my Bible I highlight, but not usually in books, but I've loved to read after Tom has enjoyed a book he has highlighted. He's now reading *George H. Meyers, His Remarkable Life Story*, and I've already highlighted. We'll see it daily here in the office bookshelf, but more importantly, we will draw life lessons from your enduring legacy of glorifying God.

CHAPTER 35
Serving Without My Life Partner

A s I reflect on my life during the nearly six decades that I was married to Dr. George Meyers, I am very thankful for all of the years we had together and his influence on my life. I realize that my greatest joy and contentment came from my commitment to helping him achieve his aspirations for life. He "finished well," and I am determined to continue on as a good steward of the gifts and abilities given to me by our loving Heavenly Father.

After he graduated to heaven August 25, 2013, my children insisted that I relocate to be nearer to them on the West Coast. My son Dan said, "It is up to me to look after you, and I can't do it if you are in Florida." He advised me to put our house on the market and I began to evaluate my possessions to determine what I should take to Oregon. Jennie came for a week to help me sort and pack with her amazing organizational skills. I definitely wanted to downsize, and it was a blessing to give away furniture and other items to people who really needed them.

Westward Ho!

As a family, we explored various options for moving my household and my car from Jacksonville, Florida, to a duplex in Harrisburg, Oregon, half a mile from Dan and his family. The decision was made for him to fly to Jacksonville to drive the U-Haul truck across the country. He took a few days of vacation along with scheduled days off for Thanksgiving.

Many friends came to lend a hand in the process. I especially want to acknowledge the incredible help I received from Danny and Mary Williams, Sonja Wagoner, and Neil and Lori Stagner in packing and loading the truck. Because of Dan's limited time for the trip, it was important for the truck to already be loaded when he arrived, and these dear friends and several young helpers made it happen.

From Jacksonville, Dan drove the 24-foot truck towing my car for two days to a planned stopover in Houston, where my granddaughter Anna and her family live. My son-in-law Mark Rice flew into Houston, and from there to California he and Dan were team drivers. Steve and Leslie offered to host everyone for Thanksgiving at their home in the San Francisco Bay area, and Jennie and the rest of their family drove there from Southern California.

After Dan left with the truck, I flew from Jacksonville to join the family and we had our turkey dinner together when the truck drivers arrived! After a day of rest and family fellowship, Mark returned home with Jennie, and I rode the rest of the way to Oregon with Dan in the moving truck. Though we were all still grieving, it was comforting to be together as a family.

837 Erica Way, Harrisburg, Oregon

Many of my grandchildren and Dan's friends stepped up to the plate to make quick work of the unloading process. It had taken many hours of hard work by the crew to load the truck in Jacksonville, but it was unloaded at my new home in 45 minutes! By prior arrangement, the truck was returned to the Eugene U-Haul site to meet the deadline of seven days. It was an incredible blessing to me to have the help of family members in getting beds set up and boxes unpacked.

George had found this duplex when it was under construction when he was on a morning walk while we were visiting Dan and Laurie some years before. Anna was the listing realtor who helped us with the purchase. It had been a rental, but now I am occupying one side of the duplex. I have good neighbors and feel safe and secure.

The first time my daughter Jennie came to visit me in my new home, she asked what I was finding the most difficult with living alone. I quickly replied that I dreaded eating by myself. That sparked an idea for her to bless me by creating a family photo wall in my dining room. She gave me a gift of collage frames and helped me acquire photos of all of my family members. Now, while I eat my meals, I look at their pictures and pray for my children, grandchildren, and great-grandchildren.

I have enjoyed being back in Oregon in an agricultural area where berries and fruit are plentiful. My first summer here I purchased a freezer to preserve the wonderful produce for winter meals and smoothies. Dan and Laurie have a mini-farm with fruit trees and berries, which they generously share. The past several years, Dan has raised gigantic Sweet Blue Hubbard squash for our whole family to enjoy and freeze for the winter, with plenty leftover to share with friends.

Picking wild blackberries always reminds me of my Grandpa Peck, who instilled in me at a young age the mandate to harvest the produce our Creator has made available for us. This past summer my good friend Jim Crumrine showed me a place near his filbert orchard where blackberries are prolific, and I enjoyed picking and preserving them for my winter provision. He also invited me to pick up walnuts in his large orchard. It was a blessing to have some walnuts to share with friends, simply for the work of picking them up, drying and cracking them. I was sad to learn that the price for walnuts was so poor that he had decided not to spend the money to harvest them.

Missionary Work

The technology of this era allows me to continue to work for Go To Nations, mostly by computer. After moving to Oregon in December 2013, I was able to embark upon a project that I had always wanted to do, but there were too many other things taking precedence. Now I can send birthday, anniversary, graduation, and new baby greetings to the missionaries, mostly by email. I thought it would be "one-way" communication, but I am often blessed to receive responses, sometimes giving me special things to pray about.

For the five years since my move to Oregon, I have traveled back to Jacksonville a couple times a year to help with hospitality for several Leadership Development Forums and other events. For the LDF, missionary leaders have come to the World Headquarters in Jacksonville to be trained and inspired for greater leadership roles. In April and May of 2018, I spent four weeks in Jacksonville helping with the GoToNationsExperience2018 and reconnecting with my Go To Nations colleagues, support partners, and friends in the area.

Member Care

In addition to my role doing assigned projects as a special assistant with the Mobilization Division at Go To Nations, I also serve with the Member Care Division. During the past two years, I have been communicating monthly with two missionary couples and one single lady in Africa, made possible by the technology of Skype or Magic Jack phone. We discuss happenings in their lives, planned ministry events, victories and disappointments, and I pray with them. It has been rewarding for me to have the close relationship and they seem to appreciate my special attention to their needs. I record the highlights of our time together on a computer report for continuity.

The Directors of Member Care, Victor and Kathie Barousse, noted my enthusiasm for the advocacy program and success with my growing relationship with my contacts. Although not mandatory, each missionary with field experience is encouraged to be an advocate for one or more others, and at the same time, another missionary is assigned as their advocate. The objective is to check on their well-being and support them spiritually, and for no missionary to be on their own without being regularly connected with someone else who is also in ministry.

Victor and Kathie asked me to consider a leadership role, and I accepted the position of Director of Advocacy for Member Care. My experience as a field missionary has uniquely qualified me for this assignment. I am now overseeing and encouraging the missionaries who have agreed to keep in touch with other field missionaries on a regular basis through this program.

GloDev, Inc.

As a successor to George's position, I serve on the board of directors for GloDev (Global Development), the relief and development arm of Go To Nations. It is exciting to see the progress Tim and Nancy Lovelace have made in the past two years; purchasing the 120-acre parcel in the Jacksonville city limits and birthing Eden Gardens Farm. By summer 2018, the land was entirely paid for and over 40 acres had been cleared. Five Aquaponic systems, two greenhouses, orchards, and raised bed gardens are built and being used. A home for the Lovelaces has been built on an adjoining property.

The whole community has been participating in helping to build out the farm and training center. There is a plan for the World Headquarters of Go To Nations to co-locate with GloDev at that site in a few years.

From Nancy Lovelace:

Janet, what you and Dr. George poured into us as missionary leaders has positioned us to lead today in both of these great global organizations, Go To Nations and GloDev, Inc. Dr. George was a patriarch in the faith and a fine example of a spiritual father and missionary leader. He taught us how to manage people and projects, how to lead and how to encourage others to do the same. Janet, you are our spiritual mother, and an exemplary model of encouragement, faith, and excellence in servant ministry.

Divine Assignments

When I asked our Father what I could do to preserve George's memory for our children, grandchildren, and great-grandchildren, the first undertaking was to write his life story. *George H. Meyers, His Remarkable Life Story* was published and distributed in 2016. The second assignment was to renovate our family cottage on the Oregon Coast. I concentrated on that project for 16 months, completing it just in time for a special family reunion in August of 2017.

When both of those assignments were completed, my family expressed concern about what I would find to do next to help me enjoy life. They didn't know that I had been considering a new hobby.

Accordion Music

My early memories of living in a Norwegian community in Wisconsin and going to dances with my folks inspired my enjoyment of accordion and fiddle music. I faintly recall playing the accordion for my own amusement when Dan was just a baby, but I don't remember how I acquired the instrument and I'm quite sure I didn't have any lessons. We purchased his accordion when he was in the third grade, more than fifty years ago. George and I sacrificed when we had limited income to give our children music lessons, including accordion lessons for Dan. He has taken his accordion to Ethiopia and later to Mombasa, Kenya, where he and Laurie served with Youth With a Mission. We are amazed at how well it has held up. He enjoys playing and opportunities to jam with others.

My cousin Elinor was visiting at the time of the Scandinavian Festival in Junction City in August 2017. We both enjoyed listening to some music groups playing polkas and ethnic folk music. I was attracted to a lady in a wheelchair who was playing the accordion. I had been thinking about learning to play, and I approached her after a concert and inquired whether she gave lessons. She responded quickly that she did not, but she referred me to her friend Darlene Ryan in Corvallis (25 miles from Harrisburg), whom she recommended as a skilled accordion teacher. I considered it a divine appointment.

I got in touch with Darlene and we really hit it off. She is not much younger than I, but a very accomplished accordionist who is in demand for local musical engagements, as well as giving lessons. Dan loaned me his accordion for a time, but before long I purchased my own so that he and I could play together. He and I went to a concert at a restaurant in Corvallis and heard Darlene play and lead several other accordion and banjo players. I have been taking lessons from her every other week for several months. She is very patient with me and an outstanding teacher.

At the Meyers/Sparhawk Annual Family Reunion on Memorial weekend, several musical family members stay up late to play together. In 2018, I was able to play along with some of the songs. I probably should have chosen an instrument that is not so heavy, but I have a cart to help when I need to transport it. I am finding satisfaction and enjoyment in learning to play.

Widows' Fellowship

In the summer of 2017, I was prompted by the Holy Spirit to consider a ministry to other widows. I acknowledge with gratitude the restoration I have received since my husband's death and I have a desire to comfort and support others who are in the same situation. The pastors at my church gave their blessing, acknowledging that it would be a perfect role for me and would fill an unmet need at the church.

As I was reviewing some files, I ran across a couple thank you notes from two widows at Christian Renewal Church in Brunswick, Georgia, where we had lived while George served with MAP International in the 1980s. Although I had forgotten about it, I had hosted a luncheon for widows nearly thirty years ago. One wrote, "What a lovely luncheon at your home. The food was good, the fellowship sweet and you are a delightful hostess. It was precious for you to minister to us as widow ladies. There are so many activities for couples and not that many for single people. Thank you, Janet!"

One thing I know, being alone is not the same as being lonely. I purposely spend time with family and friends, and now I'm hosting a group of widows once a month at my home in Harrisburg. They come from several churches and they all know me from some connection in the past. Some have been widowed for a long time; a few have lost their husbands more recently. Sometimes we have lunch together, but mostly we meet in the afternoon for a couple hours of fellowship to encourage one another. Spending time with this group of widow friends is a gratifying ministry!

CHAPTER 36
The Memorial Wall

I t was incredibly gratifying for me to have my children, grandchildren and great-grandchildren together August 5-6, 2017, to dedicate the renovation of our cottage and the memorial wall in George's honor. Although my daughter Jennie lives in southern California, she and her daughters took on the project of developing a special wall of remembrance with pictures and memorabilia from his life.

A large picture of him is on one wall with a wooden commemorative inscription above it: *In loving memory of our Dad and Granddad.* Under the picture is an eagle award from our service with Go To Nations, his military hat, and his mission statement. Another wall is covered with 8x10 pictures of him in various stages of his life, beginning with his baby picture. One wall has several pictures of our nuclear family, and another area features his military life, including a letter of appreciation for George's service to our country from the president.

I am encouraging our grandchildren to take their children to our beautiful cottage to show them the pictures and tell them about their great-grandfather, the patriarch of our family. When they are old enough, they will be able to read his life story. We want them to understand the legacy their great-grandparents have left them.

Our Cottage on the Coast

Our Family Treasure, Chapter 7 of George's life story, gave some good background about how the history of our cottage at Wi-Ne-Ma Lake on the Pacific Coast. The large parcel known as Wi-Ne-Ma Christian Camp and the town-site were acquired from the U.S. Coast Guard with some miraculous dealings occurring in the sale. We are not sure which owners built our cottage, nor do we know its exact age.

After George and I were married, my parents, Earl and Alice Peck, purchased the cabin in 1963 for $4,000 from Roy and Pearl Bierce, friends at the Newberg Christian Church. They planned for it to be a place for Mama to live in and commute the eleven miles to her teaching position, but she couldn't tolerate being in the cabin alone and soon rented an apartment across the street from the school in Hebo.

Originally our property had consisted of two lots and whoever built the house had no need to pay attention to where the house was placed on the parcel. The Houser family owns the property to the north of our cottage. When my folks purchased our cottage, Daddy was working for Houser Lumber Company in Newberg. Soon after that, Arney Houser appealed to him to sell them the northernmost lot of my parents' property to expand Housers' property and give them more land to build on in the future. Without any discussion with the family, Daddy agreed to sell the lot, and with a handshake and $2,000 the deal was accomplished. There was no survey done at the time, and neither party had any idea of the predicament it would create in the future.

We had a few fun family events there over the years and it was good to have a place at the coast to get in out of the weather. Our previous times at the beach, often enduring cold weather and wind, were not much fun and usually involved huddling under blankets around a fire. I remember one time when we roasted wieners with a cold wind blowing sand, little Steve said, "Mama, I don't like sand in my hot dog!"

Since my mother was not using the cottage as had been envisioned, my folks didn't get much enjoyment from owning it. Daddy grew weary of driving from Newberg to Wi-Ne-Ma every other Saturday to cut the grass, tend to the maintenance, and keep the blackberries from overtaking the house.

Without mentioning it to my sister Marilyn or me, my parents decided to sell the cottage. I found out about it quite by accident and appealed to George to negotiate with my dad to purchase it. George was in college at the time and we were on a tight budget, but we both saw the potential of keeping it for our family. Long story short, Daddy sold the property to us in 1967 for $6,000 on a land sales contract with payments of $50 a month plus 6% interest until it was paid off.

Important Improvements

When we became the owners, the cabin consisted of one room with a kitchen on the south end. The "bedroom" consisted of two sets of bunk beds on the north end, with curtains in front of them. There was a large porch on the west side that was under the roof line, but there were very few times when it was enjoyable to sit out there due to the weather. We decided to incorporate that space into the house. That was the first construction modification that was done, which created the bedroom and expanded the size of the living room.

At one point we considered what we might be able to do to add to the square footage and we partnered with several neighbors to have a survey done, the first step in any potential building program. The survey revealed that our house was three feet over on the lot Daddy sold to Housers. By this time my dad and Arney Houser had both died. We didn't want to leave that dilemma for our kids to solve in the future, so entered into extremely challenging negotiations with the Houser siblings to purchase 8 ft. x 80 ft., by the square inch! That made the land under the cottage ours, plus a five-foot setback on the north side. At a later date, we were miraculously able to purchase the two partial lots to the south from Wi-Ne-Ma Christian Camp.

At various times through the years when we had money and time concurrently, we upgraded the bathroom, then the kitchen, then decked the attic into a dormitory for sleeping. Pull-down stairs were replaced by the current stairway, masterfully crafted by my brother Lyle.

Family Heritage

George and I committed to the preservation of the cottage as a sacred duty and remembered its past with profound appreciation. Our goal was for it to be a resource for encouragement for our extended family in perpetuity. George developed a plan for the transfer of ownership after us and all our children and grandchildren consider it a treasure. He and I had planned for the Wi-Ne-Ma cottage to be our home in our sunset years, but after his death, our children considered the location to be too isolated for me to live there by myself. Together we decided to preserve it as a family vacation property.

In 2017 we hired Evan Carver, Carver Built Homes, as our contractor for most of the work. The cottage had never had a proper foundation and was in need of major maintenance. I knew it would require a lot of time and money, but I wanted to pass the property to my heirs in excellent condition. A new roof, new siding, and some new windows were added, including a window in the southwest corner of the kitchen giving a spectacular view of the iconic Cascade Head across Wi-Ne-Ma Lake. On the west side, from the picture windows we can see the waves of the Pacific Ocean crashing on the shore.

A vacation property doesn't need a walk-in closet, so we converted that space into a half-bath, which can be approached from the bedroom or through a pocket door on the side near the stairs. We hired Carol Cook, a new friend, to help me with interior painting and cleaning projects, including painting the kitchen cabinets white. Since the renovation, she has become the "cleaning lady" for guests who request that option.

The whole upstairs had been one room with many sleeping options, referred to as a dormitory, but it had no privacy. In the restoration, two rooms were created with a door in between. The south bedroom is decorated with Ethiopian memorabilia. The north bedroom has three single beds and storage for bedding and linens.

Tim Inman, a schoolmate of Dan's at Nestucca High School in the 1970s, did the initial excavation work to raise the house to pour a proper foundation. His final project was the creation of a parking area in our steep south lots. Tim's excavating equipment and ingenious planning combined with 30 dump truck loads of gravel have made it possible to park several cars in what used to be a blackberry patch.

My special thanks to Dan for his labor of love in sacrificing 14 weekends during 2016 and 2017 to drive to Wi-Ne-Ma with me on Friday night, working all day Saturday and sometimes Sunday. He wanted to lay the tile in the entryway, bathrooms, and kitchen, and family members and friends helped him lay new laminate flooring in the rest of the downstairs. I am very grateful for the help of some family members and friends in spite of very busy schedules. Dan did a myriad of other projects that were not assigned to the contractor. When I mentioned to him that I was going to miss those special times with him, he replied that maybe we could go out sometime just for enjoyment and NOT work.

I am pleased to make the cottage available to family members and as a refreshing get-away for missionaries and pastors. Although we don't have cable, a TV screen was added, making it possible to connect a laptop or to view a DVD on a stormy winter night.

Family Reunions

In recent times our family had been together at our Wi-Ne-Ma cottage on the 4th of July weekend in 2011, which George had enjoyed immensely. At a profoundly heartbreaking time, the family gathered together again for his graveside service in September 2013.

At our reunion in August 2017, we were 31 family members with only three unable to attend due to previous commitments. To accommodate everyone, we rented two additional houses and a few people stayed in motels. The dedication day was just for our family, but the next day we invited extended family members and about 50 people joined us for an outdoor picnic in the new parking area. Family reunions are always memorable, but this one was extra special as we dedicated the memorial wall and the extensive renovation project. We also celebrated our ownership of that property for 50 years. It meant the world to me to have my family join me for that extraordinary occasion. I'm looking forward to a similar reunion in the summer of 2019 to celebrate my 80th birthday.

CHAPTER 37
The Holy Land

George had an opportunity to visit Israel in 1998 with a group of pastors from Pennsylvania, and he declared the study trip a highlight of his life. It was a remarkable experience for him to learn from his traveling companions, one of whom had been to Israel 29 times. When he returned, he encouraged me to go. I was willing, but I wanted to wait for a time when we could go together. I was not interested in going with a large group and we never managed to have the time off from work and the funds to pay for the trip at the same time.

After George's death, I put a Holy Land visit out of my mind until one day when I was on a trip to Wi-Ne-Ma with my son Dan. I knew that he was passionate about Bible study, especially Hebrew and Greek languages, and I asked him what had motivated him to study Hebrew. He said he wanted to go to Israel sometime and be able to read the signs and speak to the people. His reply surprised me, and I began to think that I could get interested in a trip to Israel if he was my guide. Subsequently, Dan and I began to discuss the possibility of going to the Holy Land together. At that time his wife Laurie was busy helping with their grandchildren and she said she wanted to go someday, but not now.

On March 12, 2017, we flew to San Francisco and from there continued the 14-hour nonstop flight to Tel Aviv. In advance, Dan had done extensive research, recording his findings on his tablet. When we arrived at the airport, we rented a car right away and then spent two nights in Tel Aviv at Beit Immanuel Guest House. A highlight of our time in the city was a visit to Dugit Ministries. We were warmly welcomed by Avi Mizrachi and his daughter Devora. We enjoyed hearing about their ministry and prayed in the Prayer Tower, which overlooks the huge modern metropolis, home to 3½ million people, the largest concentration of Jews in the world. Avi told us that the city is a gateway to potentially reach all of Israel with the Gospel.

Tel Aviv has maintained its importance as a strategic central hub for commerce and trade. Regarding defense, everything from homeland security to the Israeli Pentagon for the military is located within the city. Dugit has many outreaches, including distribution of food and care packages to the fighting soldiers and more recently refugees from surrounding Arab countries. The house of prayer hosts many gatherings during the week with different emphases, especially praying for the government to make godly decisions.

The weather was cool, in the 60s most of the two weeks we were in the country. Our plan at each of the places where we stopped was to review the notes Dan had put on his tablet as he prepared to be the tour guide. We did a walking tour of Jaffa (Joppa), a 4,000-year-old port city, once the gateway to the land of Israel and rich in history. Jonah departed from there for his ill-fated trip. Solomon brought in logs from Lebanon for the temple. Peter had the vision of unclean animals, learning that God was interested in Gentiles as well as Jews. We drove up the coastline and toured the ruins at Caesarea, then Mt. Carmel, Mt. Hermon, Mt. Tabor (Mount of Transfiguration) and the Hula Valley, where we had our only afternoon of heavy rain.

We enjoyed Nazareth Village, but Dan decided that Jesus had left there due to the traffic congestion! I especially wanted to take a picture of Dan at Tel Dan, the site of the dreadful golden calf worship in northern Israel. That place has a dark past, but a beautiful river flows out of a giant spring there. Another place of wicked history was Banias, which is now a nature reserve.

> Banias is the Arabic and modern Hebrew name of an ancient site that developed around a spring once associated with the Greek god Pan. It is located at the foot of Mount Hermon, north of the Golan Heights. The spring is the source of the Banias River, one of the main tributaries of the Jordan River. Archaeologists uncovered a shrine dedicated to Pan and related deities, and the remains of an ancient city founded sometime after the conquest by Alexander the Great and inhabited until 1967; the ancient city was mentioned in the Gospels of Matthew and Mark by the name of Caesarea Philippi. Source: Wikipedia

We did driving tours during the day and stayed three nights in Katzrin with Elena Efrenko, a Russian friend of David and Linda Martin who would be our hosts in Jerusalem later on our itinerary. At Elena's guesthouse we enjoyed fellowship with two couples from Germany and a couple from Russia. Communication was a challenge and we were helped by the use of the translator on their cell phones. There was lots of fun as they shared life experiences and we showed pictures from our lives in Oregon. In our experience, the emotions of laughing and crying are the same language all over the world.

We enjoyed our driving tour of the Sea of Galilee area, where Jesus spent 70% of His ministry time on earth. We took a boat ride on the sea, called the Kineret by the locals, and visited Bethsaida, the Mount of Beatitudes, Tiberius, Capernaum, Tabgha, Chorazin, Gennesaret and the Yardenit, where many tourists are baptized in the Jordan River. One day we drove on the Golan Heights very near the border where attacks by Hamas are being reported in the news.

On our way to Jerusalem we visited Beth Shean, 17 miles south of the Sea of Galilee at the strategic junction of the Harod and Jordan Valleys. The fertility of the land and the abundance of water led the Jewish sages to say, "If the Garden of Eden is in the land of Israel, then its gate is Beth Shean." Source: Bible Places.com.

On March 23rd, which would have been George's 80th birthday, we thought of him as Dan floated in the Dead Sea. I took a picture of Dan in the same pose as George 19 years earlier and later featured it in my ministry newsletter. We visited Qumran, where the Dead Sea Scrolls were found, and on another day went to the Israel Museum where they are on display.

Though Dan was the guide for most of our Israel tour, we paid for a guided tour with six others on a small van to "the little town of Bethlehem." It is now a large city in the disputed Palestinian territory. There were no security issues during our half-day tour, but we felt slightly uneasy being there. We especially appreciated having a guide who was a believer in Messiah.

When we were in Jerusalem, we parked our car and traveled by public transport on buses and the light rail. We greatly appreciated our lodging with my friends David and Linda Martin, who live part-time in the German Quarter of Jerusalem and part-time in Ponte Vedra, Florida, where I met them many years earlier.

A test of my strength was a guided six-hour walking tour of the Old City of Jerusalem. There are 30,000 people living in that small space, which measures only a thousand yards by a thousand yards. We walked the Via Dolorosa, toured the City of David, and visited the Western Wall, the last remaining wall of the second Jewish Temple.

We were able to go up to the Temple Mount and view the Dome of the Rock, the third most important site in the world for Muslims. Praying is forbidden there, but how could they keep us from it? We took a shuttle to the Mount of Olives, the site of Jesus' ascension into heaven, and delighted in marvelous views of the city of Jerusalem.

The Golden Gate is the only eastern gate of the Temple Mount and has been walled up since medieval times. It was a cloudy day, but the sun peeked through just above the gate for Dan to take a spectacular picture. Our Jewish guide, not yet acknowledging His first coming, admitted that the blocked gate would not be a hindrance when the Messiah returns and enters Jerusalem. As believers we eagerly await His return and pray for the time when the Prince of Peace will reign in Jerusalem.

I don't think we missed any of the traditional touring sites, although Dan had a day trip without me, visiting the Temple Institute and Hezekiah's Tunnel, while I rested and caught up our laundry. The Yad Va'Shem Holocaust Memorial was incredibly sobering and almost more sadness than I could take. We had our picture taken at the Garden Tomb and bought some souvenirs there. We took our hosts David and Linda with us on a day trip to Masada, where we rode the tram to the top. Although it almost never rains there, that day while we were there clouds rolled in and wind brought a good rain that settled the dust. Our finale of the day was hiking in the nature reserve Ein Gedi.

Three spiritual highlights of our trip:

Our visit to the town of Magdala that was buried until 2009 when excavation revealed the oldest synagogue in Galilee. It was there that Jesus taught the multitudes and healed the afflicted, including Mary Magdalene, who made her hometown famous. A volunteer guide gave us an excellent tour and prayed with us. We were both inspired at the Encounter Chapel as we viewed a mural-sized painting of the encounter between Jesus and the woman who was healed by one touch of His garment. Dan purchased a poster replica of the mural for their home in Oregon.

One evening we worshiped with Paul Wilbur, an anointed Messianic worship leader from Jacksonville, who "just happened" to be giving a concert at the King of Kings Church in Jerusalem. I had attended many of his concerts in Jacksonville, but his anointed music was extraordinarily moving there in Jerusalem.

Our last night before departing the city, we were invited to share a meal at the home of Simontov and his wife Linda, friends of the Martins. Their apartment has a spectacular view of the Mount of Olives. We were inspired by his Shabbat communion meditation as he shared from his Jewish background and love for Yeshua. Our friend David Martin played the guitar and led us in worship with some of his original songs. A wonderful event to end our life-changing two weeks in Israel!

Coincidence?

But there was another blessing awaiting that could only have been arranged by the Holy Spirit. A day before our return to the U.S., Dan connected by Facebook with Helen Mears, a co-worker from the time that he and Laurie had worked with Youth With a Mission in Mombasa, Kenya. Helen is based in Beit Shemesh, not far from Jerusalem, with a ministry called *The Open Gateway*, a vision she had received from the Lord in 1994. That day she was in Jerusalem helping a Holocaust survivor move into sheltered housing. It happened that Helen was leaving for the U.K. from the airport the same afternoon as our departure, so we scheduled to meet her at the office where we needed to return our rental cars.

On the last leg of our journey we traveled through the Valley of Elah, best known as the place described in the Bible where the Israelites were encamped when David fought Goliath. From Jerusalem to the Tel Aviv airport is 45 miles, about an hour, a good chance for Dan and me to review our Holy Land tour. We agreed that our plan of renting a car and doing a self-guided trip was perfect.

Dan and Helen were so glad to renew their friendship, and I was pleased to meet her. During our conversation, we discovered that Helen had lived in the house next to ours in Mundri, Sudan, the year before we moved there in 1980. Dan joined in the fun of sharing tidbits of news from our ministries and mutual friends, and the pathways of our lives in the decades since Sudan and Kenya. Our time of visiting was too short as we all had to hurry to our departure gates.

Our 14-hour return trip to San Francisco was uneventful. During our long layover in San Francisco before our return to Eugene, my granddaughter Stephanie Cozzolino who lives in Half Moon Bay, met us in the airport for a good visit and chance for us to share some of our experiences in Israel. Dan is looking forward to another trip when he will be able to take his wife Laurie. In the meantime, he continues to study Hebrew, and we stay in touch with David and Linda Martin. Both the Bible and the news come alive after being in the places that are mentioned. It inspires and quickens our resolve to obey the admonition to:

Pray for the peace of Jerusalem; May they prosper who love you. May peace be within your walls, and prosperity within your palaces. Psalm 122:6,7

CHAPTER 38
The Joy of Shalom

M ost believers know that the Hebrew word *shalom* is understood around the world to mean *peace*. However, peace is only one small part of the meaning. Shalom is used to both greet people and bid them farewell, and it means much more than peace, hello or goodbye...

According to Strong's Concordance 7965, Shalom means completeness, wholeness, health, peace, welfare, safety, soundness, tranquility, prosperity, perfectness, fullness, rest, harmony, the absence of agitation or discord. Shalom comes from the root verb *shalom,* meaning to be complete, perfect and full.

Of course, there is only *one way* to find TRUE shalom – and that is in the Word of YHVH. Many search for fulfillment, happiness, and contentment in material possessions, money, sex, entertainment, etc. But those things do nothing to fill "that little hole in our soul" that only GOD can fill! Those things only serve to distract and prevent us from finding true peace...the *shalom* that can only come from Him who created and put all things into place.

The Refiner's Fire Website

Thus says the Lord, stand by the ways and see and ask for the ancient paths, where the good way is, and walk in it; And you shall find rest for your souls. Jeremiah 6:16

Excerpts from one of the last Cascade Commentaries George wrote:

Everyone needs an anchor for the soul – that part of your being that is your mind, will and emotions. Through the challenges of life, a treasure of experiences is embedded in your mind. Through reflection and concentration on your past, the memories that reinforce values and virtues can be pulled to the front to reinforce your life today...You have achieved things in life that have added value to your family, community and other relationships that make up your world.

Hang on to your positive attitude and virtues and realize that you have already entered into eternity – the abiding place of the redeemed because of the grace of God, your confession and obedience. To experience His peace, commit to covenant with your Creator who so generously lavishes grace on you and guides you in the way of His Kingdom.

We are schooled in the principles of *True Wealth – The Shalom of God, and* understand our obligation to others...The *blueprint for prosperity* is capable of expanding to accommodate our growing capacity to receive; to bring clarity to the processes of *True Wealth* accumulation; to increase our capacity for philanthropy and to maintain our equilibrium on life's journey in handling misfortune and rejoicing in success. In the transition from this life to the life to come, we can all truly rejoice that God is the One who gives us the power to obtain wealth and we are secure in Him.

I have learned so much from the TV program *Discovering the Jewish Jesus*, with teachings by a Messianic Jew, Rabbi K.A. Schneider. He reminds us that the Old Testament was the only Scriptures the early church had. At the close of every program he sings the Aaronic Blessing from the book of Numbers. George was honored to often be asked to speak that priestly blessing in various settings:

> *The Lord bless you and keep you; The Lord make His face shine on you, And be gracious to you; The Lord lift up His countenance on you, and give you peace.*
> Numbers 6:24-26

Grief Recovery

George's death was the hardest challenge I have ever had to face. During his last year of life, we both knew that his life on earth was in jeopardy, but our friend Reiss Tatum encouraged him to consider implantation of a Ventricular Assist Device to help his weakened heart. Reiss has had his VAD for eight years and is the poster boy for that special technology. He is in demand to share his experience with other medical professionals.

George's surgery in July 2013 to implant the VAD was a success and we were encouraged that he might have several more years to live. He was willing to endure the suffering of the surgery and recovery period to fulfill a goal of reaching the milestone of 60 years of marriage. He was managing his new technology well and slowly recovering. He was 76 and we had celebrated our 57th wedding anniversary on June 2nd.

During his therapy walk early on the morning of August 25, 2013, he fell in our driveway, hitting his head on the concrete. He came into the house and told me that he had tripped and fallen. At first, it didn't seem serious, and I commented that he would undoubtedly have a black eye from the abrasion just above his eyebrow. Neither of us realized during that day that his head was filling with blood. He became unconscious later in the afternoon and I called an ambulance to take him to the hospital. The doctors did a CT scan and told me that he could not recover from the trauma to his head. Having the VAD required him to be on a blood thinner, a new experience for him, which caused the unstoppable bleeding leading to his death.

Sorrow with Hope

I am trying to live from the admonition George wrote:

> Many times in my work I have felt inadequate for the task at hand, but it does help to realize that each one of us has a special contribution to make in this world. We must not try to be someone that we are not, nor try to copy others, but to be faithful to the special assignment God has called us to in our corner of the world. In our insufficiency and weakness His power is made stronger.

> In the world of hurting and suffering people, God calls us to ease the pain and to comfort the hopeless. Where there is discouragement and hopelessness, He calls us to proclaim that there is hope in Jesus. In a world of conflict, strife and war, He calls us to be ambassadors for Christ; to be channels of blessing with the ministry of reconciliation. Lord, make me an instrument of Thy peace!

The sadness of my loss has diminished in intensity as time has passed, and I am very conscious that the grieving process has helped me downplay the sorrow and embrace the memories of our 57 years together. Writing the book about George's life caused me to re-live our experiences over nearly six decades of life together and give thanks for all we had accomplished. I take comfort in knowing that our separation is not forever and that we will be together again for all eternity.

Family and Friends

The move to Oregon five years ago after George's death was definitely ordained of the Lord. Although it is usually best to let some time go by before making such a drastic change, my family recommended that I move nearer to them on the West Coast, so they could help me with the challenges of living alone. I'm very grateful for the help of Dan and Laurie, who live close by, and I enjoy family get-togethers with my grandchildren and great-grandchildren who live in Oregon. I see my California children, Steve and Leslie, Jennie and Mark and their families, less frequently, but they have been very supportive also.

My relationship with Pastor Gordon and Daisy Johnson at King's Grace Fellowship goes back more than four decades to our time in Ethiopia. They were dorm parents for Jennie when she was in junior high in 1974-76. I worship regularly at King's Grace and have many friends in the congregation. I serve on the Leadership Team and have a significant role in sharing mission news and encouraging mission involvement.

An important friendship was formed with Riyad and Salam Haddad, believers from Jordan, as a result of George's surgery in July 2013 in Gainesville, Florida. Riyad had a VAD implanted the same day and the medical staff encouraged the two men to get to know each other since they both lived in Jacksonville. Their first meeting was outside when they were in wheelchairs and being taken for a walk. They hit it off immediately and we were looking forward to getting to know them when both Riyad and George were recovering at home.

Riyad has since had a heart transplant from a 22-year old, and he loves to point out his increased vigor and vitality! I have had many opportunities to visit them and their sons Ramzy and Ronnie. I truly appreciate my friendship with them and enjoy the ethnic hospitality in their home whenever I am in Jacksonville.

Bible Study

I have come to a greater appreciation of the truth in the Torah and I purpose to study as a devoted disciple and to live my life in such a way that it will count for eternity. It is a joy for me to serve my family and others, sharing the truth that I am learning.

> *What does the Lord require from you, but to fear the Lord your God, to walk in all His ways and love Him, and to serve the Lord your God with all your heart and with all your soul, and to keep the Lord's commandments and His statutes which I am commanding you today for your good?* Deuteronomy 10:12-13

Valuable friendships in Community Bridge Fellowship have helped me as I study the Bible with emphasis on the Torah and keeping the Sabbath and Feast Days. I enjoy the fellowship at our Sabbath gatherings and have learned so much from what others have shared from their studies.

> *But you are a chosen race, a royal priesthood, a holy nation, a people for God's own possession, that you may proclaim the excellencies of Him who has*

called you out of darkness into His marvelous light...
I Peter 2:9

Measuring Success

In Mona Johnian's book *Releasing the Godly Fragrance*, there is a test about measuring your success in spiritual circumstances. I was glad to be able to respond affirmatively to the questions.

Am I growing in the knowledge of God?
Am I growing in the knowledge of His Word?
Is it easier for me to obey God quickly?
Is my temperament being replaced by His nature?
Is my affection for natural things less? Is it more for the things of the Spirit?
Do I love Jesus more than when I first came to know Him?
Am I able to overcome the adversities of life better as time goes by?

I am thankful for the guidance of the Holy Spirit that makes it possible for me to be obedient to the call of my Father to serve Him faithfully wherever I am assigned and to love people as He loved.

Quoting from "The Sweet Life," an article from my friend, Dr. Kevin McNulty:

God has done a marvelous thing for human beings! He has attached His eternal value to everything we do. We are not measured by others' opinions of what we do...only by our attitude in a desire to please Him and serve others as we do it.

Hanging above my desk is a plaque with George's mission statement. I believe he meant for it to apply to me as well, and I am making it my goal.

Through faith and wisdom acquire true wealth, mentor others and leave an enduring legacy.

I am grateful for the opportunity to share from *The Seasons of My Life* with you. I pray that reading stories from my life has confirmed truth you already knew, and perhaps opened some new vistas for you. In Sudan, we lived among people in the Anglican (Episcopal) Church. They closed every prayer time or church service with "The Grace."

The grace of the Lord Jesus Christ, and the love of God, and the fellowship of the Holy Spirit be with you all. II Cor. 13:14

Shalom!

PICTURES – C

The Peck Family – my parents and siblings

Mama and Daddy making doughnuts

With my sister Marilyn

My brother Lyle and his wife Melodie

With my newfound brother Bob

With my siblings – Lyle on the left, Marilyn and Bob on the right

On Jennie's wedding day, June 1979

My daughter, my friend – 40 years later

Our 40th anniversary

George and I on one of our many travel adventures

Still in love with that cowboy 50 years later

Our whole
family in 2005

George and I riding behind the boat in the donuts, Lake Shasta, California

Picking blackberries at Wi-Ne-Ma on the Oregon Coast

Our lovely home in Brunswick, Georgia

With our children in front of our home in Jacksonville, Florida

Serving at the book table at Go To Nations

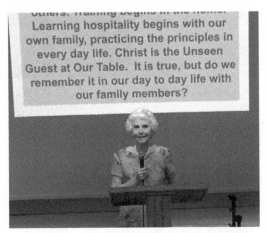

Teaching on hospitality at the Leadership Development Forum

Sharing at a Taste & See luncheon

My peers cheering as I received an eagle award for 24 years with Go To Nations at the reunion in 2017

My great-grandchildren collage is always in need of updating.
Nine precious little ones as of February 2019

Dan and Laurie

Steve and Leslie

Jennie and Mark

Tributes from My Children

From Dan:

Proverbs 31:10 *"Who can find a virtuous woman? For her price is far above rubies."* This verse describes my mother in many ways. She was a loving and supportive wife to my father through difficult circumstances at times in their various ministries and time abroad. Sudan was an incredibly tough place to live and minister and she persevered through it all. She has been a faithful and loving mother to my brother, sister and me and to our spouses. Our children and now our grandchildren have been recipients of "Grandma Janet's" love. Aside from loving her family, my mother has shown kindness to many through her amazing gift of hospitality. She also has the gift of administration and has been able to keep a lot of ministry and life projects on track. One of the very special times in my life was traveling with my mother to Israel in March 2017, a bucket list trip for both of us. We appreciate her so much and bless her on this writing of her life story.

From Steve:

My mother was a tremendous support to my father for their 57 happy years of marriage. They were each other's strength and together they accomplished more in ministry and other endeavors than each could have hoped to on their own. I have come to realize how very generous Mom and Dad were. There were always more things that I wanted than there was money available to buy them; however, we always had our needs met and they made us kids feel secure. Since Dad went to be with the Lord, Mom has continued their legacy of ministering to and serving her family and others. She is an example for others to follow.

From Jennie:

I am very grateful to my mom and dad for my happy childhood. I had the best parents in the world! Not only was I given a wonderful start in life, many enriching opportunities, and even an adventure in Africa, but I have also felt completely supported in my adult life, from advice on major decisions to their sacrificial financial help on all kinds of things, from plane tickets to houses to cars. I am especially thankful for my mom's visits to help me in times of crisis (or new babies) and for her stellar example of all a wife should be. I believe Mom and Dad were created and put on this planet for each other, perfectly suited in skills and giftings. It has been a pleasure helping Mom edit and fine-tune the book about Dad's life and now the story of the seasons of her life.

Janet E. Meyers, Author

This autobiography is a sequel to *George H. Meyers, His Remarkable Life Story,* the biography of Janet's late husband, published in 2016. The narrative continues the recounting of their international missionary adventures together, with emphasis on Janet's point of view. The stories underscore her determination to make an eternal difference in the lives of people she has influenced. Reviewing her journals and researching past communications has required her to re-live the 57 years of their marriage and eight decades of her life.

Jennifer Rice, Editor

Jennifer Rice is the daughter of George and Janet Meyers and is grateful for their example of godliness and faithfulness. Editing the book about her dad's life and now her mom's story has allowed her to revisit childhood memories and also discover new details about her parents' upbringing and international experiences. She and her husband Mark have five adult children and three precious grandchildren. They reside in Southern California, where they are active in church ministry.